THE LIVING TOGETHER KIT

by Attorneys Toni Ihara & Ralph Warner

NOLO PRESS
Courtyard Books
950 Parker St.,
Berkeley, CA. 94710

Editor:	Leslie Ihara Armistead
Production Director:	Keija Kimura
Book Design and Lay-out:	Toni Ihara
Illustrations:	Linda Allison
Illustrations:	Root Brague
Legal Research Assistant:	Catalina Lozano
Federal Tax Information:	Jeri Lee & David Brown
Photograph (Book Cover):	Lauren Elder
Type:	Koltype

ISBN 0-917316-20-7

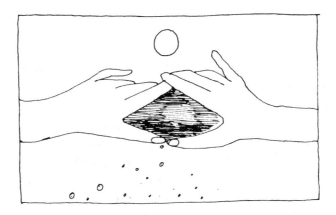

A LITTLE HISTORY

Carmen Massey and Ralph Warner co-authored the original legal guide for unmarried couples in 1974. It was entitled *Sex, Living Together And The Law* and was a successful and well-received book. In 1976 just as a new edition was being planned Carmen died. Her death was a severe blow to all who knew her: she was truly a person who gave more than she received, and whose light and good energy made her loved by many.

It wasn't until 1978 that those of us at Nolo Press felt clear enough to go on with revisions for the book. By this time *Sex, Living Together And The Law* was hopelessly out-of-date and it was necessary to create a new book. However, some of Carmen's original excellent work was still topical and an arrangement was made with her estate to include it in the new book. We feel good that some of our friend's positive ideas and common sense are still available to help people.

AND A BIG THANK YOU

Many old friends, and a few new ones, helped us make this a better book. We would particularly like to thank Anne-Theresa Ageson, Linda Allison, Leslie Armistead, David Brown, Keija Kimura, Jeri Lee, Catalina Lozano, Rosemary Nemec, Walter Warner and Milly Wohler. Special thanks to Gary Kitajo and Ron Lomax, reference librarians at the Alameda County Law Library whose kind assistance has made doing research almost a pleasure.

ABOUT NOLO

Nolo Press consists of a group of people (some lawyers, some not) who came to see much of what passes for the practice of law as being mumbo jumbo and paper shuffling designed by lawyers to mystify and confuse. Acting from the conviction "that there must be a better way", we have committed ourselves to trying to liberate the legal system from lawyers. A sane society needs a dispute resolution procedure that is cheap, fast, easy-to-understand and which is accessible to all.

Started in 1971 with *How To Do Your Own Divorce*, Nolo Press has become a positive energy force for people who want to open up our legal system and make its so-called trade secrets available to all. Nolo has now published a dozen books aimed at providing people with the information necessary to help themselves. In the process, it has helped the authors to maintain their own self-respect in a field where bank balances have often been more prominent than ethics.

Our books have been written, illustrated, designed and printed by a group of friends headquartered in Berkeley and Occidental, California. Without ever planning to, we have created our own cottage industry. We hope you get as much out of reading this book as we did in making it, and we would be delighted to get any feedback you would care to send our way.

Contents

Introduction

The purpose of this book is to help unmarried couples (straight and gay) attain mutual understanding by presenting the legal rules surrounding living together in a way that will allow them to relax and stay in touch with their love for one another. Our biases are toward simplicity and fairness.

Many people approach law as it relates to unmarried couples with hesitation, if not downright revulsion. Perhaps even the thought of introducing "unromantic" legal concepts into a personal relationship based on love and trust raises your hackles. And why not? The legal system as it now exists is commonly used in an aggressive attempt to screw every last nickel out of an adversary. Lawyers, some of whom have evolved no further than the hired guns of Dodge City, are the point men for a corrupt system having almost nothing to do with fairness, truth or the resolution of disputes.

We can't do much to change the legal system, but we can and do show you how existing rules can be used to sow the seeds of future understanding. Just as medicine need not be all pills and knives, law can be approached in a positive, conflict-avoiding way. We will show you that legal rules need not be incompatible with your best instincts and that law can be used creatively to minimize the possibility that your relationship will end in paranoia and bitterness.

Like it or not, there are many rules and regulations that apply to unmarried couples. You may ignore them for a time, but they are unlikely to ignore you. Once the rules are understood, the two of you will want to do some talking: to decide together how you and the rules can connect in a positive way. Then it will be typewriter time. We provide you with sample written agreements — living together contracts, real property agreements, wills, paternity statements, etc. It is up to you to adapt these samples to your needs. We advise you to write things down, not because we believe that most people are untrustworthy, but because we know from experience that over time, memories tend to blur. We ask you to make a small leap of faith and believe us when we tell you that sensible written agreements can do much to increase trust and harmony and that they are best made when you think that you will never need them, not when storm warnings are flying.

We believe that most unmarried couples can safely and easily master the great majority of the legal rules that affect them. We confess to our own hostility to what passes for justice in this country and to our bias against lawyers as a group. From time to time we do suggest that certain complicated situations necessitate a lawyer's advice, but you should know that there are doubtless many people who would advise you to rely on lawyers more often.

One point worthy of thought now, and as you read on, concerns the confusion of state laws relating to people living together. As you will learn, or perhaps already know, law books are full of rules everyone, including the police, ignores. Ancient laws regulating who can sleep together, when and where, are a prime example. Many of you will find that in your daily living and loving arrangement you are technically law breakers, even though you are conducting your life in what you consider to be an ethical and practical way. Perhaps you will feel, as we do, that many of these laws need changing and will realize that change will come only if lots of people make their voices heard.

In writing this book we have had some trouble figuring out the best way to organize all the material, partly because laws are often overlapping and sometimes conflicting. But it is also because people approach life from so many different directions. One person is interested in buying a house with his partner of many years, while another wants to know whether living with someone can be used against her in a contested child custody case. Much information has been included, but perhaps not in the order you might have chosen. You will find the table of contents to be a good outline of the whole subject, as well as a direction finder for any individual problem. There is nothing difficult about the information we discuss, but now and then you may find some of the technical points a little sticky. So relax, take your time and make decisions only after you have read, and re-read the sections of interest to you.

ex, Living Together, and The Law

A. DEFINITIONS

ADULTERY—voluntary sexual intercourse between a married person and any person other than the lawful spouse. A single act is called an *adulterous act* or an *act of adultery*. When two persons are living together and at least one is married to someone else, this is called *adulterous cohabitation*.

BIGAMY—the crime of marrying while one has a spouse still living, from whom no valid divorce has been effected. A *bigamist* is a person who commits bigamy. A *bigamous marriage* is a marriage contracted while at least one party was still married to another person.

BIGAMY

CHASTE—virtuous. A married person, a widow or a divorcee could be described as chaste even though such person had previously enjoyed or, in the case of a married person, is still enjoying, sexual relations, as long as these relations occurred between persons lawfully married.

COHABITATION

COHABITATION—two persons of opposite sexes living together as husband and wife without benefit of marriage. In a few states cohabitation has been defined as regular sex relations or even occasional sex relations, without living together, but this is unusual.

COMMON LAW MARRIAGE—a form of marriage valid in only a few states in which two persons of opposite sexes live together for a certain period of time with the intent of being married although they never have a marriage ceremony. In legal terms, this is called contracting a marriage.

11

COMMON LAW
MARRIAGE

COPULATION—sexual intercourse, coupling.

FELONY—a serious crime usually punishable by imprisonment for more than a year.

FINE—a sum of money that must be paid to a court by a person convicted of a crime.

FORNICATION—(1) voluntary sexual intercourse by an unmarried person with someone of the opposite sex; (2) adultery (biblical).

FINE

INCEST—sexual intercourse between persons so closely related that marriage between them is forbidden by law. Different states define incest differently, but all states legislate against marriage by children and their parents and grandparents, brothers and sisters (even if they are half brothers and sisters) and most, but not all states, include aunts, uncles and first cousins.

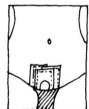

PROSTITUTION

LEWD AND LASCIVIOUS—a term used in criminal statutes to describe sexual conduct, usually short of actual sexual intercourse; obscene; inciting to lust. For example, exposing oneself in a public place.

MISDEMEANOR—a criminal offense less serious than a felony, usually punishable by a fine and/or a jail sentence of less than one year.

PROSTITUTION—the engaging in sexual intercourse for money.

SEDUCE

SEDUCE—to induce a person to surrender his or her chastity. The act of seducing is called seduction.

SODOMY—definition includes all the following: (1) "unnatural sexual intercourse"; (2) anal intercourse; (3) anal intercourse of a male with another male; (4) intercourse, anal or vaginal, of a person with an animal.

SPOUSE—either member of a married couple; one's husband or wife.

B. IF IT FEELS GOOD, IT MAY BE ILLEGAL

It is illegal to have sex with a porcupine in Florida, to have unnatural sex in Arizona, to make love with someone you are not married to in Utah, and to live together (cohabit) in South Carolina. The maximum prison sentences for these heinous crimes vary from 6 months to 14 years. Pretty silly, huh?

Whether or not it is legal for you to live with and have sex with a person of the opposite (or same) sex if you are not married depends on where you live. It is legal in

Hawaii; it isn't in Alabama. Given the puritanical roots of this country, it is not surprising that we have had a hard time shaking off the sneaking suspicion that pleasure is tantamount to sin. In the past, if it felt good, it was probably illegal no matter where you lived. Although the nation's law books are still filled with an incredible array of sexual prohibitions, this is one area of the law that is undergoing a rapid change for the better. Whether it is a direct response to the "sexual revolution" or just a pragmatic realization that it is silly to make laws regulating the private areas of people's lives, the old sexual taboos are being dropped from the books. A good thing too as we were fast becoming a nation of criminals.

Most sex law reform is being accomplished by individual state legislatures decriminalizing private consensual acts between adults. This means doing away with crimes like cohabitation, sodomy and oral copulation (see definitions). This trend has been gathering momentum over the past decade and seems likely to continue. So far the following states have made all private sex acts between consenting adults, whether straight or gay, legal:*

Alaska	New Hampshire
California	New Jersey
Colorado	New Mexico
Connecticut	North Dakota
Delaware	Ohio
Hawaii	Oregon
Illinois	South Dakota
Indiana	Washington
Iowa	West Virginia
Maine	Wyoming
Massachusetts	Vermont
Nebraska	

Because the law in this area is changing so fast, this list may not be completely up-to-date by the time you read this. If your state is still worried about how you fit your bodies together, check with your state legislator to find out if there are any current bills pending on decriminalization of consensual acts. A letter in support can't hurt. Obsolete laws are dangerous and unfair especially when you are the one violating them. While it is true that the comic book sex codes of most states are not rigorously enforced, every once in a while one of those old statutes falls off a shelf and hits somebody on the head. If it happens to be your head — you won't think it's very funny.

Another approach to wiping all sex laws off the books has been promoted by civil libertarians for years. Instead of approaching the problem one state at a time they have been trying to get a decision by the United States Supreme Court prohibiting all laws regulating the private consensual behavior among adults on the theory that such laws are an unconstitutional invasion of a citizen's right to privacy. The Supreme Court has yet to make this decision and many people feel that the present nine elderly, male

---

* In most states minors within a year or two of majority may live together with parental approval, but will face the strong possibility of action by juvenile authorities if parents are opposed.

justices are unlikely to do so. Like mountains, and almost as slowly it sometimes seems, Supreme Court Justices do change eventually, and there is hope that a future Court may be less rigid. Recently, the New Jersey courts have voided that state's fornication and sodomy laws on the grounds that they violated the right of privacy under both the state and federal constitutions.* In its landmark decision in State v. Saunders the New Jersey Supreme Court said: "We conclude that the conduct statutorily defined as fornication involves, by its very nature, a fundamental personal choice. Thus, the statute infringes upon the right of privacy." Hopefully, the Supreme Courts in other states that have not gone the legislative route of decriminalization will follow the New Jersey example.

You may be wondering how a fornication case came before the New Jersey Supreme Court in the first place. It happened like this. The defendant was originally charged with rape. He successfully defended his case on the theory that the alleged victim consented to the intercourse. He was acquitted. He was then charged and found guilty of fornication. We have found several other prosecutions for fornication or cohabitation in the last few years, but for the most part, the number of prosecutions for these kinds of "crimes" is low. If both of you are over 18, and neither is married to anyone else, you can practically speaking consider yourself safe from criminal prosecution for all common, heterosexual, sexual activities, no matter what your living arrangements. Local police departments and district attorneys have far better things to do with their time. Most sex laws are never used or are used only to harass gay people. Remember that we are not talking about violent sexual acts, sexual acts with children and prostitution and its associated activities. Laws against these activities are enforced, and at least in the first two categories, should be. We are also not talking about bigamy (more than one marriage without a divorce) and incest (sex with relatives). They are punishable under the laws of all states, although bigamy, except in cases of fraud, is seldom prosecuted and incest is defined differently in different states.

---

* State v. Saunders, 381 A. 2d 333 (1977) and State v. Ciufinnni, 395 A. 2d 904 (1978).

Cohabitation, fornication and sodomy are still crimes in many states. These are the crimes that most affect people who are living together and so we include the following table indicating the states which still have valid statutes proscribing these acts:

Sex Laws in the United States

	OUTLAWS FORNICATION	OUTLAWS COHABITATION	OUTLAWS SODOMY AND/OR ORAL COPULATION BETWEEN CONSENTING ADULTS
Alabama	No	Yes	Yes
Arizona	No	Yes	Yes
Arkansas	No	No	Yes
Florida	Yes	Yes	Yes
Georgia	Yes	Yes	Yes
Idaho	Yes	Yes	Yes
Kansas	No	Yes	Yes
Kentucky	No	No	Yes
Louisiana	No	No	Yes
Maryland	No	No	Yes
Michigan	No	Yes	Yes
Minnesota	No	No	Yes
Mississippi	No	Yes	Yes
Missouri	No	No	Yes
Montana	No	No	Yes
Nevada	No	No	Yes
New York	No	No	Yes
North Carolina	No	Yes	Yes
Oklahoma	No	No	Yes
Pennsylvania	No	No	Yes
Rhode Island	Yes	Yes	Yes
South Carolina	Yes	Yes	Yes
Tennessee	No	No	Yes
Texas	No	No	Yes
Utah	Yes	Yes	Yes
Virginia	Yes	Yes	Yes
Wisconsin	Yes	Yes	Yes
Washington, D. C.	Yes	Yes	Yes

If you would like to find out more information about laws (and penalties for violators) regulating fornication, cohabitation, sodomy, oral copulation and assorted unnatural acts in your state, go to your local law library and look in the penal code under the index headings you are interested in.

C. COMMON LAW MARRIAGE

There is a widespread belief among many that if you live with a person for a certain period of months or years, you are automatically married. In the great majority of states, including California and New York, this is simply not true. A few states still recognize what are called "common law marriages". A state that recognizes such marriages requires that both persons **intend** to enter into a common law marriage; the length of time you live together is not in itself important, but may be considered insofar as it tends to show intent. Thus merely living together doesn't create a common law marriage even in those states where it is recognized. And, if one or both parties are married to someone else, no amount of intent and living together can create a valid common law marriage.

There is one little trick in this area, however. A state that does not provide for common law marriage within its own boundaries will recognize such a marriage which was properly formed in a state that does recognize it. For example, if Bob and Carol started living together in Los Angeles in 1927 and are still living together and have never moved from the state of California, they are not legally married, even if both parties thought they were.* However, if Ted and Alice started living together in Colorado in 1965 with the intention of forming a common law marriage and have been living together since that time, both Colorado and California will recognize the marriage as valid.

The following chart indicates the laws of the different states regarding common law marriage. If you have any questions regarding the status of your relationship, you would be wise to do some research as to the law in your own state. Frequently the question of whether there was sufficient "intent" to form a marriage is tricky. There are no specific laws as to what conduct shows "intent to be married". Intent, or lack of it, is normally found from the facts of each situation. Such things as using the same last name, filing joint income tax returns, and holding yourselves out to the community to be married, etc. would be important. If you want to protect what you consider a marriage, or prevent yourself from being married against your wishes, it is better to do this now than to wait until you break up. If you do decide to split, a common law marriage must be ended by divorce, just like a marriage with a ceremony, and you cannot legally marry another person until that common law marriage has been terminated by legal proceedings or death.

---

* Many states that do not recognize common law marriage give certain property rights to people who are living in situations similar to marriage or who falsely believe that they are married. Often a person living in this kind of situation is called a "putative spouse". See Chapter 7.

16

STATES RECOGNIZING COMMON LAW MARRIAGE

Alabama	Iowa	Oklahoma
Colorado	Kansas	Pennsylvania
Columbia, District of	Montana	Rhode Island
Georgia	Ohio	South Carolina
Idaho		Texas

STATES NOT RECOGNIZING COMMON LAW MARRIAGE

Alaska	Maine	New York
Arizona	Maryland	North Carolina
Arkansas	Massachusetts	North Dakota
California	Michigan	Oregon
Connecticut	Minnesota	South Dakota
Delaware	Mississippi	Tennessee
Florida	Missouri	Utah
Hawaii	Nebraska	Vermont
Illinois	Nevada	Virgin Islands
Indiana	New Hampshire*	Washington
Kentucky	New Jersey	West Virginia
Louisiana	New Mexico	Wisconsin
		Wyoming

*However, living together for at least three years until one spouse dies results in a valid marriage for inheritance purposes.

ractical Aspects of Living Together

A. GETTING TOGETHER

When people come together to walk the same path for awhile, they bring not only themselves and their love for one another, but tend also to drag along all sorts of objects, debts, animals, relationships, etc. We will let you work out your own problems involving the goldfish, Great Danes, and former mothers-in-law, but will give you a quick rundown of your rights in more mundane areas:

1. Debts

By living with someone you take absolutely no responsibility for their debts. Your wages cannot be attached and your property cannot be threatened to pay for your friend's overdue bills. If your friend's creditors contact you, a good chuckle should handle the problem. Should your friend declare bankruptcy, your property will not be taken, **as long as you have kept it separate.**

WARNING: If your friend is having debt problems, be very careful not to mix property together in a joint bank account, in joint ownership of a car, or in any other way. Do not enter into an agreement to share and pool earnings and accumulations. In this situation it would be advisable to sign a contract keeping everything separate (such as Contract I in the Appendix) so that there can be no possible confusion as far as your friend's creditors are concerned. Because, if your property does become commingled (say in a joint bank account) with that of your friend, you will, at the very least, have problems explaining to your friend's greedy creditors that some of it is yours and you may end up losing out in the confusion.

2. Property Acquired Before Getting Together

Each person retains complete ownership of all possessions owned prior to getting together. We include as part of the contracts set out in the Appendix a page where the separate property of each party can be listed (see Chapter 4). One person can, of course, give the other objects of his (her) property, or a part interest in a particular piece of property. If a major item is given, a little note setting forth the facts would be helpful. We have seen a lot of problems where people disagree as to what was or was not a gift.

3. Property Acquired After Getting Together

Generally, it is our opinion that the easiest and cleanest way to handle your economic affairs is to keep them separate. As we noted above, it is imperative to do this if one of you is having debt problems. But even when this is not the case, a lot of potential complications can be avoided by each of you maintaining your financial independence and keeping your property and debts separate. If you keep three simple plans in mind, you will have a smoother relationship with fewer bitter feelings at the end. These plans are:

☯ Enter into an agreement keeping your earnings and accumulations separate as in Contract I in the Appendix (see Chapter 4).

☯ Do not have joint accounts or make joint purchases unless absolutely necessary. Do not mix money or business affairs together except in emergencies. Always keep your own bank account and do not add extra signatures to your charge accounts. Continue to use your own names and do not pass yourself off as husband and wife. Do not cosign loans or credit agreements unless you are completely willing to assume all payment obligations if your friend cannot or will not pay.

☯ If you do purchase expensive items that you intend to belong to both of you, write out an agreement that sets out your understanding. This should include how the items are being paid for, what will happen to them if you break up and what will happen if one of you dies (see Chapter 4, Section B for sample joint purchase agreements). Be sure that each of you signs the agreement and that a copy is attached to your over-all, keep-things-separate contract. If you buy a house together, you will need a more formal document as outlined in Chapter 6. If you jointly purchase an automobile, there are certain additional registration procedures to follow (see Section F below).

If you each have adequate income and each of you pays your share of the expenses, the above plans should be simple to follow. However, if you have a relationship where one of you works and supports the other, it is just as important that you have written understandings, although they may be a bit more complex (see Chapter 4). This is especially true if one of you works and the other has free access to the money and makes purchases and pays bills. At the end of such a relationship, there should never be the need for one person to say, "I supported him (or her) for ten years; he (or she) did not contribute anything and now the lazy bum has gone off and left me." Whatever your financial understanding, it should be absolutely clear that each person is free and equal in the living arrangement, whether the person happens to bring home the bacon, or cooks it and cleans up the mess afterward.

Remember, you entered the relationship freely. Each of you has the right to leave it freely. If you feel you are being taken advantage of, examine your own head and the situation. If you are unhappy, perhaps it is time to dissolve the living arrangement.

B. SHARING BANK ACCOUNTS

Our advice to anyone considering sharing a bank account, either checking or savings, is: DON'T. If each person has his (her) own account and pays the agreed-upon expenses, there is no possibility of confusion. Canceled checks serve as receipts. Our experience has been that joint accounts often lead to confusion, paranoia and bitterness. Of course, we are definitely prejudiced in this matter. We give the same advice to married couples.

There are no legal problems associated with opening joint accounts. Banks will be happy to take care of your money under any name or names. If you insist on having joint accounts, the bank will assist you in deciding how many signatures will be necessary to write a check or make a withdrawal from a savings account. You may decide that either one of you should be able to get money by signing for it, or you may decide that it is necessary for both of you to sign. Remember, if you do have a joint account, you are both responsible for all checks drawn on the account even if the other person takes all the money and disappears. Further, if your partner takes all the money out of the savings account and leaves, the bank is not responsible unless two signatures were required for withdrawal.

C. CHARGE ACCOUNTS AND BUYING ON TIME

You and your friend may want to buy on credit or establish joint charge accounts. Again, if you were to ask us if this is a good idea, we would say NO. If you are both working, there is no reason why you cannot each have your own account. This means that you each deal with your creditors on your own terms, and you do not have to worry about the purchases of the other party. However, in spite of this practical advice based on experience and many tales of woe and dismay, many people are enamored of the idea of credit and like to carry around a large number of magical credit cards. Some of these same people are determined to share "everything" with their partners and will stop at nothing to obtain joint credit accounts. The following sections are included on the theory that if we can't talk you out of it, we may as well give you a hand.

This is also a good place to tell you that the best one-word definition we know for most cosigners is: "IDIOT". A cosigner is a person who by signing his name fully obligates himself to pay another person's debt if that person fails to do so, whatever the reason. The cosigner gets none of the benefits of the transaction (often a loan) and often all of the burdens. Should the primary debtor default, the cosigner can be sued if he or she doesn't pay voluntarily, and is subject to wage garnishments if he or she doesn't pay the judgment. A person should cosign only if he or she is fully prepared to pay the debt if the debtor defaults.

D. HOW TO APPLY FOR CREDIT

There are still some stores that will not set up joint accounts for unmarried couples. Although this is a somewhat murky legal area, it is the opinion of staff members of the Federal Trade Commission that such a denial would be a violation of the new Equal Credit Opportunity Act (see Section E). However, after conferring with representatives of a number of national retail chains, we have found that credit discrimination against the unmarried couple is mostly a thing of the past. Most of the major stores will open joint credit accounts for unmarried couples if they have joint accounts at all.* After all, it is to their advantage to have as many persons as possible responsible for a debt. If you should run into a situation where joint accounts are limited to married couples, do not pretend to be married to qualify. A little misstatement now can cause big problems later, especially if you ever have to file for bankruptcy. In this case your creditor could claim you obtained credit by fraud and prevent you from getting rid of the debt.

When you are dealing with a store that is happy to issue you a joint charge account, remember that you are both legally responsible for all charges made on the account by either of you, or by the person that has the consent of one of you to make charges. This means that if Keija allows her cousin Floyd to use the joint charge card that she has with Felix and Floyd runs up a bill for $1,000, Keija **and** Felix are both responsible for the debt even if Felix opposed or did not know about Floyd's use of the card. Also, if Felix leaves Keija and uses the charge card on a spending spree across the country, both Felix **and** Keija are legally responsible for all charges made by Felix.

If, in spite of our warnings, you and your partner do open joint credit accounts, we suggest that you arrange the account so that both of your signatures are required in order to charge. In addition to guaranteeing that the card is not abused, this may serve as a brake on impulse buying.

IMPORTANT: If the two of you do break up, be sure to inform all your joint creditors that you wish to close out your account immediately. We have seen many cases where friends forgot to do this and ended up paying for an ex-lover's purchases. It is not a good idea to simply divide the accounts and agree one person can use some of the accounts while the other person uses the others. Remember, you are still liable for all purchases if your name is still on the account, even if your relationship is over.

E. CREDIT AND CREDIT AGENCIES

A store or a lending institution need not lend to any particular person. Of course, stores normally lend to people they consider good financial risks and refuse to lend to poor financial risks. However, no one seems to agree on just what a "poor financial risk" is, and what factors contribute to determining the financial responsibility of an applicant for credit. If a person has no apparent source of income, he is not a good risk. If a person has a history of being unemployed for long periods of time, he is not a good risk. If a person has immediate plans to leave the country, he is not a good risk. If a person has a low income and a lot of dependents or a lot of expenses, it is reasonable to assume that he is not a good risk. But what about factors that are seemingly unrelated

---

* Montgomery Wards and some other large stores handle the problem by not issuing joint accounts to anyone. Obviously, if they don't issue joint accounts to married couples, they can't be thought of as discriminating if they don't issue them to the unmarried. Almost all stores, including Wards, do allow a cardholder to authorize additional signatures on his or her account. This works the same as a joint account for some, but by no means all purposes. For example, only the person whose name is on the account is legally liable to pay the store.

to income or ability to pay?

Congress has passed laws which say that creditors cannot discriminate against certain groups or classes of people. As of March 23, 1977, it has been unlawful for creditors to discriminate on the basis of "race, color, religion, national origin, sex , marital status, or age, or because all or part of a person's income derives from any public assistance program."* Some creditors apparently claim that "marital status" only refers to whether you are married or single and does not prevent them from discriminating against unmarried couples. As noted in the previous section, the people that we talked to at the Federal Trade Commission seem to disagree, but there are no court decisions backing them up as yet.

This sounds pretty good, especially since the law also says that a creditor who fails to comply with this law may have to pay an individual who has been discriminated against $10,000 plus any money that individual actually lost as a result of the discrimination. (If a large group of people wins a suit against the creditor for unlawful discrimination, the creditor may have to pay up to $500,000 for violating the law.) But, and this is the big "but" that always seems to be present when we try to solve human problems by legislation, the law becomes very complicated as it attempts to define "discrimination". For example, an inquiry into a person's marital status is not discrimination if "such inquiry is for the purpose of ascertaining the creditor's rights and remedies applicable to a particular extension of credit, and not to discriminate in a determination of creditworthiness." This sounds like a pretty fine line to us. Also, state property laws may be considered by a creditor in deciding whether to extend credit. This means that a creditor's decision in one state may be OK while it would violate the law in another state.

---

* This is called the "Equal Credit Opportunity Act", Public Law 93-495 (Title 5),1977 Amendment Public Law 94-239.

ons issued to the Federal Reserve System say specifically that a cre-
quire use of a married name, but must allow credit to be issued in either
iven name or a combined surname. The regulations also say you can be
o reveal alimony and child support payments that you are required to make,
payments you receive, unless you are relying on them to establish your income
edit purposes. A creditor may not completely ignore your income from child
pport or alimony payments in determining your creditworthiness, but may consider
now likely they are to be paid. A creditor may not completely ignore income from a
part-time job. A creditor may not ask you questions about your birth control practices,
or whether you intend to have children. A creditor cannot terminate your account or
require a re-application if you change your name or marital status unless there is
evidence you are unwilling or unable to pay your bill. Also, if the creditor denies you
credit, he must inform you of the reason for the denial.

There haven't been many cases testing the effect of the Equal Credit Opportunity
Act. However, under this law, it has become much easier for married women to buy on
credit without having their husbands involved in the credit transaction. It is also
easier for unmarried couples to open accounts either joint or separate. If you feel you
were discriminated against, contact the nearest regional office of the Federal Trade
Commission (for non-bank related credit problems) or the Federal Reserve Board (for
bank-related credit problems). If you feel that yours is a clear case of discrimination,
you may wish to contact an attorney (you could inquire through women's organizations or the ACLU) to bring a lawsuit on your behalf.

REMEMBER: Being refused credit is often a cloud with a silver lining, since what
is credit really other than a license to buy lots of things you can probably do without at
prices that exceed their true worth to you while paying unreasonable amounts of
interest for the privilege?

Some organizations specialize in keeping credit files on individuals. Normally,
these "credit bureaus" are part of, or have close working relationships with, bill
collection agencies. Creditors and other sources contribute information to these files
and prospective creditors can then contact the agency and obtain the information
contained in your file for a small fee. Some of these agencies claim that they keep
information only as to past performance in paying debts, but this is not true. All sorts
of personal information, completely unrelated to financial matters routinely appears
in these files.* Some of these agencies also claim that they do not cross-index unmarried persons living together (husbands and wives are always filed together) but this
may not be true. In some cases, a bad credit rating on the person with whom you are
living will also show up on your credit rating and may prevent your obtaining of
credit. Your file will contain every name you have been known by and, if Keija has
applied for credit as "Mrs. Felix Finnegan", Felix may find the bills listed under his
name even if he did not sign for the account. This is especially true if the couple has
consistently represented itself to creditors as "Mr. and Mrs. Felix Finnegan".

---

* For a good rundown on credit bureaus and collection agencies and a thorough discussion of your rights, see *The
California Debtors' Handbook — Billpayers' Rights*, Honigsberg and Warner — coupon side back cover.

24

IMPORTANT: Under the Federal Fair Credit Reporting Act you have the right to go to a credit bureau (there may be more than one in your area) to find out what is in your file. If false information is in the file, you have the right to get it corrected and may also put information in the file to explain your point of view, where you believe a wrong impression is being made.

If you do decide to open a joint account, be aware that not only **your** "sins" but also the "sins" of your partner may haunt you for a long time. If your friend takes off, leaving a large debt behind that you pay despite the fact that you are not legally obligated to do so, your slow payment record will still remain in your file. Again, do not represent yourself as married if you are not. Give only correct information on your application. Credit is not worth the problems that can follow from this kind of deception.

F. BUYING A MOTOR VEHICLE

Occasionally, a couple may decide to jointly purchase a motor vehicle. If only one of you has signed the loan from the lending institution but both of you are contributing funds toward its purchase, an agreement should be prepared like the one found in Chapter 4, Section B. When the vehicle is registered with the state, you may register it any way you choose. If your intention is that the vehicle belongs to both of you, you should register it in both your names. If your intention is that the vehicle belongs to one of you, then register the car only in the name of that person. Again, the important point is that you agree **before** you make the purchase as to who shall own and use the item and who shall pay for it. In most states there are three types of joint ownership of motor vehicles:

1. Vehicle registered in the form "Felix Finnegan **or** Keija Adams". If this form of registration is used, then if one person dies the ownership certification and registration card can be reassigned to the surviving joint tenant by the Department of Motor Vehicles without the necessity of going through a probate proceeding. **However,** this type of joint ownership allows either party to sell the vehicle at any time without the knowledge or consent of the other joint tenant.

2. Motor vehicle registered in the form "Felix Finnegan **and** Keija Adams". If this form of registration is used, the signatures of both parties are required to transfer the title of the vehicle. However, if one party dies, the other party may have to go through probate proceedings in order to obtain title to the vehicle. We say "may" because some states such as California exempt estates from probate when they are small. If you use this form of ownership, a will is necessary to pass your share of the property to your friend if you die (see Chapter 11).

3. Motor vehicles registered in the form "Felix Finnegan **and** Keija Adams, JTRS" (Joint Tenancy with Right of Survivorship). If registration is in this form, both signatures are required to transfer title to the vehicle, but, at the death of one party, the survivor may obtain title to the vehicle from the Department of Motor Vehicles without going through probate proceedings.

NOTE: Before relying on this information, check with the government agency in charge of registration for your state. They should be able to advise you about the different methods available.

G. TRAVEL

Looking over the next hill, just across an ocean, or perhaps for the end of a rainbow seems to be one of our great national joys (some would say diseases). How you will travel, whether strapped into a great silver bird or wandering slowly down a country road, is less important than the fact that almost certainly, you will travel. When you move about together, you are bound to experience those funny (sometimes scary) moments when, with pen poised in hand over hotel or motel register, you freeze — absolutely don't know what to write. You probably don't want to break laws unnecessarily, but you also don't want to be hassled, especially don't want the poetry of your trip ripped off.

But how to register? In some places only one name is necessary. The number of persons that will be occupying the room must be stated, but only one signature is required. It is sensible to start by registering in this way and to let the motel employee ask for more specifics if he or she wants them. Where both persons must sign or be identified, the question arises as to whether you register as "Keija and Felix Finnegan" or "Felix Finnegan and Keija Adams". Many places prefer that you register under the first alternative. They may not care if you are married or not, but they like to have the appearance of caring. Some places may hassle you if you register under the second method, and, if the issue is forced, refuse to give you lodging. However, we have found in recent years that greed has triumphed over conventional "morality". The sheer volume of business due to unmarried couples traveling is an economically persuasive argument to stop hassling. As part of doing this book we talked to a number of national and international hotel chains including Hilton and Hyatt and found that they have adopted an official policy of "not inquiring" into the status of a couple, even if they register using separate last names.

Sometimes travel discount rates are available only to married couples. It is more common these days that they are extended to any two adults traveling together, but you may still run into a chance to save money by saying that you are married. Do you run any legal risk by doing this? No. For purposes of tours, tickets, etc. you are safe enough claiming the status that will get you the cheapest rates. As lots of married couples use different last names these days, no one is likely to hassle you.

H. DISCRIMINATION IN EMPLOYMENT

Many private employers will not be aware of your living situation unless you are in an extremely important or sensitive position. If you are unlucky enough to have an employer who threatens your job when he discovers you are living in an unmarried state, you may wish to consult an attorney about whether or not you can do anything to protect yourself. In most cases, the attorney will probably advise you that there is little that can be done. Traditionally, private employers are not required to hire or retain particular employees. They are free to terminate employment just as an employee is free to resign and move on. Recently, however, many national corporations have announced policies of not discriminating on the basis of marital status. If such a policy has been announced by your employer, you have a legal right to rely on it.

However, the situation is somewhat different for employment in state, county and city jobs. Police departments, school boards, post offices are all subject to the principles found in the Fourteenth Amendment of the Constitution. Unfortunately, the most recent U. S. Supreme Court decision in this area is a horrible one in which the court, over Justice Marshall's eloquent dissent, refused to consider the case of Rebecca Hollenbaugh and Fred Philburn, who were fired from their employment at the Carnegie Free Library in Connesville, Pa., for living together.* The lower federal courts held that, while there needed to be some relationship between the reason for the firing and the performance on the job, that this test was met because the couple was living in a state of "open adultery". However, in a much wiser decision, the more enlightened California Supreme Court has just ruled that gay employees of private public utilities can't be fired for living together.** This case is being read by many as establishing the right of all people, straight and gay, to live with whomever they wish free of any employment discrimination. It's about time.

Court decisions protecting unmarried couples have traditionally been strongest in the area of federal employment. In 1967 a postal clerk in California was dismissed from his job because his living with a women he was not married to constituted "immoral conduct". He appealed and the Federal District Court of Northern California decided that his dismissal was unconstitutional becasue the post office had failed to show that his private sex life had any connection with the responsibilities of his position so that his firing was arbitrary and a denial of due process. Also, the post office had failed to show a "compelling reason" to justify the invasion of his Ninth Amendment right to privacy. Other court decisions have gone on to clearly establish that the private living arrangements of public employees is not normally relevant to their jobs.

---

* 99 X. Ct. 734 (1978).

** In the case of *Gay Law Students Association* v. *Pacific Telephone and Telegraph,* _____.
In another move toward sanity, the Virginia Supreme Court recently upheld the right of a woman to become an attorney even though she had a live-in lover. *Cord v. Gibb,* 254 S. E. 2d 71 (1979).

However, there is one area of public employment where living together can still cause problems. This is in education, especially at the primary and secondary level in conservative areas of the country. As recently as 1975 a school teacher was dismissed from her job in a small town in South Dakota for "gross immorality" because she was living with a man without benefit of marriage. She appealed to the Federal District Court of South Dakota where the judge said that although the school board had to show a connection between the proscribed conduct and the workings of the educational system, the fact that she was a "bad example" for her students was sufficient. He upheld her dismissal. Apparently in many localities the policy is not to hassle teachers living together if they are reasonably discreet. Having a baby while living with someone is almost always judged to be indiscreet.

If the federal government, or a state or local government is discriminating against you because you are living with someone, your best bet is to contact your local American Civil Liberties Union (ACLU) or a lawyer who handles these kinds of cases. The ACLU has handled several of these cases successfully in the past. If you believe that your job is being threatened because of your race, ethnic background or sex, you may have a claim against the employer and you should contact an attorney, the branch of the United States Equal Employment Opportunities Commission (EEOC) nearest you, or the agency in your state or city that deals with such matters. Don't delay, start protecting yourself as soon as you see you have a serious problem. If you feel you are entitled to money damages, first contact a private attorney as he can do more in this area than can the governmental agencies.

I. PAYING YOUR TAXES

The American Income Tax system is incredibly complicated and not always logical. In the world of business many actions are not even planned without a consultation with a tax lawyer and an accountant. More to the point, many persons of normal intelligence with high school or college educations are so intimidated by forms and regulations and laws that they hire an agency or "expert" to prepare their returns. Part of the confusion arises in classifying income, taking deductions and claiming exemptions and credits. However, even when all this is done, two persons with identical incomes may end up paying different amounts of taxes. How does this happen? Different persons pay different **rates** of income tax, depending upon their marital or family status.

For example, an unmarried person may file as a single person or, in certain cases, qualify as an "unmarried head of household"; a married person may either file a joint return or a married person's separate return or, in certain cases, qualify to file as an "unmarried head of household". What difference does it make how one files? Suppose Susan Hall has two dependents including herself; during 1977 she had a tax table income* of $10,000. If Ms. Hall uses Form 1040A (the Short Form) in computing the amount of tax she must pay on these earnings rather than itemizing her deductions, she might be required to pay any of the following amounts:

---

* Tax table income is the amount you pay income tax on and is almost always different from the total amount of income you earned. If you do not itemize your deductions, it is the same as "adjusted gross income" which is basically the amount you earn minus what it cost you to earn that money. If you itemize your deductions, tax table income is adjusted gross income minus your excess itemized deductions (the amount of your itemized deductions less the standard deduction).

If wage earner is:	She must pay:
Single	$1051
Married (files joint return)	757
Married (files separate return)	1279
Unmarried Head of Household (claiming standard deduction)	975

Does this mean that married persons are always better off tax-wise? NO, most often they are not. Consider the following examples.

Keija and Felix are living together. Each had a tax table income of $12,000 in 1977. Each has only one dependent (himself or herself). Using the Short Form and filing as a single person, each would have to pay a tax of $1,666 or a total of $3,332 for both of them. It Keija and Felix were married in 1977 so that their joint income was $24,000 and they filed a joint return (Short Form) claiming two dependents (each of them is a dependent) they would have to pay a total tax of $3,997 or $665 more than if they had not married. Legally, they cannot file as single persons. They could each file a separate return as a married person. If they filed this way and each claimed one dependent and $12,000 of adjusted gross income, each would have to pay a tax of $2,050 or a total of $4,100, so this possibility doesn't help them. Now let's suppose that Keija and Felix cannot use the short form because they each have incomes over $20,000. In 1978 Keija had a taxable income of $21,000 and Felix had an income of $32,000. If they are both single they may each use the $2,200 deduction (or itemize deductions, if they will be higher than $2,200). After allowing each of them the personal exemptions of $750 and the new "general tax credit" (Schedule TC, for use with long form), Keija will then pay $4,348 and Felix will pay $8,783, for a total of $13,131. O.K., now let's say that Keija and Felix are married and file a joint return without itemizing deductions, in which case their returns automatically take into account a $3,200 married couple standard deduction.* After allowing $1,500 (2 x $750) for the two personal exemptions for themselves, and applying the general tax credit, their income tax liability on their combined income of $53,000 is $16,030. This is a whopping $2,899 more than they would pay in taxes if they were single!

Even if Keija and Felix were to itemize deductions, the situation would still be pretty much the same. If Keija had itemized deductions of $3,000 (as opposed to a $2,200 standard deduction) to offset her $21,000 income, she would, if single, pay $4,075 in federal income taxes. If Felix had itemized deductions of $3,500 to offset his $32,000 income, he would pay $8,198. The total federal income taxes for this unmarried couple are now $12,273. If they are married, though, they pay $14,380 if they file a joint return and $14,588 ($4,810 for Keija and $9,778 for Felix) if they file as "married filing separately". Again, they pay a lot, namely $2,107, for being married.

One couple in similar circumstances was quite aware that the federal government was taxing their marriage, or rather, would pay them to get a divorce and live together, depending on how you look at it. They saved well over $2,000 in taxes each year by

---

* Notice that the $3,200 standard deduction allowed a married couple is smaller than two times the $2,200 standard deduction allowed single individuals. Married taxpayers filing separately fare even worse, with only a $1,600 standard deduction.

flying South for the winter to Haiti each December to get a "quickie" Haitian divorce. They then enjoyed their annual vacation at this Caribbean resort, after which they would fly back home to get married again the following January. By being able to file as single taxpayers at the end of each year, they saved more than enough money to pay for the vacation! The couple was so thrilled about their discovery that they decided to tell a nationwide TV audience about it on CBS' "60 Minutes". An angry Internal Revenue Service, not to be denied the last word, rushed through a new ruling. "The tax laws do not contemplate a sham transaction that manipulates year-end marital status for federal income tax purposes," said an IRS spokesperson. The IRS said in a retroactive ruling that it would no longer recognize divorces obtained solely to reduce a couple's taxes. But how would the IRS know whether tax-dodging was the reason for the divorce? What about the couple who really gets a divorce because they can't stand each other but later get back together for a trial period? This happens every day. How can the IRS, short of bugging a divorced couple's bedroom (or seeing the couple tell it on TV), learn the true motives behind the divorce, or even learn if the couple has in fact remarried? The IRS replied, "We will apply the ruling only when we have reason to believe it (the divorce) was obtained solely for the purpose of getting more favorable tax treatment." As for unmarried couples who live together and avoid marriage, even if only for tax reasons, the IRS spokesperson stated that these individuals are single people entitled to file their returns that way. We wonder why a couple would ever remarry each January rather than just remain single and living together? If it was for religious reasons, they could have simply gone through a religious ceremony without getting another marriage license, and remained single in the eyes of the law and the IRS, but married in the eyes of God.

Do all these examples mean that tax-wise it is always better not to be married? No. Consider the following examples.

In 1978 Sarah and Michael are single and living together. Sarah had an adjusted gross income of $14,000 and Michael had an income of $1,000. As a single person with one dependent (herself), and not itemizing deductions, Sarah must pay federal income tax of $2,187. Michael, of course, does not have to pay any tax. If Sarah and Michael get married and they file a joint return claiming themselves as two dependents and not itemizing deductions, the total taxes owed are only $1,481, or $706 less than Sarah would pay as a single person. (If Sarah were to file as "married filing separately" she would owe $2,675, which is much more than she would pay if she were single.)

Now suppose that in 1978 Sarah had an income of $26,000 and Michael had an income of $4,000. Sarah must pay a tax of $6,230 and Michael must pay a tax of $114, for a total of $6,344 if they live together and file separately. If they get married and file a joint return on this combined income of $30,000, then the income tax liability is $5,939, or $405 less than if they were single.

Consider one further example. Theresa and Andrew are single. They live together with Theresa's five children from a prior marriage. Andrew has no dependents other than himself. In 1978, Theresa had no income and Andrew had an income of $18,000. As a single person using the Short Form, Andrew must pay an income tax of $3,348. If Theresa and Andrew had married and filed a joint return and claimed five children (plus themselves), then the income tax liability would be only $1,471, or $1,877 less than if Theresa and Andrew were not married.

Whether there is a tax advantage to living together or being married, and whether a couple that is married is better off filing separate returns of married persons or a joint return, depends on your family composition and who earns what. If two persons are living together and each person earns anywhere near the same amount as the other person, there is probably a tax *disadvantage* if the two persons marry. However, if the two persons living together have incomes which are widely disparate, there is probably a tax *advantage* if the two persons marry. This advantage will be increased if the person with the lower income has dependents.*

Can you file a joint return with the person with whom you are living if you are not married? NO. This is illegal and **may** result in your having to pay money back to the government **and** at least in theory in criminal sanctions (prison or fine) being imposed on you. As a practical matter the government doesn't usually know whether you are married or single and lots of people have been claiming to be married when they are not and getting away with it, but it's not a course of action that we can recommend.

May you claim your roommate or your roommates' children as your dependents even if they are not related to you? Only if they have lived with you for the entire year as members of your family, you have provided more than one-half of their support, they have not earned more than $750 each, they have not filed a joint return with anyone else, and they meet certain residency requirements. For details, see the Internal Revenue Service guidelines.

For those of you who can understand things better when presented graphically we include the following chart created by our friend and colleague Dave Brown.

FEDERAL INCOME TAX (BENEFIT OF LIVING TOGETHER UNMARRIED)

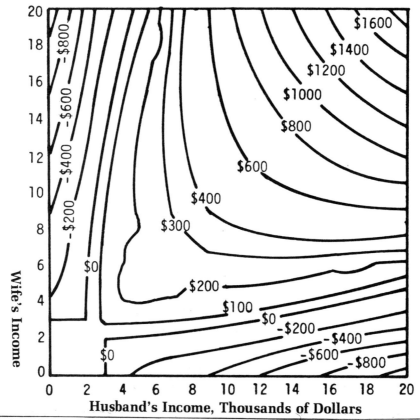

Husband's Income, Thousands of Dollars (x-axis)

Wife's Income (y-axis)

---

* Unmarried couples who have accumulated considerable property ($175,000 or more) and who face the death of one member of the couple may wish to consider marriage. Federal and state estate tax rules grant large tax exemptions for the surviving spouse which are not available to couples living together. If you are worried about this, check the federal estate tax rules or see an accountant.

To figure out your joint savings simple take a ruler and draw two lines. One starting from the husband's income and one from the wife's. Your tax saving as a result of living together will be at the point where the lines intersect. A negative number means that you're better off being married.

Of course, we hope that people do not get married solely for the tax advantage but, if you do, be sure to consult the tax tables for the current year as you may find yourself surprised by the results.

J. WELFARE, FOOD STAMPS, MEDI-CARE

Welfare regulations are much like quicksand. What looks safe, solid and reliable one minute can gobble you up the next. Changing rules seem to be part of a system that has never found a comfortable place in the American consciousness. So before you rely on what we say here, check with your local social services agency.

If a person (usually a woman) receiving welfare under the Aid For Dependent Children (AFDC) Program starts living with a man, can she continue to receive her monthly check? Yes, as long as the man is not actually contributing to her support or the support of the children, welfare will not be cut off or reduced. Some welfare departments will require considerable proof that money is being kept separate, others are not so tight. The welfare department is not supposed to be interested in the physical relationship between the mother and the man, only in what he contributes. It is always wise to call and find out exactly what local procedures are so that you can adjust your situation to fit any technicalities.

Both the AFDC mother and the unrelated male will have to sign a welfare department statement stating under penalty of perjury the amount of money, if any, he pays. Most welfare departments have a requirement that a man who has income contribute at least the fair cost of his monthly expenses to the family unit. In many states this is assumed to be about $120. A man who does this should be sure that his contributions are kept separate and are only used for his own expenses. He has no legal duty to contribute to the support of either the AFDC mother or her children, and the welfare department cannot legally force him to do so. If they do subtract money from the mother's grant because he is living in the house, an appeal should be taken (called a fair hearing). To do this, see your nearest legal aid or welfare rights group for help.

HINT: Find out what the minimum monthly contribution for a male for his own expenses is in your state. Document that the man pays this much and no more and does not contribute to the expenses of the woman or her children. This will result in the AFDC mother keeping most or all of her grant. If you report that the man pays more than the minimum, you will lose welfare benefits.

EXAMPLE: Sara and her two children are receiving a monthly grant under the AFDC Program. Ben, who makes $1,000 per month, moves in and contributes $120 per month for his rent and household expenses (Sara has checked to see that this is the minimum in her state). Sara can keep the majority of her grant as long as Ben doesn't provide additional money for her support or for the support of the children. Sara should keep detailed records as to income and expenditures to prove that she is independent. As long as the records are neat and seem sensible, the welfare department is unlikely to demand proof for every item.

Rules on food stamps are a little tighter. If Sara is living with Ben, it will be assumed that they are eating together. Since Ben has a substantial income, food stamps will be cut off. However, if Sara can prove that she buys and stores her food separately and doesn't share with Ben, she can also keep her food stamps.

HINT: The amount of money received under your AFDC check is quite large in comparison to the value of the food stamps. You may be wise not to be "too greedy" and press for food stamps too. If you do, you risk the authorities taking a closer look at your situation — something many people on welfare find that it is wiser not to encourage.

Medical benefits are figured the same way AFDC benefits are. This means that you can live with someone and keep the medical card for you and your children as long as the person who you are living with doesn't contribute to your support.

K. SERIOUS ILLNESS

We are often asked what happens if one member of an unmarried couple becomes seriously ill or is involved in an accident and medical authorities need someone to O.K. a treatment decision. Probably this problem is more imagined than real, as doctors will just go ahead and do what they think is best in a genuine emergency, but it is annoying that spouses are routinely consulted, but living together partners are not. Here is a form that may be of some use, both for treatment emergencies and for hospital visitation privileges. We don't guarantee that this sort of authorization will be accepted everywhere, but it is a lot better than nothing. It would also be a good idea to carry a card in your wallet listing the person you live with as your closest friend and asking that they be notified in case of an emergency.

MEDICAL EMERGENCY AND VISITATION AUTHORIZATION

In the event that I am ill, injured or otherwise incapacitated, I hereby authorize _____ (name) _____ to make all decisions relating to my medical treatment. This includes any necessary x-ray, examination, anesthetic, medical, surgical, or other procedure carried out under the supervision and upon the advice of a physician or surgeon licensed to practice medicine.

Further, I hereby authorize _____ (name) _____ to visit me at any time in any hospital, convalescent home, or other facility where I may be undergoing treatment.

This authorization is good from _____, 19____ to _____, 19____.

_____
DATE   SIGNATURE

(Notarization is optional, but advisable)

arvin v. Marvin

A. A LITTLE HISTORY

In the old days, couples who lived together existed pretty much in a legal vacuum. They lived together because they liked each other and let the details take care of themselves. What little law there was held that money and property belonged to the person who earned it, while agreements between unmarried couples were viewed with alarm. But law, perverse creature that it is, abhors a vacuum and on December 27, 1976, the California Supreme Court rendered a decision in a case involving film actor Lee Marvin that profoundly affects the several million people who share their lives without the benefit of a marriage license.* As you will soon see, law, but not necessarily order, has been brought to the realm of the unmarried couple.

NOTE: As we discuss in section D, below, there has also been a subsequent trial court decision in April, 1979, actually dividing the Marvin's property. The sensationalism of the trial that proceeded this second Marvin decision has led many to conclude that it is legally important. The first Marvin decision at the Supreme Court level is the one that has great meaning to all unmarried couples.

The *Marvin* case is important not only because it is law for Californians, but because it is symbolic of a judicial trend across the nation. The California Supreme Court is extremely influential and it is likely that most states will follow its lead. Indeed, the Minnesota Supreme Court has already done so. In a case involving an unmarried couple who had lived together for 21 years, they approved a division of the real and personal property accumulated over that period and quoted at length from the *Marvin* opinion in support of their decision.** The Oregon Supreme Court also quoted from *Marvin* when they ruled on April 18, 1978 (Beal v. Beal, 577 P. 2d 509), that Oregon courts will uphold the explicit and implicit contracts of unmarried

---

* *Marvin v. Marvin,* 557 P. 2d. 106 (1976). We urge you to read the entire opinion which you can get at any law library if you are interested in a history of the law as it applies to the unmarried couple. You may also be interested in an article entitled *Marvin v. Marvin: Preserving The Options,* Kay and Amyx, California Law Review, Vol. 65, No. 5 (1977).
** *Carlson v. Olson,* 256 N.W. 2d 252 (1977).

couples, and Illinois and New Jersey appellate courts have followed the *Marvin* rationale in upholding an unmarried couple's right to contract.*   It is our best estimate that the appellate courts of close to twenty states have accepted the *Marvin* rationale and that about four states led by Georgia in the case of *Rehak v. Mathis*, 238 S. E. 2d 81 (1977), have rejected it, finding that the immoral nature of the living together relationship prevented the participants from forming a contract.

The legal rules that the *Marvin* case sets out are not particularly revolutionary or radical. In fact, they were fairly predictable once courts got around to recognizing that unmarried couples and alternative families were here to stay. What the California Supreme Court did was to recognize the capacity of unmarried couples to contract between themselves, just as they are capable of contracting with anyone else. In addition, the Supreme Court stated that courts have the power to look at an unmarried couple's relationship to make sure that property is divided according to their reasonable expectations. They also adopted a presumption that members of an unmarried couple intend to "deal fairly with each other". Doesn't sound like much of an advance, but for years the validity of such contracts was questioned by sanctimonious judges who didn't want to extend contract rights to people who were "living in sin". Well, you know "the times they are a changing" when even as establishment a body as the California Supreme Court admits that "the mores of the society have indeed changed so radically in regard to cohabitation that we cannot impose a standard based on alleged moral considerations that have apparently been so widely abandoned by so many".

Because of the significant impact the *Marvin* case has upon unmarried couples throughout the United States, and because a great deal of misinformation has been reported, let's take a look at what "really" happened. The story begins in October of 1964 when Lee Marvin and Michelle Triola decide to live together. But from this time on Lee and Michelle have different recollections as to what was said and agreed to. As in so many situations where people break up, Lee and Michelle seem to look at the past through different windows. Michelle alleges that from the beginning she and Lee "entered into an oral agreement that they would combine their efforts and earnings and would share equally in any and all property accumulated as a result of their efforts whether individual or combined". Michelle further claims that she agreed to give up her lucrative career as a singer and entertainer in order to devote her full time to Lee as companion, homemaker, housekeeper and cook in return for Lee'spromise to provide for all of her financial needs for the rest of her life. Lee doesn't have quite the same recollection of their "agreement", especially where it involves Michelle's right to half of his accumulated property and his duty to support her indefinitely. Indeed, Lee can't seem to remember agreeing to anything more than that he would pay their joint living expenses while they were together.

Lee and Michelle actually lived together for six years. She eventually took his last name (this is perfectly legal, see Chapter 2). While they lived together Lee allegedly accumulated over a million dollar's worth of property — all in his own name. The

---

* *Hewitt v. Hewitt*, 380 N. E. 2d 458 (1978), *Kozlowski v. Kozlowski*, 395 A. 2d 913 (1978).

relationship ended in 1970. Lee asked Michelle to move out, but continued to pay her $800 a month in support for over a year after their separation. The payments stopped and Michelle brought suit for half of the property accumulated while they had lived together under the legal theory that she was entitled to it under the original oral contract. The trial court denied her claim based on the authority of a number of old cases limiting the right of people "living in sin" to form contracts at all. Michelle appealed. Enter the Supreme Court of California.

B. WHAT THE MARVIN CASE DECIDED

The Supreme Court begins their opinion with the conclusion and so will we.

> "We conclude: (1) The provisions of the Family Law Act do not govern the distribution of property acquired during a nonmarital relationship; such a relationship remains subject solely to judicial decision. (2) The courts should enforce express contracts between nonmarital partners except to the extent that the contract is explicitly founded on the consideration of meretricious sexual services. (3) In the absence of an express contract, the courts should inquire into the conduct of the parties to determine whether that conduct demonstrates an implied contract, agreement of partnership or joint venture, or some other tacit understanding between the parties. The courts may also employ the doctrine of quantum meruit, or equitable remedies such as constructive or resulting trusts, when warranted by the facts of the case.*"

Yes, this is about as easy to understand as Sanskrit. But if we look at their conclusion, part by part, perhaps we can decipher what the Court is getting at. Hang in there — this is important.

1. Unmarried Couples Are Not Covered By Rules That Affect The Married

The first part of this decision is a recognition of a legal conflict which has arisen over the past 15 years due to the substantial increase in the number of couples living together without marrying. The legal controversy occurred when one partner died or the couple separated and a court had to decide how the property acquired during the relationship was to be divided. Some courts said that when a nonmarital relationship looked enough like a married one, the Family Law Act of California required an equal division of the property according to community property principles. That is, if the unmarried couple used the same last name and acted as if they were married, they would be treated as if they were by the courts. The part of the *Marvin* decision marked (1) expressly rejects this interpretation. The California Supreme Court is saying that you are either married or you are not, and that it is not up to the courts to pretend you are if in fact you have not met the marriage requirements. However, as we shall see, even though the Court does not allow unmarried couples an equal division of property under the community property laws, the same result (an equal division of the accumulated property) can be reached under the *Marvin* decision using other theories.

---

* In another part of the decision the California Supreme Court specifically stated that they were not deciding the question of whether a party to a non-marital relationship is entitled to support payments and that this question would be decided in a future case. However, to add confusion to an already mixed-up set of circumstances, Michelle's award of $104,000 in the subsequent trial court decision for "rehabilitation purposes" sounds an awful lot like a lump-sum alimony payment. See section D below.

2. Unmarried Couples May Contract

The part of the decision marked (2) states simply that unmarried couples may make "express" contracts between themselves concerning their property. Express contracts can be written or oral, but they do require the direct words of the parties and are different from contracts implied from the circumstances of the relationship which we discuss in the next section. Elsewhere in their opinion the justices indulge in a brief historical discussion of previous decisions concerning contracts and the "meretricious couple" (that wonderfully legal term describing people who shack up). In the past, the California Supreme Court had invalidated many contracts because of the "immoral" character of the relationship. Instead of admitting directly that its previous decisions didn't make much sense, the Court stated that they "hovered over the issue in the somewhat wispy form of the figures of a Chagall painting". They then proceeded to reverse old cases and state the following simple rule:

"The fact that a man and woman live together without marriage, and engage in a sexual relationship, does not in itself invalidate agreements between them relating to their earnings, property, or expenses. Neither is such an agreement invalid merely because the parties may have contemplated the creation and continuation of a nonmarital relationship when they entered into it. Agreements between nonmarital partners fail only to the extent that they rest upon a consideration of meretricious sexual services.*...Adults who voluntarily live together and engage in sexual relations are nonetheless as competent as any other persons to contract respecting their earnings and property rights...They may agree to pool their earnings and to hold all property acquired during the relationship in accord with the law governing community property; conversely, they may agree that each partner's earnings and the property acquired from those earnings remain the separate property of the earning partner (a great variety of other arrangements are possible, see Chapter 4). So long as the agreement does not rest upon illicit meretricious consideration, the parties may order their economic affairs as they choose and no policy precludes the courts from enforcing such agreements."

3. A Court May Imply A Contract From The Circumstances Of A Living Arrangement

And so we come to the third and final part of the decision which is marked, appropriately enough, (3). It is here where, if laws can be likened to worms, the Court has opened up a very large can indeed. The Court says, in effect, that even if a written or spoken contract doesn't exist, judges can still poke around into the facts and circumstances of a couple's relationship to decide whether or not an implied contract or partnership agreement existed. And even if the judge can't find an implied agreement, he or she may still decide to employ one of those formidable sounding doctrines known as "quantum meruit" or "constructive or resulting trusts" in order to avoid the "unjust enrichment" of one of the partners.

What do these exotic sounding remedies mean? Unfortunately, there are no simple answers because their definitions have been cannily crafted over centuries by the convoluted intellects of lawyers. However, a brief description of the elements involved may help make these muddy waters a trifle clearer.

NOTE OF SANITY: As you read through these cumbersome explanations you may feel yourself beginning to lose track of where one worm ends and another begins. If so, keep in mind that there is no need to have a detailed understanding of any of this legal gobbledygook if you have the foresight to write out your agreement. An express written property agreement is the first thing a court will recognize. Only in its absence will a judge start to sift through the worms (sample contracts are set out in Chapter 4).

---

* This means that if you put in your contract that it is based on one or both persons performing one or another sexual acts the contract is invalid. As you can see the Court is liberated, but not that liberated.

a) Implied Agreements

As we noted above, a contract that has not been spoken out or written down can sometimes be inferred from the actions of the parties. The possible subject matter of implied contracts can be as broad as that covered by written or spoken agreements. Co-ownership, partnerships or trusts are all possible. For example, agreements to compensate for domestic services may be inferred from one party's request that another perform the services. A judge will look at how a couple has arranged their economic affairs to see if their intentions and expectations add up to a contract. At this point there are no cases setting out what things a judge will or will not take into consideration, but it is safe to say that the individual judge will have considerable discretion in making a decision and that his or her personal feelings and prejudices will play a part.

EXAMPLE: Ben asks Sara to live with him. Sara is working and Ben has a full-time job. Ben asks Sara to do a majority of the work in the home. She does so for the five years that they live together. Absent any written or oral contract, a court might well imply that one existed in this situation and find that Sara had the right to an economic return for her labors.

b) Implied Partnerships

When the *Marvin* Court suggest the possibility of finding an implied partnership or joint venture, they refer to a Washington State Supreme Court decision, *Estate of Thornton*, 499 P. 21 865 (1974). Here the Washington Court upheld the right of a woman to claim an implied partnership on the basis of the couple having lived together for sixteen years while the woman shared equally in the running of two farms held in the man's name and in the enhancement of the couple's economic status. Their situation could be likened to that of a business enterprise where capital was provided by one partner with the other acquiring her interest by providing services.

c) Resulting Trusts

A resulting trust is a device that courts use for the most part when real property is held in the name of one person only, but in fairness (equity) and by the intent of the unmarried couple, the other should have a share. Before *Marvin* there was a legal presumption in California and in many other states, that when people were "living in sin" and one was working and the other was taking care of the house, the value of domestic services could not be used as the basis for a resulting trust. *Marvin* changed this rule. Now, the economic value of the homemaker is recognized and the resulting trust theory may provide relief where one party has contributed the domestic services while the other party pursued outside employment and acquired assets and earnings. If it is possible to conclude as a matter of circumstantial evidence that property was intended by the parties to be held by one of them for the benefit of both, a resulting trust is established. There are two very limiting requirements to the establishment of this kind of trust. First, proof of intent must be clear and convincing and second, the valuable contributions of the person asserting the trust must have been used in the purchase price of the property. In this legal area Texas has been more liberated than California. Almost 70 years ago a Texas court approved such a trust in a living together situation. The Court said that if a woman could show that the money with which a piece of land was purchased was acquired in whole or in part by her labor before the time when the land was purchased, then she should be entitled to a share in the land in the proportion that her labor contributed in producing the purchase money.

d) Quantum Meruit — Unjust Enrichment

First we talked about written and oral contracts and then about implied agreements based on a court being able to guess at the couple's intentions through their conduct. Now we go one step further. The *Marvin* Court stated that, even where conduct doesn't imply an intention to contract or compensate, the law may impose a remedy where one person has greatly benefited at the expense of another. For example, a person who accepts the benefits of housekeeping without paying for them could be deemed to be unjustly enriched even if that person never asked that the services be performed. According to *Marvin*, the person who provides these homemaking services, if he or she has an expectation of monetary reward, may recover under the legal theory of "quantum meruit" for "the reasonable value of household services rendered less the reasonable value of support received".

EXAMPLE: Sara moves in with Ben. Ben goes off to work every day and Sara stays home. Gradually Sara falls into the habit of doing all the cleaning, cooking and shopping. Although Ben never asks her to do so, he is delighted to take advantage of her services and tells his friends that "I am lucky to live with such a great little homemaker". Although Sara has never asked to be paid for her work, she feels that in some way she is an economic partner in their living together arrangement.

e) Constructive Trusts

As with "quantum meruit", "constructive trusts" do not depend on the couple's intention to contract. Using this theory a judge can look at the entire relationship in light of all the circumstances and impose a trust to force one person to restore money or property to the other if the first person, in fairness and good conscience, ended up with something that belongs to the other. Contributions of valuable assets and contributions of valuable services can both be taken into account to determine the relative interests of a man and woman who acquire and enhance financial resources during their life together.

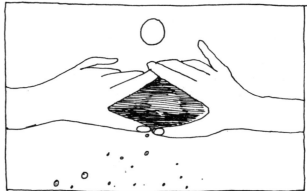

42

C. PROOF REQUIRED BY THE MARVIN CASE

It is probably apparent to you, if anything is apparent at this point, that the problem with all of these remedies is proof. Not surprisingly, proving a legal claim or theory is always more difficult than alleging it. To make matters worse, most of the relevant proof required in a dispute between unmarried couples has to do with what one or the other person "intended" months or years ago. Where intentions have to be proven, most of the actual evidence will probably be subjective and conflicting. A good case in point involves the *Thornton* case which we mentioned above. After upholding the woman's legal right to claim an implied partnership, the Supreme Court of Washington sent the case back to the trial court to decide whether she could prove her case. Given conflicting evidence, the trial judge decided that she had failed to establish the existence of a partnership, a joint venture or a constructive or resulting trust. Instead, the judge (a man) found her to be a "managerial employee" of Mr. Thornton and refused to give her a half interest in the remaining property.

Proving domestic services will surely be a tricky business especially when there is conflicting evidence of who did what and in what proportion. In addition, the value of **support** provided is certain to be difficult to figure out since it will involve the quality of such things as food, clothing and entertainment. The proof is in the pudding so to speak and given the nature and consistency of the ingredients, one who is dependent upon this kind of remedy is liable to end up with little but a slightly unsavory aroma.

LET US SAY IT AGAIN: All of these old contract doctrines that the *Marvin* Court has dragged out of some law school attic can be safely left to gather cobwebs if you take a little time to read the following chapters and devise your own written agreement.

D. THE PRACTICAL CONSEQUENCES OF MARVIN

When the Supreme Court of California made its ruling in 1976 upholding Michelle's right to sue on a contract, the case was sent back to the trial court to decide whether or not a contract in fact existed. After a lengthy and sensational trial during which every aspect of the Marvin's relationship was gobbled up and spewed out by the ever-hungry media, the trial judge finally issued his decision. Who won? Each side claimed victory. The judge found that there was no contract, either oral or implied so Lee was happy. Michelle received an award of $104,000 based on the equitable remedies available to the judge for "rehabilitation purposes" to ease her re-entry into the labor market — so she at least claimed that she was happy even though the award was far less than she requested. But what should be stressed about this trial decision is that it is just one decision on one set of circumstances (and the Marvin's circumstances were far from your common garden variety living together situation). The decision that is important is the California Supreme Court decision made back in 1976 which recognized the unmarried couple's right to contract with each other. The practical consequences of this decision are just now being felt.

Unfortunately, the original Supreme Court *Marvin* case is a rickety framework for regulating the property rights of people living together. We believe that it is a confusing decision that is likely to create more problems than it solves. After properly recognizing that living together is a blossoming social phenomenon of our times and that it encompasses people from all walks of life with a wide assortment of reasons and needs for their decisions to live together, the Court has fashioned guidelines that are more than a trifle on the vague and misty side. Perhaps the Court set itself an impossible task. Unmarried couples include people who wish to avoid the permanent commitment of traditional marriage, people who can't afford to dissolve a former marriage, people who view living together as a preparation for marriage, those who see it as an alternative to marriage as well as those who, under a mistaken belief that common law marriage exists, believe themselves actually married. Only the broadest sort of rules could cover such a diverse group. Unfortunately, overbroad rules don't meet anyone's specific, personal needs and tend to confuse everything.

Right now we can't tell you what the *Marvin* case really means. The big question mark floating around in everyone's minds is — just what conduct, circumstances, or factors will be regarded as having created an implied agreement to share mutually acquired property? Tacit agreements can be implied or inferred from a multitude of facts. When two people live together they engage in numerous cooperative acts — which ones will indicate the intent to "apportion fairly"? And if an implied agreement isn't found, what factors should be considered in the fashioning of an equitable property settlement? What weight should be given to the length of the relationship, existence of children, etc.? In a California trial court decision that did not receive national attention, a woman was awarded half the value of a condominium which had been accumulated during a three-year living together relationship. The judge ruled that an "implied contract" existed between the couple when the condominium was purchased to share it equally even though title was taken in the man's name only. In two different New York decisions, two different trial courts went in opposite directions when faced with two different *Marvin*-type cases. The first involved a situation which closely resembled a traditional marriage. The couple had lived together for 28 years and held themselves out as man and wife and raised three children. The court adopted the *Marvin* rationale in deciding that the couple's conduct evinced an implied contract to share their assets. The second case involved rock star Peter Frampton being sued by the woman he had lived with for six years based on an oral agreement to share. The judge in this case dismissed the suit ruling that an oral agreement was insufficient and any agreement to share property must be made in writing. This New York *Marvin* dilemma will obviously have to be resolved in the future by the appellate courts.

Remember, the California Supreme Court rejected prior legal reasoning which divided the property equally between the parties when a relationship closely resembled that of a traditional marriage. Under *Marvin* it is not necessary to look like a traditional family for a court to hold that the earnings and accumulations of both people belong totally, or in part, to both. But what is necessary? On one side of the spectrum there are the kinds of relationships that look and smell like marriages but aren't. The unmarried couple who behaves no differently than the married couple. They have children, hold joint credit cards, bank accounts, file joint returns, and generally conduct their business as husband and wife. In their relations with each other they conform to the traditional roles, one bringing home the paycheck and the other taking care of the house and kids. Given facts like these, courts using the *Marvin* standard of trying to fulfill the expectations of the unmarried couple would probably find an implied agreement to mutually share accumulations. But what about situations where the conduct of the parties is not so clear? Let's take a look at two different examples of living together situations and make a guess at what the outcome under *Marvin* would be.

EXAMPLE:* Carol and Bill decide while in college to live together. Bill goes on to medical school and though she intended to go to veterinary school, Carol postpones her education, drops out of school and goes to work to support the two of them until Bill graduates from medical school. After six years of living together, just when Carol is free to enroll in vet school, Bill moves out and decides he wants to marry Evelyn. Carol is left with all the property they accumulated during their relationship (a leaky waterbed and a 15-year old T.V.). What are Carol's rights under *Marvin*? Beginning with the assumption that they intended to deal fairly with each other, at least at the start of their relationship, what can we deduce from Carol and Bill's conduct? One reasonable interpretation might be that Carol expected, that since she had put Bill through med school, he would pay her expenses while she went to vet school. If there had been an "express" agreement (written or oral) to that effect, it would certainly be enforced. If no express agreement existed, or if Bill denied that an oral agreement was ever spoken, it is not certain whether a court would imply such an agreement, although we feel that Carol has a pretty strong case. What do you think? Another approach that Carol might take would be to characterize Bill's medical education as the only asset produced by the efforts of both of them during their cohabitation. Carol could argue that her investment in Bill's future earning capacity ought to be recognized under a theory of "unjust enrichment" or "constructive trust".

EXAMPLE: Cathy is divorced with two children and owns her own clothing boutique. John, also divorced, works as an accountant for a large firm. He pays alimony and child support to his prior family. Having both been burned, Cathy and John decide that marriage is not for them. They live together in a house they acquired in joint tenancy. They maintain separate bank and credit accounts and contribute to the mortgage and monthly living expenses in proportion to their incomes. Cathy makes about twice as much as John. After living together for eight years, Cathy decides to move her business to Paris. John wants to stay in California. Cathy is willing to let John buy her share in the house, but contends that the cost ought to reflect the 2 to 1 ratio of her contributions to the purchase price, not just half of the present value of the home. Neither claims any interest in the property the other accumulated during their relationship. Cathy and John are on the opposite end of the spectrum from the tradi-

---

* These examples are drawn from the article by Kay and Amyx, supra.

tional marriage type of relationship. They have been careful to keep their assets separate and to remain financially independent. Their attitude is typical of that which exists among many people who have been married before and who are self-supporting. If one of them changed his or her mind and asked (without an express agreement) for a share of the other's property, a court would examine their overall conduct and almost certainly conclude that they had a separate property agreement regarding their accumulations.

In fact, Cathy and John simply have a dispute involving the house which was the only property that they acquired jointly by pooling their assets. Since they took title to the house in joint tenancy rather than as tenants in common (see Chapter 6 for a discussion of joint tenancy, tenancy in common and how to make a contract to own a house in unequal shares and avoid this problem), the court would probably interpret this as an express agreement that each party was to have an **equal** interest in the house.

These are only two of the almost numberless variations of living together situations that will probably appear in the courts soon. Given the vagueness of the guidelines set down in the *Marvin* decision, it is hard to predict the exact outcome in most situations. Two factors that will probably be examined closely are choice and dependency. Did the couple expressly reject the institution of marriage on principle? If so, a judge may find a tacit understanding that they consider their property separate. Is one partner dependent on the other for support at the same time that he or she is rendering uncompensated services? The *Marvin* case found it to be an "unfair" situation where the homemaker partner is left with nothing at the end of the relationship while the income producing partner keeps the property acquired in his name during the relationship; hence the recognition of the economic value of services in the home. In many traditional relationships, a court that implies an expectation of reward for taking care of the home and family by the dependent partner will be accurate in its determination of the couple's understanding. However, many women reject traditional marriage precisely because it limits their freedom and independence and they don't want to be cast in what they consider to be old-fashioned sexist roles. Women with this view may not assert any property claims at the end of a relationship. However, if they do, courts will probably not be generous. It is hard to see how a "liberated woman" who deliberately rejects the "barefoot, pregnant and in the kitchen" image can turn around and portray herself as a dependent partner who is entitled to a share of the man's accumulated property.

The one thing that all this ambiguity means for certain is more work for lawyers. This is not surprising since the judges making the decision are all trained as lawyers and believe that law and lawyers are equipped to solve disputes between unmarried couples. As the massive failure and organized legal corruption in the divorce area clearly show, this isn't true. Somehow the California Supreme Court doesn't seem to have gotten the message that in many cases people are living together precisely in order to escape lawyers. Pardon us if we believe that personal disputes can only be solved well by the people involved and that domestic disputes of all kinds should be removed from the adversary court system. We need conciliators and mediators and

forums where former lovers can meet in an atmosphere conducive to compromise and accomodation. We do not need more lawyers. In the meantime, the best thing you can do is to carefully read the rest of this book with special emphasis on Chapters 4 and 6 and write out your own living together agreement.

Jotting down your expectations at the beginning of your relationship is the one clear way to avoid paranoia. Writing a contract may turn out not to be as bad as you think and it is certainly better than having the courts write one for you.

The seeds of doubt that the *Marvin* case have sown in the realm of the unmarried couple has prompted not only California legislators but state legislators across the nation to respond by introducing various bills that would limit the potential impact of *Marvin* and would set guidelines for when and how it should be applied. One such bill would, if enacted, create the presumption that property and earnings of an unmarried couple remain separate unless acquired jointly or under some sort of formal agreement. At the rate we are going people may have to go to law school before they can safely live together.

ontracts

The wonderful thing about contracts is that they can mean as much, or as little, as you want them to. They can cover things as small as a teapot, or as large as a lifestyle. Unlike a legislative act that applies to everyone but fits no one perfectly, contracts belong to you and you may construct them to fit your needs. Legally a contract is no more than a promise (or promises) to do something in exchange for someone else's promise (or promises) to do something in return. Pretty simple. And there is no need to become intimidated by visions of fine print clauses and incomprehensible jargon. These have to do with lawyers and their love for mumbo jumbo and obfuscation, not with contracts themselves.

One reason for a lot of people's general apprehension when it comes to contracts results from the fact that their prior experiences have occurred in situations where they are powerless — insurance contracts, bank loans, major installment purchases, leases, etc. You want or need what the seller is offering and have to accept the one-sided contract that goes with it. Who ever heard of anyone calling up Henry Ford and getting him to add a few months to the warranty? Fortunately, living together contracts need not be written like these standard form monsters. You are free to design the contract to say exactly what you want in words that you can understand. With a little care and attention you should be able to design it to fit like a glove, not a handcuff.

Lawyers notwithstanding, there is nothing illegal about writing a contract in simple English. The simpler it is, the easier it is to understand. For example, you know your friend's name so why not use it instead of calling him the "party of the second part"? When your contract is done, you want to be able to understand it — not have the meaning escape somewhere between the second "wherefore" and the third "pursuant".

STEP 1 — MAKE YOUR AGREEMENT

Writing your understanding down is basic, but there is something that is even more basic — arriving at a good personal understanding as to what you want to do. When people get married, they automatically receive a contract as to their property — rules and regulations set down by state legislatures and courts in legal codebooks and judicial decisions. People who live together are provided with no prepared-in-advance understanding. They are free to create their own rules and regulations by contract. With the *Marvin* decision and the increasing readiness of courts in every part of the nation to recognize the property rights and obligations of unmarried couples, it is almost essential that people living together have a written understanding of their economic relationship with one another.

We have no magic advice about how to reach an understanding. This is up to you. As two people who live and work together, we arrive at ours more from the flow of what's happening than from a structured business meeting or encounter group approach. But we don't set ourselves up as models for anything. We are as capable of arriving at misunderstandings as the next person. We do suggest, however, that before you try to tie all the details of your agreement down on paper that you carefully read the rest of this book to make sure you understand the basic rules. Oh, and one more thing — don't put off making your contract until you have a fight — the best time to agree is when you are feeling so mellow that no agreement seems necessary.

STEP 2 — PUT IT IN WRITING

This is the most important part of this book. If you write your understandings down, all of the complicated remedies described in the discussion of the *Marvin* case in Chapter 3 can be avoided.* If you have a written understanding you are extremely unlikely to ever end up fighting in a courtroom. And if you do, the judge will be interested only in interpreting your written agreement. A court won't normally start inferring and presuming unless you have no written agreement.

From a down to earth, practical perspective, almost nothing gets resolved in court. Those of you who have been through a divorce already know this — those of you who haven't are lucky. Any money or property that exists at the start of a court dispute almost always gets consumed by the lawyers. And then there is the time, emotional pain and bitterness that are so much a part of our adversary domestic relations court process. Have we convinced you? Do you have your pen and paper out? With a written agreement as to who owns what and how property is to be divided if you separate, all of this can be avoided.

NOTE: The agreements that follow are mostly written assuming heterosexual couples. The great majority of this material (except that dealing with having children) also applies to gay couples. Gays should read Chapter 12 carefully before proceeding and then adapt the sample contracts printed here to their needs.

---

* No one has put it better than the French legal scholar Beaumanoir in his *Coutumes de Beauvaisis*, written in the year 1283. "For the memory of men slips and flows away, and the life of man is short, and that which is not written is soon forgotten."

STEP 3 — DESIGN YOUR CONTRACT

Perhaps this step should come before the previous one. Certainly before you write something down, you must know how to do it.

There is a wide variety of economic arrangements that can be made by people living together. This freedom and flexibility to order your life in the way you want, free from the traditional institutional rules of marriage, is one of the reasons why living together has become so popular. You can create your agreements to reflect this freedom by carefully designing them to meet your circumstances. Property agreements can be simple or complex, two sentences or twenty pages. Many people live together precisely because they don't want to share their property, while others operate on the assumption that what belongs to one belongs to both. A couple may agree to keep their earnings separate, but compensate one person for services of benefit to the other. They may choose to pool a part, but not all, of their earnings, or form a partnership, or hold property as "joint tenants", or agree to any one of countless other plans. Living together contracts can also include everything that is relevant to the living together arrangement including division of housework, whether or not to have children, the name to be used, property division at separation, and even who takes the dog out for its nightly stroll. However, contracts are normally only enforceable in a legal sense to the extent that they refer to personal property and real property. Provisions relating to children will only be enforced by a court if the court, in its independent judgment, believes that the contract terms are in the best interests of the children (see Chapters 8 and 9). Contract provisions having to do with the personal conduct of the couple are not enforceable. Courts will simply not tell you or your friend to put the cap back on the toothpaste or not to piss on the toilet seat.

REAL PROPERTY NOTE: We discuss buying houses and other real property in Chapter 6. Real property has its own specialized rules and is usually, but not always, handled in a separate agreement. Several sample agreements are set out in Chapter 6.

MARRIED PERSONS NOTE: We have gotten many inquiries from people who are still married but in a living together situation with someone else as to the legality of any living together contract they enter into. In most states there exists a legal provision whereby the property accumulated after a married couple *separates* (a divorce decree is not the crucial point) becomes the separate property of the spouse that acquires it. Therefore, a living together contract would be perfectly valid as to any property accumulated with a living together partner even though one or both partners are still married to someone else. This is almost sure to be true in the states which have made all conduct of consenting adults legal (see Chapter 1). It is possible that there could still be some problem in states that still outlaw adultery.

A. FILL-IN LIVING TOGETHER CONTRACTS

In the Appendix at the back of this book we have included two fill-in, tear-out contracts. One is designed to keep property separate, the other to pool and share it. Read these carefully but don't make any choices until you have read the other alternative contracts in this chapter and the rest of this book with special emphasis on Chapters 2 and 6. The two contracts in the Appendix are fairly thorough and cover most areas of concern to the average unmarried couple. Assuming that one of these reflects many of your concerns, choose it as your basic draft. You are likely to find that you will want to make some additions or deletions based on your circumstances. Fine — here is how to do it.

❷ Deletions

Deletions can be handled by simply crossing out and initialing the offending provisions. If you make a number of changes it will be neater to re-type the whole contract. Simply use regular 8 1/2" x 11" typing paper.

Additions

Additions are a bit more complicated — you have to write or type out the new provision and add it to the contract. We have left a space before the signatures for you to do this. If you decide not to use this space, it would be wise to cross it out with a large X. When you read through the other examples of living together contracts in this chapter you may find provisions that you would like to add to the basic contract, or perhaps substitute for an existing provision. Go right ahead. Remember, your goal is to create a contract that feels comfortable and right to you.

If your substitutions, deletions and additions begin to eat up the original, you may want to have your finished product checked by an attorney. This is a particularly good idea if you have a lot of money or property. But be careful when dealing with attorneys — many charge outrageous prices and have little experience with the problems encountered by unmarried couples. Do some investigating before you make an appointment and be sure to get the fee set in advance. Remember, you have already done most of the work and you are only asking a lawyer to check it. A fee of $35-$50 should be adequate for this service (see Chapter 13).

Signing The Contract

In the Appendix we have provided one copy of each contract. When you have decided which one you are going to use, or have designed your own, xerox your final draft. Both of you should then sign and date both copies of the contract. Notarization is optional unless your contract involves real property and you need to have it recorded at the County Recorder's office. Failure to notarize doesn't make your contract any less legal, but notarization does serve to prove that your signatures are legitimate and not forged in the unlikely event that anyone might question their validity.

Relax

One last word. Many people find that filling out or creating a contract like this forces them to deal with the very guts ot their relationship. This is surely a healthy thing to do, but it can also at times be trying. Take your time and don't expect to do the whole job in an evening. Remember too that a good contract normally involves a spirit of compromise and accomodation. If you both feel that you have given up a little more than you received you are probably on the right track. Preparing your contract should be an affirmative act, but it's up to you to make it so. If you get too bogged down in trading this for that and start wondering why you are dealing with all of this legal bullshit, try writing each other a poem.

B. SHORTFORM PROPERTY CONTRACTS

For those of you who do not feel the need to be as thorough as the agreements in the Appendix contemplate, we have designed simple, one-page statements to the same effect. The rest of this chapter contains contracts designed to fit a variety of lifestyles and circumstances. Read them carefully. You may find something that will work for you.* Let's start with a shortform agreement designed to keep all property separate followed by one which puts it all together.

SAMPLE AGREEMENT (SEPARATE)

Keija Adams and Felix Finnegan agree as follows:

1) That they have been living together and plan to do so indefinitely;

2) That Keija and Felix will share their love and good energy, but they agree that the income of each, and any accumulations of property traceable to that income, belong absolutely to the person who earns the money. Any joint purchases shall be made under the terms of paragraph 6 below;

3) That in the event of separation neither Felix nor Keija has a claim upon the other for any money or property for any reason unless there is a subsequent written agreement to the contrary under paragraph 6;

4) That Felix and Keija shall each use his/her own name and will maintain his/her own bank accounts, credit accounts, etc.;

5) That the monthly expenses for rent, food, household utilities and upkeep and joint recreation shall be shared equally;

6) That if, in the future, any joint purchases are made (such as a house, car, boat, etc.) the joint ownership of each specific item will be reflected on the title slip to the property, or by use of a separate written agreement which shall be signed and dated. Joint agreements to purchase or own property shall only cover the property specifically set out in the agreement and shall in no way create an implication that other property is jointly owned.

7) That this agreement replaces any and all prior agreements whether written or oral and can only be added to or changed by a subsequent written agreement.

_____	_____
Date	Keija Adams
_____	_____
Date	Felix Finnegan

---

* For another good source of alternative living together contracts, see Weitzman, Lenore, *Legal Regulation of Marriage — Tradition and Change*, Vol. 62 Calif. Law Review, p. 1169.

SAMPLE AGREEMENT (TOGETHER)

Phillip Mendocino and Ruth Alameda agree as follows:

1) That they plan to live together commencing March 1, 19   and to continue to live together indefinitely;

2) That all property earned or accumulated prior to Phillip and Ruth getting together belongs absolutely to the person earning or accumulating it;

3) That while they are living together all income earned by either Phillip or Ruth and all property accumulated with the earnings of either person whether real or personal, belong in equal shares to both and that should they separate, all accumulated property shall be divided equally;

4) Should either Phillip or Ruth inherit or be given property, it belongs absolutely to the person receiving the inheritance or gift;

5) That should Ruth and Phillip separate, neither has any claim for money or property except as set out in paragraph 3.

_____
Date

_____
Phillip Mendocino

_____
Date

_____
Ruth Alameda

C. AGREEMENTS COVERING JOINTLY ACQUIRED ITEMS

Most people who have consulted us or who have attended our lectures or workshops want to adopt a basic keeping-things-separate approach. Often, however, there will be a major item, or several major items, that they want to own together. As you will see from reading either the contract in the Appendix or the short form contract, we have provided a structure for you to do this. Here is a sample agreement covering a specific item that you can modify to fit your needs.

AGREEMENT COVERING A JOINT PURCHASE

Cerena Takahashi and Sam Armistead agree as follows:

1) That they will jointly acquire and own a stereo system valued at $900;

2) That should they separate and both want the stereo, they will agree on a fair price and then flip a coin, with the winner keeping the stereo after paying the loser the agreed-upon price;

3) If on separation neither person wants the stereo or if they can't agree on a fair price, it shall be sold to the highest bidder and the money equally divided.

Date _____	Cerena Takahashi _____
Date _____	Sam Armistead _____

56

Sometimes only one of you will legally make a joint purchase. This can occur because only one of you has good credit or for some other reason. Even though only one name is on the contract with the seller, you may wish to own the property together. Here is a sample agreement to accomplish this:

AGREEMENT

Joseph Benner and Josephine Clark hereby agree that:

1) Joseph has entered into an agreement with Sears, Roebuck and Company to purchase a bedroom set consisting of one king-size bed, one double dresser, two nightstands, and two lamps at a total cost of $900, and

2) Joseph has agreed to pay to Sears said sum in monthly installments of $90 for ten months, due on the first of every month beginning January 1, 19   , and

3) It is the intention of Joseph and Josephine that this bedroom furniture shall be owned equally by both and that both shall pay one-half the cost, and

4) Each shall make one-half the payments on the furniture. Each payment shall be made directly to Sears, on or before the date the payment is due, and

5) Should one person fail to make his or her payment, the other shall have the right to make the payment and the amount of the payment shall be added to the share in the furniture of the person who makes it, and

6) Each shall keep a record of all payments made. All payments shall be made by check or money order, and

7) Upon the death of either, the interest of the deceased in the furniture shall immediately belong to the person surviving. That person shall pay all monies, if any, due and owing on the furniture. If either Joseph or Josephine should make a will, this provision will be incorporated in said will, and

8) If Joseph and Josephine should stop living together, either person may buy the interest of the other in the furniture at a sum agreed upon, taking into consideration the money, if any, still owing on the furniture, and

9) If Joseph or Josephine cannot agree as provided in paragraph 8, the furniture shall be sold. Upon the sale each shall be entitled to one-half the net proceeds realized from the sale unless payments have been made under paragraph 2 of this agreement, in which case each shall be entitled to that percentage of the net proceeds which corresponds to the percentage of the payments he or she has made of the total payments.

Date	Joseph Benner
Date	Josephine Clark

NOTE: If one of you signs a credit agreement to purchase an item, only that person is legally obligated to pay the creditor. This is true even if you and your friend sign an agreement among yourselves to share ownership and payments. Of course, the creditor will take the payments from anyone and properly credit your account, but if a payment is not made, he will go after the person (or persons) whose name is on the account (see Chapter 2).

D. AGREEMENTS COVERING JOINT PROJECTS

John and Marsha live together. They have no property to speak of, but they have a dream. They want to build their own boat and sail around the world. They foresee that it will take a lot of time, energy and cooperation and they want to protect their vision should any of life's disappointments affect their relationship.

AGREEMENT

John and Marsha agree as follows:

1) That both desire to construct a 30-foot sailboat following plans to be jointly agreed upon, to be jointly owned upon completion.

2) That each will contribute $5,000 for the purchase of necessary supplies.

3) That each person will work diligently on the boat (this means at least 20 hours per month).

4) Should they separate, Marsha shall have the opportunity to buy out John's share for an amount of money equal to John's actual cash investment plus $7 per hour for each hour he has worked on the boat.

5) At separation, should Marsha decide not to buy John's share under the terms of the previous paragraph, John shall have the opportunity to buy her share on the same terms.

6) Should neither John nor Marsha elect to purchase the other's share of the boat at separation, the boat shall be sold and the proceeds divided equally between the two parties.

7) If either fails to put in 20 hours of work per month for three consecutive months on the boat, the other may buy out his (her) share under the terms set down in paragraph 4.

8) Should either John or Marsha die, the other becomes sole owner of the boat. If either John or Marsha makes a will, this provision will be incorporated in said will.

_____	_____
Date	John Mason
_____	_____
Date	Marsha Deere

E. AGREEMENTS COVERING HOMEMAKER SERVICES

Ted is 45 and divorced with custody of his two children. He is a lawyer with an annual income in excess of $40,000. Joanne is 38 and also divorced with custody of her child. Her ex-husband consistently refuses to meet his support obligations. Ted and Joanne decide to live together and agree that Ted will earn the money and that Joanne will take care of the three children and of the household on a full-time basis. They are interested in a contract that will protect both of them, providing Joanne with fair compensation for her housework and childcare, but not giving her any rights to Ted's property should they separate.

AGREEMENT

Ted Corbett and Joanne Lewis agree that:

1) Ted shall continue to work as a lawyer with the expectation that he will work a 40-50 hour week and shall have little time or energy to devote to taking care of the home;

2) Joanne will work in the home supervising the children and taking care of all domestic chores including cleaning, laundry, cooking and gardening. Ted will pay Joanne $125 a week for her services over and above the costs of running the home which are set out in paragraph 5. These payments shall be adjusted from time to time to reflect changes in the cost of living;

3) Ted will make Social Security payments for Joanne as his employee and will pay for complete medical coverage for her and her son, Tim;

4) All property shall be owned by the person earning or accumulating it. The house and its furnishings will be provided by Ted and will be owned solely by him. All property purchased by Joanne with her earnings belongs to her;

5) Ted will provide reasonable amounts of money each month to provide food, clothing, shelter and recreation for the entire family as long as they live together. By doing this Ted assumes absolutely no obligation to support Joanne or her child upon termination of this agreement (see paragraph 7);

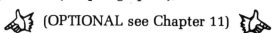 (OPTIONAL see Chapter 11)

6) Ted and Joanne each agree to assume full responsibility for the other's children in the event the other dies during the time this agreement is in effect. Ted agrees to make provisions for Joanne and the children in his will;

7) Either Ted or Joanne can end this agreement by giving the other two months' written notice. Joanne will be entitled to severance pay at the rate of two months for every year the agreement has been in effect. This money shall be paid in a lump sum at the time of separation. Neither Ted nor Joanne shall have any financial obligation to the other upon separation.

Date	Ted Corbett

Date	Joanne Lewis

F. AGREEMENTS COVERING HOUSEHOLD EXPENSES AND PERSONAL IDIOSYNCRASIES

Annie and Clem have been seeing each other for over two years before they decide to live together. Annie is a fashion model and Clem is a private detective. They both have adequate incomes and decide to keep their earnings and property separate.

AGREEMENT

Annie Auburn and Clem Black agree as follows:

1) That they plan to live together for the indefinite future;

2) Each will use his or her own name;

3) Neither will use the credit of the other and both will maintain separate bank and credit accounts;

4) The earnings and other assets of each shall be kept separate and each shall keep absolute ownership of his or her property and shall be responsible for his or her own personal expenses including clothing, medical and dental bills, long distance telephone calls, entertainment, car, cleaning, laundry, etc. If Clem and Annie acquire any property jointly, they shall make a separate agreement to cover this property and what happens to it if they separate. However, the financial obligations relating to the management of the joint household, which include rent, utilities, food and cleaning supplies, shall be payable using a "joint funds" system which shall work as follows:

Each year on January 1, Clem and Annie will tell one another the amount of their current annual income after taxes (minus any alimony or child support paid for prior family obligations). The two income figures shall then be added together and a ratio arrived at by dividing the total into Annie's net income and then dividing the total into Clem's net income. Household expenses shall be paid according to this ratio. (For example, if Annie clears $15,000 and Clem $10,000 — they would add these figures together and get $25,000. Then they would divide $25,000 into $15,000 and $10,000 respectively. The result ot these equations is that Annie earned 60% of the total combined income and Clem 40% and the household expenses would be divided accordingly.)

5) Each shall be responsible for domestic tasks. However, certain daily tasks will be assigned based on the following realities: Annie has no sense for food and cooking while Clem is not too neat and does not require as high a standard of order and cleanliness as does Annie.

a) Clem will do food shopping and cooking and will take care of all the plants.

b) Annie will wash dishes and do the cleaning including general straightening, sweeping, dusting and keeping the bathroom in order.

6) Neither Clem nor Annie wants children at this point in their lives. Since the most effective mutually acceptable birth control methods on the market today are female contraceptives, Annie will take responsibility for birth control. However, if in the future a safe and effective oral male contraceptive becomes available, Clem agrees to use it.*

7) In the event that Annie gets pregnant, she will get an abortion which will be paid for jointly.*

8) Clem and Annie agree that each shall make a valid will, revocable upon the ending of this agreement, providing that all of their property will pass to the other in the event of death (see Chapter 11).

9) Either Clem or Annie can terminate this agreement by giving the other a 30-day written notice. Upon separation, each shall take his or her separate property and any jointly held property will be divided according to the separate written joint ownership agreements.

10) Neither Clem nor Annie will have any financial or other responsibility to the other after separation and division of the property.

_____	_____
Date	Annie Auburn
_____	_____
Date	Clem Black

* Agreements to have or not to have children are only expressions of intention and are not legally enforceable. See Chapter 8.

G. AGREEMENT DESIGNED FOR STRUGGLING ARTISTS

Terri and Chris are a lesbian couple who have lived together on and off for three years. They decide to enter into a living together agreement which would give each time to pursue her own interests. Terri is a potter and Chris is a musician, but both have had to take ordinary part-time jobs in order to make ends meet. Now they wish to take turns supporting each other, so that the person being supported can do her thing full-time.

NOTE: Just as this agreement could be used by a straight couple, most of the agreements in this chapter were designed for use by both gay and straight. The language used may indicate that most are only for straight couples, but as you will see by reading them carefully, this is not the case. See Chapter 12 for a discussion of contract issues facing gays and for another sample contract.

AGREEMENT

Terri McGraw and Chris Macklin agree as follows:

1) Both of us will keep whatever property we presently hold as separate property. But any property or income from property including salaries or financial returns from artistic pursuits, which either of us acquires while we live together will belong equally to both of us and will be jointly shared. These funds will be kept in joint savings and checking accounts;

2) We both agree to take turns working at regular full-time jobs in order to earn enough money for both of us to live on. Terri will work for the first six months of this agreement, and Chris the next six months and so on for alternating six-month periods for the duration of this agreement;

3) All household expenses and personal and medical expenses of both of us will be assumed by the one who is employed at the time the expense is incurred;

4) If one of us wishes to end the living arrangement and the other does not, prior to the dissolution of this agreement, both of us agree to participate in conciliation sessions with a mutually acceptable third party. If, after a minimum of three sessions, one of us still desires to end the agreement, then it will be so terminated. Upon separation, each of us will take our separate property (property we owned prior to living together) and all joint property (property acquired while we lived together) will be evenly divided. No financial or other responsibilities will continue between us after separation.

_____	_____
Date	Terri McGraw
_____	_____
Date	Chris Macklin

H. AGREEMENT FOR PEOPLE IN SCHOOL

Carol plans to be a veterinarian and Bill is an aspiring dentist. To maximize both career opportunities and their personal relationship they decide on a contract with the following provisions:

AGREEMENT

Carol Thayer and Bill Fugimoto agree as follows:

1) That they are living together and plan to continue to do so indefinitely;

2) That they will take turns going to school so that the person not going to school can support the other until he/she gets a degree. To decide who will go to school first a coin will be flipped. The loser will be solely responsible for the winner's educational expenses and support for the next four years. When this period is up, the person who goes to school first assumes these same responsibilities for the following four years for the other person. If their living together relationship should dissolve at any time during these first eight years, they stipulate that the financial obligations shall not be affected. This means that if dissolution occurs during the first four years, (and Bill has won the coin flip), Carol will continue to pay Bill's tuition and pay him an additional $3,000 per year for living expenses. At the end of the first four years, Bill shall then pay for Carol's tuition for four years and her living expenses at $3,500 per year. If they separate after Carol starts her schooling, Bill will pay Carol's remaining tuition (up to four full years in a school of veterinary medicine) and pay her $3,500 per year in living expenses. All living expenses are to be paid in 12 equal monthly payments.

3) During the first eight years that Carol and Bill live together all of the income and property of either person, excluding gifts and inheritances, will be considered to be jointly owned by both. The income-producing person will have management and control over the funds. After the first eight years an inventory will be taken of all the accumulated property and it shall be equally divided. Thereafter, each person's earnings shall be his or her separate property and neither will have any rights to any interest in the present or future property of the other. Should Carol and Bill separate before the end of eight years, all accumulated property shall be equally divided according to the fraction of time each has provided the support (if Carol supports four years and Bill two years, Carol is entitled to two-thirds of the property). If a separation occurs, neither person shall have any continuing financial obligations to the other except as set out in paragraph 2 above.

4) Both Carol and Bill will retain their own surnames.

5) If there are children, both Carol and Bill agree to submit to at least three conciliation sessions before ceasing to live together. If a decision to dissolve the relationship is made, both Carol and Bill agree to submit to binding arbitration if they are unable to reach a mutual decision regarding the issues of child custody, child

support and property division. It is the strong conviction of both Carol and Bill that they wish to avoid any battles over custody and support and want to stay away from courts and lawyers if possible.

_____   _____
Date   Bill Fugimoto

_____   _____
Date   Carol Thayer

I. ENFORCEABILITY OF CONTRACTS

As we have previously stated, agreements between unmarried couples are generally enforceable in a court of law to the extent that they apply to real property, personal property (money, insurance policies, stocks, etc., as well as stereos, cars, ice boxes, etc.) and payment for services. They are generally not enforceable when they involve conduct that normally has little or no monetary value. Thus, if you contract to pay your friend $200 per month for two years in exchange for putting you through school, your agreement will be recognized by a court, but if you contract to feed Nectarine, the pet turtle, every afternoon if your friend gets up early to make the coffee, a judge isn't likely to be very interested if you file a lawsuit saying that your friend overslept.

NOTE: In four states there is some doubt that any contract entered into by members of an unmarried couple is enforceable. Why? Because the courts in these states still think that it's sinful for people to live together and that allowing unmarried adults to contract about living together somehow encourages the "nasty practice." These states are Arizona, Arkansas, Florida and Georgia. If you are in one of these states, see a lawyer before signing on the dotted line.

J. ARBITRATION OF DISPUTES

By adding an arbitration clause to any contract, you free yourself of the need to go to court if a dispute arises. You solve your dispute by following the arbitration procedure that you have set out in your contract. The essential bankruptcy of our overpriced, overcomplicated, and time-wasting court system is leading more and more people to prefer arbitration which is normally faster, cheaper and less hostile when compared to court. Business has used arbitration to settle disputes for years at least in part as a result of the realization that getting a dispute settled quickly can be as important as who wins and who loses.

Here is a sample arbitration clause which can be added to any of the written agreements in this book, including the ones in the Appendix. There are many other arbitration alternatives which you may want to check out yourself at a law library.*

Any dispute arising out of this agreement shall be arbitrated under the terms of this clause. The arbitration shall be carried out by three arbitrators, with each person having signed the Living Together Contract designating one arbitrator and the two designees naming a third. The technical details of the arbitration shall be carried out as follows:

a) The complaining person shall inform the other of the nature of the dispute in writing at the same time that he or she names one arbitrator;

b) Within five days from receipt of this notice, the other person shall reply in writing naming the second arbitrator;

c) The two arbitrator designees shall name a third arbitrator within ten days from the date that the second arbitrator is named;

d) An arbitration meeting shall be held within two days after the third arbitrator is named. Each person shall be entitled to present whatever oral or written agreements he or she wishes and may present witnesses. Neither person may be represented by a lawyer or any third party;

e) The arbitrators shall make their decision in writing within five days after the arbitration hearing. The decision of a majority is controlling;

f) If the person to whom the demand for arbitration is directed fails to respond within the proper time limit by naming an arbitrator, the person initiating the arbitration must give the other an additional five days written notice of "intention to proceed to arbitration." If there is still no response, the person initiating the arbitration may proceed with the arbitration before the arbitrator he or she designated and his or her award shall have the same force as if it had been settled on by the full board of three arbitrators;

g) If the arbitrators designated by the two parties can't agree on a third arbitrator within ten days, arbitration shall be held before three arbitrators appointed by the American Arbitration Association and following their rules;

---

* See *Cluing Into Legal Research*, Honigsberg (information at back of this book).

h) The arbitrators shall be entitled to charge at a rate of $20 per hour (you can change this up or down) for their time in addition to any necessary expenses involved in the arbitration itself. This cost shall be borne by the parties as the arbitrators shall direct as part of their award;

i) The arbitration award shall be conclusive on the parties, and shall be set out in such a way that a formal judgment can be entered thereon in the court having jurisdiction over the dispute if either party so desires.

_____	_____
DATE	SIGNATURE
_____	_____
DATE	SIGNATURE

K. A LIVING TOGETHER CERTIFICATE

When you go to the marriage license clerk and fill out all of the papers necessary to get married, you are in reality paying the government a tax for permission to live together. There is nothing wrong with this. However, you should be aware that if you ever want to get another permission slip to end the marriage, the fees will be vastly higher.

When it comes to living with your lover, you need no permission slip and you pay no tax. However, there is something in a lot of us that loves certificates. We filled one out and hung it over the stove — half as a joke and half to remind ourselves that we are serious about our relationship. You don't have to get married to get some official-looking papers or certificates — you can make your own. Why not? Papers and ink are cheap and your local printer can doubtless help you make up a wonderfully official-looking (or kooky) certificate for less money than the county clerk will charge. And isn't being independent and creative what living together is all about? We include, at the back of the Appendix, a living together certificate designed by Toni and illustrated by Linda Allison.

enting and Sharing a Home

GOBBLEDY-GOOK DEFINED:

EVICT—to legally force someone to move out of an apartment, house, etc. This is accomplished by the landlord suing the tenant and obtaining a court order that the tenant remove himself (or herself) from the premises.

LANDLORD (MALE), LANDLADY (FEMALE), LANDPERSON (NON SEXIST)—the person who owns property which is rented to a tenant.

LEASE (as a noun)—a written agreement by which the landlord agrees to rent certain property for a specified period of time (commonly one year) in exchange for a certain amount of money; the lease may contain many other agreements and restrictions for each party; (as a verb)—to enter into such an agreement. (See Section I, below.)

LEASE

LESSOR—the person who leases the property to the tenant.

LESSEE—a person who has the right to possession of property under a lease.

LIABLE—legally obligated; if a person is "liable," a court can make an order as regards the obligation; for example, liable for the payment of the rent or liable to pay for all damage caused by any person on the premises.

RENTAL AGREEMENT—If you don't have a lease and pay rent, you probably have a rental agreement. This is a contract between a landlord and a tenant whereby the tenant agrees to make periodic payments (usually monthly) of rent in exchange for the right to have possession of certain property. Typically, a rental agreement will contain many other agreements and restrictions for both parties. A rental agreement may be either written or oral (see Section B, below).

RENTAL AGREEMENT

SUBLESSEE—a person who leases from a lessee (tenant) rather than from the original landlord. Most leases require getting the permission of the original landlord.

TENANT—a person who rents property.

A. RENTING A HOME

This is the nitty gritty, isn't it? If you are going to live with someone, you have to go through the mechanics of getting a place. We can't do much to help you find a beautiful, cheap flat right across from a rose garden, but we can give you some hints about the legal implications of dealing with the landlord and each other if you do find it. This chapter is primarily about the special legal problems encountered by people renting together and does not discuss all aspects of landlord-tenant law. The best available general information in this area is found in the *California Tenants' Handbook* (see coupon at back of this book).

There are all sorts of landlords. Little old men who raise African violets and don't add so well may have rental property right next to that of a large real estate corporation. Obviously, their attitudes toward life (that includes you) will be vastly different. We can, and do, give you a lot of information about your legal rights, but you will have to do the more important job of arriving at a good human understanding of the person with whom you are dealing.

Most landlords are more interested in your money than your morals. As long as you pay rent on time, keep the apartment clean and don't fight with the neighbors, they don't care which beds you sleep in. There are, of course, exceptions — property owners who still refuse to rent to unmarried couples. Some (despite the divorce statistics) base their refusal on the belief that unmarried couples are inherently less stable than married ones. Others don't even try to be logical — they simply will not rent to unmarried couples because they don't like them.

What are your legal rights to rent a place if you are discriminated against? Are unmarried couples given any sort of protection? Since there is no federal law barring discrimination against unmarried couples, it depends on the state, city or county in which you live. Most have no laws barring this sort of discrimination — a landlord can legally refuse to rent to you because you can't produce a marriage license. In the few backward states that still make it a crime to live together (cohabitation) this sort of refusal will obviously stand up (see Chapter 1). However, as Victorian attitudes toward living together begin to change, some states such as California and many cities including New York have moved to enact laws prohibiting discrimination on the basis of marital status.* Anti-discrimination laws are pending in many other areas as we go to press. To get up-to-date information for your area, call your local District Attorney's office, or go to the library and get a copy of both your state laws and your county and city ordinances. Check the index under "Housing Discrimination".

If you live in an area where there is no anti-discrimination law to protect you, you will have to decide whether you want to confront the landlord with your lifestyle and make an issue of it, or whether you want to try to slide by. Here are some suggestions that others have found helpful:

Do not flaunt the fact that you are not married. Many landlords will not care. Many will assume you are and not ask.   Depending upon your own personality and how conservative an area you are in, you may want to do the old wedding ring routine. It is not illegal to wear a ring that looks like a wedding ring.

In every city and most large towns there are geographic areas where lots of people aren't married. Often this is particularly true near universities. Ask around and go with the flow if possible.

Assume an air of responsibility and respectability (financial and personal references help). This can relax later.

Do not rent from a landlord who obviously disapproves of you or who is likely to disapprove of you when he or she finds out more about your lifestyle. This is especially important if he or she lives nearby. Life is too short for all the hassles you are inviting. Keep looking until you find a landlord whose head is in the twentieth century. It's worth it in the long run.

But what if the landlord asks if you are married? If you say no, you may lose the apartment. If you say yes, what are the consequences? Practically, probably none — if you are otherwise good tenants, the landlord will be unlikely to hassle you. Legally, if the landlord discovers later that you were not married, he or she might have sufficient cause to evict you in some states. There is no chance that a criminal prosecution would result.

How does a woman sign the lease or rental agreement in a situation where you would just as soon have the landlord believe you are married? If both of you are using the same last name, no problem. If you have different names, there are legal implications. In California, New York and in almost all other states, a person can legally use any name he or she wants, as long as the name is not used for the purpose of fraud and

---

* The federal government bans discrimination on the basis of marital status in public housing by regulation of the Department of Housing and Urban Development (Standards for Establishment and Administration of Admission and Occupancy Regulations).

the new name is used consistently.*But if Clem Lawrence and Julie Renoir sign a lease or rental agreement as Clem Lawrence and Julie Lawrence and if Julie does not commonly use the name Lawrence, is Julie getting herself into a legal mess? There is almost no legal authority on this point, but our educated guess is there should be no practical problem. If Lawrence and Renoir regularly pay their rent, the landlord has suffered no financial loss.

Worrying about how to sign your name is pretty dismal, isn't it? However, as society becomes more tolerant of varying lifestyles, the problem should become less frequent. In the end, "good business" will probably win over "good morals" and landlords will resign themselves to renting to those who can pay at the first of each month without regard to their participation, or non-participation, in civil ceremonies. Hopefully, that day is almost here.

B. LEASES AND RENTAL AGREEMENTS**

There are three common methods of renting property:

🌓 The Lease — a written lease normally provides for a payment of a specific rent for a specific period of time (typically one year). Most leases also contain a long list of rules and regulations governing occupancy.

🌓 The Written Rental Agreement — a written agreement which provides that rent be paid periodically (usually once a month) in exchange for the right to live on the property for the same period. A rental agreement differs from a lease in that the agreement may be ended by either party or the rent raised on very short written notice (usually 30 days). As with a lease, there are normally written rules and regulations which are part of the agreement.

🌓 Oral Rental Agreement — the same as a written rental agreement, but nothing is written down. Even with an oral agreement you need a **written** notice (normally 30 days) to terminate the tenancy in California, New York and most other states.

Before signing anything, carefully examine the fine print rules and regulations (covenants) section of your lease or written rental agreement. Many of these rules are extremely restrictive and many are downright illegal. This is because many of the lease forms are out-of-date and still contain provisions that have been outlawed. For example, many lease forms purport to give the landlord the right to evict you immediately without getting a court order should you fail to pay rent on time. This is illegal — only a judge has the legal authority to order that you be moved out. We don't have the space here to list all illegal lease provisions, but if you see something that rubs you the wrong way, check it out; unmarried couples will particularly wish to check for a clause prohibiting "immoral behavior". In states where living together is

---

* See *How To Change Your Name* (California edition, coupon inside back cover).
** Most leases and rental agreements are prepared by landlords or their attorneys and are very one-sided (guess which side). A tear-out lease and rental agreement fair to both sides and good in all states is available in the *California Tenants' Handbook*. This book also contains a list of lease provisions which have been outlawed under state law, but which still appear in leases and rental agreements.

legal this sort of clause is now meaningless, but in states that still outlaw cohabitation it could cause a problem if the landlord tries to use it to evict you. It would be a good idea to ask the landlord to cross out any "immoral behavior" language. If he or she refuses, it is probably a good indication that you would be happier renting elsewhere.

IMPORTANT: Keep copies of all leases, rental agreements and communications with your landlord in a safe place just in case a misunderstanding does develop. In dealing with landlords it is wise to act in a friendly, courteous manner and hope for the same treatment in return; at the same time you should be prepared for the worst, if it happens. As in dealing with people generally, you can normally catch more flies with honey than by hitting them over the head with a mallet.

C. MOVING IN TOGETHER

1. Legal Obligations Of The Tenants To The Landlord

If both Julie and Clem enter into a lease or rental agreement (written or oral), they are each on the hook to the landlord for **all** rent and **all** damage to the apartment. It makes no difference that Julie used Clem's last name when she signed the lease, she is still personally liable to the landlord for **all** rent and damages.

EXAMPLE 1: Clem and Julie rent a place using the names Clem and Julie Lawrence and both sign a rental agreement providing for a $300 total monthly rent. They agree between themselves to each pay one-half. After three months Clem refuses to pay his half of the rent (or moves out with no notice to Julie and the landlord). In either situation Julie is legally obligated to pay all the rent as far as the landlord is concerned. Clem, of course, is equally liable, but if he is unreachable or out of work, the landlord will almost surely come after Julie for the whole amount. Since Clem and Julie have rented under a month-to-month written rental agreement, Julie can cut her losses by giving the landlord a written notice (30 days in most states) of intention to move. She can do this even if Clem is lying about the place, refusing to pay or get out.

IMPORTANT: If either Clem or Julie ends up paying the landlord more than his or her fair share of the rent, the person who paid too much has a right to recover from the other. If payment is not made voluntarily, this can best be done in Small Claims Court.*

EXAMPLE 2: The same fact situation as Example 1, except that this time there is a lease for one year. Again, both partners are independently liable for the whole rent. If one refuses to pay, the other is still liable unless a third person can be found to take over the lease, in which case both partners are off the hook from the day that a new tenant takes over. Because of the housing shortages in most parts of the country, it is reasonably easy to get out of a lease at little or no cost, by simply finding an acceptable new tenant and steering him or her to the landlord. A newspaper ad will usually do it. The landlord has an obligation to limit his or her damages (called "mitigation of damages" in legal slang) by renting to a suitable new tenant as soon as possible. Should the landlord fail to do this, he/she loses the legal right to collect damages from the original tenants.

2. Legal Obligations Of The Tenants To Each Other

People living together usually have certain expectations of each other. Sometimes it helps to write these down. After all, you expect to write things down with the landlord almost as a matter of course, so why not do the same with each other? Nothing that Clem and Julie agree to among themselves has any effect as far as the landlord is concerned, but it still may be helpful to have something to refresh their own memories, especially if the relationship gets a little rocky. Here we give you a

---

* See *Everybody's Guide To Small Claims Court*, Warner, Nolo Press, $5.95.

sample agreement which only covers a rented living space. Many unmarried couples will prefer to incorporate this type of provision in a more comprehensive living together contract such as those discussed in Chapter 4.

AGREEMENT

Julie Renoir and Clem Lawrence, upon renting an apartment at 1500 Peanut Street, Falfurrias, Texas, agree as follows:

1. Julie and Clem are each obligated to pay one-half of the rent and one-half of the utilities, including the basic monthly telephone charge. Each person will keep track of and pay for his or her long distance calls. Rent shall be paid on the first of each month, utilities within ten days of the day the bill is received.

2. If either Julie or Clem wants to move out, the one moving will give the other person and the landlord 30 days' written notice and will pay his/her share of the rent for the entire 30 day period even if he/she moves out sooner.

3. No third persons will be invited to stay in the apartment without the mutual agreement of both Julie and Clem.

4. If both Julie and Clem want to keep the apartment but one or the other or both no longer wishes to live together, they will have a third party flip a coin to see who gets to stay. The loser will move out within 30 days and will pay all of his or her obligations for rent, utilities and for any damage to the apartment.

Here is an alternative for Number 4

4. If both Julie and Clem want to keep the apartment but no longer wish to live together, the apartment shall be retained by the person who needs it most. Need shall be determined by taking into consideration the relative financial condition of each party, proximity to work, the needs of minor children, if any, and (list any other factors important to you). The determination shall be made by a third party who both Julie and Clem agree (in writing) is objective. The determination shall be made within two weeks after either party informs the other that he or she wishes to separate. After the determination is made, the person who is to leave shall have two additional weeks to do so. The person who leaves is obligated for all rent, utilities and any damage costs for 30 days from the day that the original determination to separate is made.

Date	Julie Renoir

Date	Clem Lawrence

D. MOVING INTO A FRIEND'S HOME

Perhaps just as common as two people looking for their home together is for one person to move in with the other. This can be simple and smooth where the landlord is relaxed and sensible, but can raise some tricky problems and is not recommended where the landlord is a neanderthal idiot who despises unmarried couples. The best advice we can give you when it comes to getting into arguments with idiots is, don't. It makes far more sense to use the same time and energy looking for a place to live where the landlord is pleasant.

In some situations where the landlord is not in the area or is not likely to make waves, it may be sensible simply to have the second person move in and worry about the consequences later. But is this legal? Is a tenant required to tell his landlord when a second person moves in? It depends on the lease or rental agreement. Read the agreement carefully. If no mention is made as to the number of persons allowed in the apartment, use your own discretion and knowledge of your landlord. Some don't care or (like parents) would prefer not to know.

Although moving in with no notice to the landlord is often the easiest thing to do, we suspect that it is commonly not the most sensible. The landlord will probably figure out what is going on before long and may resent your sneakiness more than he or she resents your living with someone. We advise you to:

● Read the lease or rental agreement to see how many people are allowed to live on the premises and if there are any restrictions. Sometimes additional people will be allowed for a slight increase in rent. Many landlords who do have their heads in the twentieth century will not care whether you are married, living together or joined by the toes with rubber bands, but will expect to collect more money if more people live in their rental unit.

● Contact the landlord to explain what is happening. If you can't do this in person, you might send a letter such as this:

```
                                    1500 Peanut Street, #4
                                    Falfurrias, Texas

                                    June 27, 19___


    Smith Realty
    10 Jones Street
    Falfurrias, Texas

    Dear Sirs:

        I live at the above address and regularly pay rent to your office.  As
    of July 1, 19___, there will be a second person living in my apartment.
    As set forth in my lease I enclose the increased rent due which now comes
    to a total of $300.  I will continue to make payments in this amount as
    long as two people occupy the apartment.

        Should you wish to sign a new lease to specifically cover two people,
    please let me know.  My friend, Julie Renoir, is regularly employed and
    has an excellent credit rating.



                                    Very truly yours,



                                    Clem Lawrence
```

REMEMBER: A written rental agreement can be terminated on short notice (30 days in most states) without any reason being given. Thus, a landlord who wants to get rid of you can do so easily unless you have a lease. However, in our experience, if you have a good payment record and are cooperative, it is not likely that the landlord will bother putting you out even if he/she prefers people who have mumbled "until death do us part". If you live in one of the areas where discrimination on the basis of marital status is illegal (see Section A above), the landlord can't legally put you out because you are living together. If he/she tries to do so, you should file a complaint with the local or state agency charged with enforcement of the anti-discrimination law. Of course, the landlord may make up some phony reason to get rid of you to disguise his or her real reason. If you suspect this, file your complaint and let the landlord try to explain why he/she found you to be an adequate tenant while you were living alone and wants to evict you only after you began living with someone.

If you have a lease, you are probably in a little better position to bargain with the landlord if a friend moves in. This is because, to get you out before the lease expires, he/she would have to establish that you have violated one or more lease terms.* If your lease has a provision allowing occupancy by only one person, your landlord probably

---

* In New York, a court has ruled that sharing an apartment with a person of the opposite sex does not constitute grounds to terminate a tenancy, *Fraydun Enterprises v. Ettinger*, 388 N.Y.S. 2d 855, (1976). New York courts have also ruled that if a tenant allows a man to stay overnight a couple of times a week that does not establish grounds to end a lease early, *Messiah Baptist Housing, Etc. v. Rosser*, 400 N.Y.S. 2d 306, (1977).

has the right to terminate your tenancy if a second person moves in without his or her permission. However, if he or she accepts rent with the knowledge that you are living with someone, many courts would hold that he/she can no longer enforce that right. If the lease simply says that the premises shall not be used for "immoral or illegal purposes", it is highly questionable whether the landlord can terminate the lease simply because you are living with someone, unless you are in a state which still makes cohabitation illegal. If the matter were pursued as far as a court eviction in such a state (which is unlikely), the answer would probably depend on the biases and prejudices of the judge. In any case, the landlord could not be sure of winning and would probably hesitate to go through the time and expense of an eviction action if you continued to pay your rent and otherwise were a cooperative tenant. Of course, the landlord can wait until your lease runs out and simply refuse to renew it. His/her refusal would be legal unless you were living in an area that prohibits discrimination on the basis of marital status and you could show that his or her reason for refusing to renew the lease was because you were not married.

1. What Is The Legal Relationship Between Person Moving In And Landlord?

If Julie moves into Clem's apartment, what is the relationship between Julie and Clem's landlord? Is Julie obligated to pay rent if Clem fails to pay? What if Clem moves out, but Julie wants to remain? If Clem ruins the paint or breaks the furniture, does Julie have any obligation to pay for the damage?

The answer to these questions is that Julie starts with no legal rights or obligations regarding the rent, or the right to live in the apartment. She has entered into no contract with the landlord.* Clem is completely liable for the rent and also for damage to the premises whether caused by Julie or himself, because he has entered into a contract which may be in the form of a lease, written rental agreement or oral rental agreement. If Clem leaves, Julie has no right to take over his lease without the landlord's consent.

Julie can, of course, enter into a lease or rental agreement contract with the landlord which would give her the rights and responsibilities of a tenant. This can be done by:

● Signing a new lease or rental agreement which specifically includes both Clem and Julie as tenants.

● Making an oral rental agreement with the landlord. Be careful of this one as an oral agreement can consist of no more than a conversation between Julie and the landlord in which she says she will pay the rent and keep the place clean and he says OK. There may be some legal question as to whether an oral agreement between Julie and the landlord is enforceable if there is still a written lease or rental agreement between the landlord and Clem which doesn't include Julie, but it is our belief that most judges would bend over backwards to give Julie the rights and responsibilities of a tenant if she seemed to be exercising them.

---

* Of course, if she damages the property, she is liable just as a visitor, a trespasser, or a thief who caused damage would be liable.

◑ The actual payment of rent by Julie and its acceptance by the landlord especially if it is done on a fairly regular basis. As in the preceding paragraph, this would set up a month-to-month tenancy between Julie and the landlord and would mean that either would have to give the other a written notice (30 days in California, New York and most other states) of intention to end the tenancy.

IMPORTANT: Rental agreements, leases, evictions, etc. can get fairly complicated and confusing. If you get into a real problem area, see the *California Tenants' Handbook,* which contains much useful information applicable to all states. Also, you a might consider seeing a lawyer for a one-time consultation. This need not be expensive and you can then decide whether you want to pursue the dispute (see Chapter 13).

Should the situation ever arise that Clem wants to move out and Julie remain, it is important that the legal relationships be clarified. Clem should give the landlord written notice of what he intends to do at least 30 days before he leaves. If he does this, he is off the hook completely in a written or oral rental agreement situation. If a lease is involved and Clem is leaving before it runs out, he is still OK because the landlord has a legal duty to take steps to limit his/her loss as much as possible (mitigate damages). This means finding a new tenant to pay the rent. In our example, as long as Julie is a reasonably solvent and non-destructive person, the landlord would suffer no loss by accepting her as a tenant to fill out the rest of Clem's lease. If the landlord refuses Julie without good reason, Clem is still legally off the hook and any loss is legally the landlord's problem, not his.

(For use if you have a rental agreement)

```
                                        1500 Peanut Street, #4
                                        Falfurrias, Texas

                                        June 27, 19___


    Smith Realty Company
    10 Jones Street
    Falfurrias, Texas

    Dear Sirs:

        I live at the above address and regularly pay rent to your office.  On
    July 31, 19___  I will be moving out.  As you know, my friend, Julie Ren-
    oir, also resides here.  She wishes to remain and will continue to pay
    rent to your office on the first of each month.

        We will be contacting you soon to arrange for the return of my damage
    deposits of $100, at which time Julie will give you a similar deposit.
    If you have any questions, or if there is anything we can do to make the
    transition easier for you, please let us know.

                                        Very truly yours,


                                        Clem Lawrence
```

(For use if you have a lease)

1500 Peanut Street, #4
Falfurrias, Texas

June 27, 19___

Smith Realty
10 Jones Street
Falfurrias, Texas

Dear Sirs:

I live at the above address under a lease which expires on October 30, 19___. A change in my job makes it necessary that I leave the last day of February. As you know, for the last six months my friend, Julie Renoir, has been sharing this apartment. Julie wishes either to take over my lease or enter into a new one with you for the remainder of my lease term. She is employed, has a stable income and will, of course, be a responsible tenant.

We will soon be contacting your office to work out the details of the transfer. If you have any concerns about this proposal, please give us a call.

Very truly yours,

Clem Lawrence

---

2. What Is The Legal Relationship Between Person Moving In And Person Already There?

Alas, it seems all too common that big-brained monkeys go through violent changes in emotional feelings. A relationship that is all sunshine and roses one minute may be more like a skunk cabbage in a hurricane the next. Sometimes, when feelings change, memories blur as to promises made in happier times and the nicest people become paranoid and nasty. Suddenly, questions such as "whose apartment is this, anyway?" may turn into serious disputes. We suggest that when feelings are relaxed (preferably at the time that the living arrangement is set up), both people make a little note as to their mutual understandings, either as part of a comprehensive living together arrangement or in a separate agreement. If this is done in a spirit of making a writing to aid the all too fallible human memory, it need not be a heavy experience. We include here an example that you might want to change to fit your circumstances.

AGREEMENT

Julie Renoir and Clem Lawrence make the following agreement:

1. Clem will move into Julie's apartment and will give Julie one-half of the monthly rent ($150) on the first of each month. Julie will continue paying the landlord under her lease and Clem will have no obligation under the lease.

2. Clem will pay one-half of the electric, gas, water, garbage and monthly telephone service charges to Julie on the first of each month. Julie will pay the bills.

3. Should Clem wish to move out, he will give Julie as much written notice as possible and will be liable for one-half of the rent for two weeks from the time he gives Julie written notice. Should Julie wish Clem to move out, she will give him as much written notice as possible, in no case less than two weeks. In any case of serious dispute, it is understood that Julie has first choice to remain in the apartment and Clem must leave on her request.

Date	Julie Renoir
Date	Clem Lawrence

IMPORTANT: If you get into a serious dispute with your friend involving your shared home and have no agreement to fall back on, you will have to do the best you can to muddle through to a fair solution. Here are a few ideas to guide your thinking:

❷ If only one of you has signed the agreement with the landlord and that person pays all the rent, then that person probably has the first claim on the apartment, especially if that person occupied the apartment first. The other should be given a reasonable period of time to find another place, especially if he or she has been contributing to the rent and/or has been living in the home for any considerable period of time.

❷ If you have both signed a lease or rental agreement and/or both regularly pay rent to the landlord, your rights to the apartment are probably legally equal, even if one of you got there first. Try to talk out your situation letting the person who genuinely needs the place the most, stay. Some people find it helpful to set up an informal arbitration proceeding with a neutral third person who will listen to the facts before making a decision. If you do this, make sure that the arbitrator is not a close friend as the person who loses is likely to have hard feelings. Lean over backwards to be fair about adjusting money details concerning such things as last month's rent and damage deposits. Allow the person moving out a reasonable period of time to find another place. **We have found that the best compromises are made when both people feel that they have gone more than half way.**

● Each person has the right to all his or her personal belongings. This is true even if they are behind in his or her share of the rent. Never lock up the other person's property.

● It is a bad idea to deny a person access to his or her home except in the most extreme circumstances. If you are going to lock a person out, you should also be ready to sign a formal police complaint because it may come to that if your former friend tries to get in by using force. In most cases, except where a person has no right to live on the premises (has not paid rent, has not signed a lease, has not been living with you long), locking a person out is not legal and you can be sued for damages.

E. DEPOSITS

Getting cleaning and security deposits returned can be a problem for all tenants - not just the unmarried. **To avoid deposit trouble and to handle it when unavoidable you must have good documentation.** By this we mean making a written and photographic record of what the place looks like at the time you move in and then again when you move out. Witnesses - people you know who would be willing to examine your place and then speak out if necessary - are also extremely valuable.

Let's assume now that Clem and Julie move into a rented flat and pay $400 ($200 each) for cleaning and security deposits. What should they do to be sure that they will get those deposits back?

STEP 1: First, they should document any problems that exist when they move in. Dirty conditions, damaged rugs or appliances, and scratched walls or floors are examples of conditions that should be noted. The best way to do this is to fill out the landlord-tenant checklist which is included at the end of this chapter. If the landlord doesn't wish to do this or drags his or her feet, Julie and Clem should be on notice that self-protection is essential. They should have a friend or better yet, friends, check the place over and take pictures of offending conditions. The person taking the pictures should write his or her name and the date on the back.

STEP 2: Before Clem and Julie move out, they should invite the landlord over to discuss any conditions that might lead to misunderstandings about deposit return. Clem and Julie don't have to leave the place exactly as they found it — part of their rent is to cover normal wear and tear. If there is a problem over and above what might be considered normal — say Julie burned a counter top with an iron — Clem and Julie should get all of their deposits back less the cost of replacing the counter top. If the top was already somewhat damaged from other causes, this should be taken into consideration. Assuming that Clem, Julie and the landlord do come to an agreement, they should write it down and sign it. This can be done as part of the same landlord-tenant checklist mentioned in Step 1 or in some other form.

Now and then a tenant gets advance warning that a landlord never returns deposits voluntarily. This could come from a former tenant, or perhaps even directly when the tenant tries to have a reasonable conversation with the landlord. If you are in this situation, you may wish to take affirmative steps to protect yourself. This is particularly true if you plan to move out of town so that suing later in the local Small Claims Court would be difficult or impossible. Perhaps the simplest way to protect yourself is to withhold the payment of the last month's rent, or that portion of the last month's rent which equals the deposits. If you do this, be sure that you notify the landlord in writing of what you are doing and make sure that you do, in fact, have the place clean and undamaged when you leave. Here is a sample letter:

```
                                        1500 Peanut Street, #4
                                        Falfurrias, Texas

                                        June 1, 19___


Smith Realty
10 Jones Street
Falfurrias, Texas

Dear Sirs:

    As you know, we occupy apartment #4 at 1500 Peanut Street, Falfurrias,
Texas and regularly pay rent to your office.  As we notified you previous-
ly, we will be moving out on July 15, 19___.

    In speaking to other tenants in the building, we have learned that
from time to time, the return of cleaning deposits has been the subject
of disputes between your office and departing tenants.  Accordingingly,
we have decided on the following course of action.  Instead of sending
you the normal $300 rent check for June rent, we are sending you a check
for $50 to cover rent for both June and July and are requesting that you
apply our cleaning and damage deposit of $400 to cover the rest of the
rent owed for this period.

    We will leave the apartment spotless.  We have no intention of causing
you any loss or other problems.  If you should doubt this, or want to dis-
cuss this matter further, please give us a call so that we can make an
appointment to check the apartment over.  We think you will be satisfied
that we are dealing with you honestly and in good faith and that the apart-
ment, which is clean now, will be spotless when we leave.


                                        Very truly yours,



                                        Julie Renoir
                                        Clem Lawrence
```

STEP 3: If Clem and Julie move out and have no understanding with the landlord, they should be very careful to document the condition of the premises. After they clean up, they should again get friends to inspect the place and take pictures. It is also wise to keep copies of receipts for cleaning materials.

Clem and Julie should receive their deposits back within a maximum of two weeks after moving out. If they don't, they should first write a letter and then sue in Small Claims Court. The letter would look like this:

---

800 Walnut St.
Pampa, Texas

August 1, 19____

Smith Realty Co.
10 Jones St.
Falfurrias, Texas

Dear Mr. Anderson:

On July 15, 19____ we vacated the apartment at 1500 Peanut Street, #4. As of today we have not received our $400 cleaning and security deposits.

We left our apartment clean and undamaged, paid all of our rent and gave you proper notice of our intention to move. In these circumstances, it is difficult to understand your oversight in not promptly returning our money.

Perhaps your check is in the mail. If not, please put it there promptly. Should we fail to hear from you in one week, we will take this matter to court.

Very truly yours,

Julie Renoir
Clem Lawrence

If this doesn't work, the next step is to go to Small Claims Court. In most states, the amount that can be sued for is at least $750 which should take care of most deposit cases. But Clem and Julie shouldn't just assume that they will win automatically. The landlord may show up claiming that they left the place a mess. To counter this they will need their pictures, witnesses and cleaning receipts (see Steps 1-3 above). Julie and Clem might present their case in the court something like this:*

---

* In most states no one occupies the witness box in Small Claims Court. All testimony is given from a table which faces the judge. Each person who has something to say says it himself/herself and there is no cross-examination such as you have become so expert at, watching Perry Mason cutting up Sergeant Tragg on T.V.

JULIE: Good morning, your Honor, my name is Julie Renoir and this is Clem Lawrence. From May 15, 1979 until July 15, 1980, we lived at 1500 Peanut St., #4 here in Falfurrias. When we moved out, the Smith Realty Co. refused to refund our $400 cleaning and security deposits even though we left the place spotless. We carefully cleaned the rugs, washed and waxed the kitchen and bathroom floors, washed the insides of the cupboards and the windows.

CLEM: Your Honor, I can testify that everything Julie said is true. We worked a full day to get that place really clean. I would like to show you some pictures that were taken of the apartment the day we moved out. These were taken by our neighbor, Mrs. Edna Jackson, who is here today and will testify. Also, I would like to show you these receipts for a rented rug shampooer and waxer plus receipts for other cleaning supplies. They total $22.00. I don't have anything else to add except that Mrs. Jackson and Ms. Kimura are here to testify.

After the witnesses are sworn in and give their names and addresses, their testimony should be brief and to the point.

MRS. JACKSON: Julie and Clem asked me to check their place on Peanut St. over on July 15, the day they moved. It was very clean and neat. I took those pictures that you looked at, your Honor - the ones with my name on the back. I would have been delighted to move into a place as clean as that.

MS. KIMURA: Your Honor, I didn't take any pictures, but I did help Clem and Julie clean up and move out and I can say the place was spotless. I know because I did a lot of the work, including helping with the windows, cleaning the bathroom, putting that smelly oven cleaner on, etc.

CHECKLIST

The following is a summary of the condition of the premises at

_____, California,

on the dates indicated below.

	CONDITION ON ARRIVAL	CONDITION ON DEPARTURE
LIVING ROOM		
Floors & Floor Covering		
Drapes		
Walls & Ceilings		
Furniture (if any)		
Light Fixtures		
Windows, Screens & Doors		
Anything Else		
KITCHEN		
Floor Covering		
Stove & Refrigerator		
Windows, Screens & Doors		
Light Fixtures		
Sink & Plumbing		
Cupboards		
DINING ROOM		
Floor & Floor Covering		
Drapes		
Walls & Ceilings		
Furniture (if any)		
Light Fixtures		
Windows, Screens & Doors		
BATHROOM(S)		
Toilet(s)		
Sink(s)		
Shower(s)		
Floor, Walls & Ceiling		
Light Fixtures		
Windows, Screens & Doors		
BEDROOMS		
Floors, Floor Covering		
Walls & Ceiling		

Furniture (if any)		
Windows, Screens & Doors		
Light Fixtures		
OTHER AREAS		
Floors & Floor Covering		
Windows, Screens & Doors		
Walls & Ceilings		
Furnace		
Air Conditioning (if any)		
Lawn, Ground Covering		
Patio, Terrace, Deck, etc.		
Other		

Checklist filled out on moving in on_____, 19____, and approved by

_____ and _____.
              Landlord   Tenant

Checklist filled out on moving out on_____, 19____, and approved by

_____ and _____.
              Landlord   Tenant

uying a House

GOBBLEDY-GOOK DEFINED:

CLOSING COSTS—costs associated with buying a house; these costs include realtor fees, recording fees, notary fees, penalties for paying off a loan early, past due taxes, etc.

CONVENTIONAL LOAN—a loan, normally made by a bank or savings and loan company, that is not guaranteed by FHA, VA, or some other governmental agency.

DEED OF TRUST—a kind of mortgage used in some states

DOWN PAYMENT—a percentage of the total purchase price that is paid before title is transferred; with a conventional loan, the down payment is usually 10-25% of the purchase price. If the loan is guaranteed under a governmental program, the down payment may be less than 10%.

DOWN PAYMENT

DEED—the legal document by which one person or persons transfer title (recorded ownership) to real property to another person or persons. If the transfer is by a *grant deed,* the person transferring title makes certain guarantees or warranties as regards the title. If the transfer is by *quitclaim deed,* the person transferring does not make any guarantees, but simply transfers to the other person all the interest he has in the real property.

DEED

ESCROW—in real estate jargon, the process by which two parties deliver documents or money to a third person (escrow agent) who then completes delivery; for example, the seller will deliver a deed to the third person; the buyer or his agents will deliver the money to the same third person. When the third person has received all the money and the deed and other necessary documents, he delivers the deed to the buyer and the money to the seller. CLOSING OF ESCROW refers to the time when all documents and money have been delivered.

ESCROW

FHA—Federal Housing Authority.

INDENTURE—a fancy word for written contract or agreement.

MORTGAGE—Since people rarely have the cash to purchase a home they end up borrowing most of it—this is called taking a mortgage. Technically, it is the security interest that a seller or lender retains in property where recorded ownership (title) has been transferred to a buyer, but the buyer has not paid the whole purchase price. In practice, it is common for a financial institution to pay off the seller immediately and become the mortgage holder; as a verb—to convey or place property under mortgage.

A. FINDING A HOUSE

There may come a time when you and your friend decide to purchase a house or other real property. For many of us property ownership is symbolic of rootedness, of having a sense of place and belonging. Most societies, including our own, have honored the acquisition of land and the process of building with ceremonies, often spiritual. Even though this planet has been here five and a half billion years, and, measured against such an immensity of time, the concept of owning land is laughable, in our human time frame it can make great sense. Perhaps if we think of ourselves as stewards of our land and living spaces, rather than owners, we can connect both to our need for foundation and place as well as recognizing that, in a larger view, our presence on the land (or in the house) is a momentary one and that we owe something to those who are yet to come as well as to the land itself.

Sadly, as the earth has become more crowded and building supplies scarcer, the availability of decent living spaces has decreased. Even in the past few generations we have seen the death of America's founding dream — each family with a good home on good land and room to grow. Now many of us rent from necessity and many others express their desire to be homeowners with cooperative apartments or condominiums. Still, more than in most parts of the world, the possibility of home ownership exists despite high land, construction, and interest costs and property taxes that are so exorbitant that they might as well be called rent.

Here we will give you both general information about buying a house and specific ideas that unmarried couples will find of value. From time to time we will suggest that legal advice on some detailed point would be helpful. Before seeing a lawyer, however, we suggest you read Chapter 13.

In some states, sales of real property (land and/or buildings) are handled in close consultation with an attorney. In most, a real estate broker handles all of the transactions and attorneys are not normally involved. In all the states, the individual has the right to handle the purchase or sale himself and should certainly make sure he has the best possible deal. There are several paperback books on the market which discuss buying and selling a house without a real estate broker. With a good deal of study, effort, and care, buyer and seller working together doing things themselves can save at least 10% of the sale value of real property. Because the financial community (banks, real estate brokers, title companies, lawyers, etc.) is interrelated, it often happens that one or more of these interest groups will make it difficult for you if you don't patronize all of them. Difficult is not the same as impossible, however, and if you are interested, check with your bookstore or library for helpful materials. You want to look for books that relate to your state particularly, as opposed to those that pretend to be of national scope.

For the unmarried couple, buying a house generally involves four distinct steps:

1. Finding the house.

2. Financing the purchase.

3. Transferring ownership (taking title to the house).

4. Working out a sensible agreement between the buyers.

Finding a house normally involves no special problem for the unmarried couple. The overwhelming majority of sellers will not care about your marital status. If you use a realtor, you are particularly unlikely to have problems as the realtor will not receive his commission unless he sells the house, and is thus generally willing to encourage the owner to sell to anyone. But what happens if, despite good business and common sense, the owner of a house or condominium refuses to sell to you because you are not married? In most states nothing happens because there are no laws stating that it is illegal to discriminate on the basis of marital status in the sale of real property. Such discrimination is illegal in Oregon, New Jersey, Delaware, Minnesota and New York City.*

NOTE: In Chapter 1 we discuss the fact that cohabitation (living together in a relationship that includes sex) is itself a crime in some states. Does this mean that an unmarried couple will have difficulty buying a house in these states? No. As noted, the anti-cohabitation laws are not enforced and it seems no more difficult for an unmarried couple to buy property in these states than in the others.

You may have read that some local communities have enacted zoning ordinances preventing more than a specified number (usually 2-4) of unrelated persons from living together (excepting household help, of course) in an attempt to eliminate communes from their neighborhoods. While some legal scholars feel that such ordinances discriminate against unmarried persons and are unconstitutional in that they deny equal protection of the laws to such persons, the United States Supreme Court does not agree. In the case of *Village of Belle Terre v. Boraas*, 416 U.S. 1 (1974) the Supreme Court held that anti-group living ordinances are constitutional. This means that they allowed the village of Belle Terre to say that no more than two unrelated people could live in the same house. But what does all of this mean for unmarried couples? Very little — the Supreme Court has approved zoning ordinances that prohibit **more** than two unrelated people from living together: The Court has not said that it is constitutional for a neighborhood or town to ban unmarried couples. Indeed, the language of the *Belle Terre* case seems to indicate that, if faced with such a case, the Court would prohibit a community from discriminating against unmarried couples.

---

* Several other cities and counties have enacted gay rights ordinances which prohibit discrimination in housing on the basis of sexual orientation. The wording of some of these ordinances is broad enough to protect both straight and gay couples. See Chapter 12J.

The *Belle Terre v. Boraas* case was decided by the Nixon Supreme Court — men who for the most part see the world through starched lace curtains. Hopefully the Court will loosen up a bit with future appointments. *Belle Terre* is the law now, however, so if you are living with more than one person and you are not related by blood or marriage, a local community can keep you from renting or buying through their adoption of zoning laws.

B. FINANCING YOUR HOUSE

Very few people are able to pay cash for a house. Most of us have to borrow money and accept the conditions imposed by the lender. Sometimes the realtor will tell the buyer that he can arrange for the financing of the house. This can be helpful, for the realtor may be able to persuade a bank or other lending agency to loan you money when you would not otherwise be able to obtain a loan. However, realtors often have working relationships (business habits) with certain lending insitutions that can result in your being referred there even though better interest rates are available elsewhere. Often, too, the realtor may simply be lazy and not know the practices of banks other than the ones he usually deals with. So before accepting an offer of help, shop around and compare the interest rates and fees of different lending institutions. Several careful research studies have shown that lending practices, fees*, and interest rates can

* Yes, most banks charge you a fee for the privilege of borrowing money from them. This is in addition to the interest you pay for the use of money.

vary considerably even within a small geographical area. For most people a house is the most expensive purchase they will ever make, and the property should not be bought or financed without careful attention to all details (interest rates, repairs, taxes, etc.).

How much can you afford to pay for a house? People who have thought carefully about this generally state that the purchase price should not exceed three times the annual gross income of a family. This is probably a good rule for unmarried couples as well. A larger purchase price may well result in house payments that are unrealistically high. In figuring the purchase cost you must add not only the cost of the house itself, but also the cost of the structural repairs you will be required to make (in some cases the seller makes these repairs and the cost is reflected in the purchase price), the closing costs*, and at least one-half of the redecorating costs you plan to incur in the first year. Some lending institutions may require repairs to be made before the loan will be granted. Financial institutions are also concerned with the portion of net income that it will take to pay mortgage installments and taxes — generally they will not loan unless the monthly total is less than 33% of net monthly income.

In most cases you must pay a cash down payment for at least 10-25% of the purchase price and the closing costs. The rest of the money for the purchase of the house will be loaned to you by a bank or other lending institution which will retain the "mortgage" or similar legal interest in the property until you pay the entire purchase price (this may take 25 years or more). When you buy a house, you must be able to afford the monthly payments on the house as well as the initial down payment. The charts below show monthly payments that will have to be made on various loans at different rates of interest for various lengths of time. As you can see, a 1% difference in the interest rate can result in a large difference in the total amount of money you end up paying for a house. A $30,000 loan can easily cost you $80,000 in total payments over a 30-year period.

In order to pay off a loan of $20,000 in 25 years, you will have to make the following monthly payments at the specified interest rate:

5%	116.92	9%	167.84
6%	128.87	10%	181.85
7%	141.36	11%	196.02
8%	154.37	12%	210.65

In order to pay off a loan of $30,000 in 25 years you will have to make the following monthly payments at the specified interest rate:

5%	175.40	9%	251.80
6%	193.30	10%	272.70
7%	212.10	11%	294.03
8%	231.60	12%	315.97

* These can easily equal a couple of thousand dollars and the buyer and seller must agree ahead of time as to how they will divide the costs.

In order to pay off a loan of $40,000 in 25 years you will have to make the following monthly payments at the specified interest rate.

5%	233.90	9%	335.70
6%	257.80	10%	363.50
7%	282.80	11%	392.05
8%	308.80	12%	421.29

In order to pay off a loan of $50,000 in 25 years you will have to make the following monthly payments at the specified interest rate.

5%	293.30	9%	419.60
6%	322.15	10%	454.35
7%	353.40	11%	490.06
8%	385.40	12%	526.61

To look at the problem another way, suppose you want to know how large your payments must be to pay off a loan over different lengths of time. For example, to pay off a loan of $20,000 at 9% interest you will have to make the following monthly payments during the length of the mortgage:*

LENGTH OF MORTGAGE IN YEARS	PAYMENT PER MONTH	LENGTH OF MORTGAGE IN YEARS	PAYMENT PER MONTH
1	1749.03	15	202.86
5	415.17	20	179.95
10	253.36	25	167.84

In order to pay off a loan of $30,000 at 9% interest you will have to make the following monthly payments during the length of the mortgage:

LENGTH OF MORTGAGE IN YEARS	PAYMENT PER MONTH	LENGTH OF MORTGAGE IN YEARS	PAYMENT PER MONTH
1	2623.60	15	304.30
5	622.80	20	270.00
10	380.10	25	251.80

In order to pay off a loan of $40,000 at 9% interest you will have to make the following monthly payments during the length of the mortgage:

LENGTH OF MORTGAGE IN YEARS	PAYMENT PER MONTH	LENGTH OF MORTGAGE IN YEARS	PAYMENT PER MONTH
1	$3498.10	15	405.80
5	830.40	20	359.90
10	596.80	25	335.70

* Rates of interest have been experiencing wide swings in recent years. Interest tables are available at the reference desk at your public library so that you can accurately determine the amount you will have to pay if the interest rate is more or less than 9%.

In order to pay off a loan of $50,000 at 9% interest you will have to make the following monthly payments during the length of the mortgage:

LENGTH OF MORTGAGE IN YEARS	PAYMENT PER MONTH	LENGTH OF MORTGAGE IN YEARS	PAYMENT PER MONTH
1	$4372.50	15	507.10
5	1037.90	20	449.80
10	633.40	25	419.60

You must also take into account the fact that you will be paying taxes and fire insurance as well as monthly loan payments. In some cases these costs will be added to and included in the monthly payments you make, with the lending institution then purchasing the insurance and paying the taxes for you. Often lending institutions don't purchase the most reasonably priced insurance; sometimes they charge a fee for paying the property taxes. Normally, it is cheaper to handle these things yourself. If you are directly responsible for making the payments, the lending institution will surely retain the right to make the payments (and add the cost to the mortgage) if you fail to do so.

EXAMPLE: Felix and Keija are an unmarried couple. Felix is a teacher and earns $22,000 yearly before taxes and other deductions are subtracted from his checks. After deductions he brings home $1350 per month. Keija manages a restaurant and earns $18,000 every year before deductions. She brings home $1100 per month. Each of them has a savings account of about $12,000. Each of them intends to continue working and sees a gradual increase in income in the future. Their annual gross income is $40,000. Taking both incomes together, they could afford a house with a cost in the range of $100,000-$130,000 without strain.

Felix and Keija find a house that is advertised for sale for $100,000. They offer $90,000 to the seller and the seller agrees to sell for $95,000.* Felix and Keija accept this "counteroffer" and then find a bank that will loan them 80% of the purchase price at the rate of 10% for 25 years. The taxes are $950 per year and the fire insurance will cost $250 per year. The seller will pay for all repair work that must be done on the structure. Felix and Keija will want to repaint the inside of the house and remodel the kitchen. They plan to do the painting themselves; the supplies will cost $800, and they have an estimate from a contractr that remodeling the kitchen will cost $6,000. Their cost of obtaining title to the house (closing costs) is $3,500.

---

* As a general rule, a seller asks more for a house than he thinks he can get. A buyer never offers to pay the asking price, but offers to pay a somewhat lower price. A little back-and-forth dance of offer and counteroffer takes place which, if successfully played out, ends with both parties compromising a bit and thinking they got a good deal.

Total cost of house equals:

Purchase price	$95,000
Closing costs	3,500
Half of remodeling costs ($3,000 + $400)	3,400
	$101,900

Total monthly payments equal:

Loan payment (25 year loan at 8 1/2% interest on 80% of $65,000, or $51,000)	$690.61
Monthly taxes ($1,400÷12)	79.17
Monthly fire insurance ($200÷12)	20.83
	$790.61

The monthly payments will be $790.61, or slightly over 32% of Felix and Keija's total net monthly income. In addition, Felix and Keija must pay a down payment of 20% of the purchase price. This comes to $19,000 plus closing costs of $3,500, or a total of $21,500. Keeping all these costs in mind, plus the costs of maintenance on the home, they have a big decision to make.

Suppose Felix and Keija decide that they are willing to invest their money in this house. The next problem facing them is how to obtain a loan for the 80% of the purchase price that they can't pay in cash.*

WARNING: In shopping around for the money to finance your house, beware of institutions which will loan you money at a fluctuating rate of interest. Some loan agreements are structured so that, while the borrower makes regular payments on the house, the rate of interest he pays changes according to some criterion outside the loan (usually the prime interest rate), so that the amount of the payment that is actually applied to the loan (principal) changes from month-to-month. The idea behind this kind of loan is that the lending institution profits because its money is always loaned out at the optimum rate, and the borrower profits because, if the prevailing rate goes down, he will automatically start paying a lower rate of interest without having to obtain another loan. Of course, the borrower suffers if interest rates go up. We have seen numerous cases where borrowers have had their monthly payments increased or have found that at the end of their 25 year loan period, they still owe money because rising interest rates have resulted in an insufficient amount of their payments being

---

* Sometimes a seller is willing to carry the mortgage himself, but most commonly he/she wants his or her money, or most of it, right away, making it necessary to get outside financing. Sometimes a lending institution will not lend the buyer enough to completely pay off the seller even when the loan is added to the down payment. This means that a second mortgage to make up the difference is necessary. Sometimes a seller will provide the second mortgage directly. If not, it may be necessary to borrow from family or friends.

applied to the principal. We believe the average borrower is better off with the certainty of a fixed interest rate.*

You may also have heard of "variable rate mortgages" or "flexible rate mortgages". The federal government and the lenders are experimenting with mortgages which allow the borrower to make smaller payments in the earlier years and bigger ones later. The idea is that many younger people with families who can't afford to buy houses because of the high initial payments under a standard mortgage will be able to buy with a "variable rate plan". When you think for a moment, it's a very American plan — consume now, pay later. Unfortunately, the sugar plum dreams of constantly rising incomes which are supposed to make it easy for us to pay those big bills that we put off until tomorrow don't always come true. For too many people, it's consume now, choke later. So be careful — if someone shows you a "variable rate mortgage" plan that seems too good to be true — it probably is. Of course, if you only plan to live in a home a few years a low initial rate be just what you are looking for. By the time the big bills come in you will be long gone.

In deciding whether or not to loan money on real property, all financial institutions look carefully at two factors: (1) the value of the property itself; and (2) the personal financial circumstances of the borrower. Some lenders are more concerned with the value of the property on the theory that their investment is well protected, even if the borrower fails to make his payments, as long as the property is worth more than their loan. Other lenders put more emphasis on the financial situation of the borrower, only lending to people in excellent financial shape. Institutions which look more to the credit of the borrower do so because they do not want to be bothered with the legal complications of regaining property and the hassle of collecting overdue payments. They simply want to be sure that the money comes in every month.

Traditionally it has been difficult for unmarried couples to get mortgage loans. Financial institutions have long adopted the attitude that they are unstable. People who work in banks tend to be conservative and to think that everyone who doesn't follow all of society's traditional formalities (like marriage) can't be trusted to pick up candy wrappers, discipline their children, or more important, pay their bills. In practical application this attitude used to mean that banks would not lend jointly to both members of an unmarried couple. They usually insisted that the loan be solely in the name of the person with the highest income, and would only consider that person's income in measuring ability to repay. In effect, the bank was pretending that the unmarried couple didn't exist. More than one couple was told that, if they wanted both incomes considered and wanted both names on the loan and deed, they would have to do one very simple thing — get married.

Fortunately, hostile attitudes toward lending to unmarried couples have been mellowing over the last few years. Much of this change for the better is traceable to the fact that so many more unmarried couples are buying houses, but much is also the result of the Fed.Equal Credit Opportunity Act, which forbids credit discrimination based on sex or marital status. This act means that a woman, whether single or married, is entitled to receive credit on the same basis as a man with a similar credit

---

* As this book goes to press, interest rates are so high that some may feel that they are more likely to go down than up. If you believe this, you may want to disregard our advice but remember, if you are wrong, you will be paying even higher rates.

profile.* Banks now cannot act as if unmarried couples don't exist. In preparing this book we talked with a number of bankers. Most indicated (at least to us) that they had no negative attitudes toward unmarried couples, but we did find hostility among a few. "We know we have to deal with them, but we don't have to like it," one man told us. There is an old saying: "Don't try to push a river, especially if it's going in the wrong direction." Check with unmarried friends to see who in the banking or real estate business is going your way.

When Felix and Keija get a loan (mortgage) it means two things: the real property itself is liable (can be foreclosed on) to pay off the debt, and Felix and Keija are personally obligated to pay the entire amount. Assuming that the loan is made to Felix and Keija together, **both** are on the hook to pay it all back. Felix can't excuse his failure to pay by claiming that Keija has not made her share of the payments. **Let's say it again, because it is important:** Felix and Keija are each independently liable to repay the whole debt. Indeed they are both required to pay back the loan even if they transfer (sell) the property to a third person who agrees to make the payments **unless** the bank agrees to release them from their obligation and allows the new person to "assume" the mortgage. Even if something happens to the house (fire, flood or other catastrophe), Keija and Felix are still legally on the hook to repay the bank loan. But because banks know that people don't like to pay for things that no longer exist, they will require that Keija and Felix take out insurance that will at least cover the amount of the bank loan (see Chapter 7).

1. F.H.A. Financed Housing

The Federal Housing Authority (F.H.A.) guarantees loans on certain types of houses, typically tract or development homes build after World War II. This means that financial institutions will lend to people (often with a low down payment) who might not otherwise qualify for a home loan. The Authority also administers some special programs in which they loan money, sometimes with a subsidy, to low-income persons.

You may have heard that it is difficult for unmarried couples to qualify tor F.H.A. guarantee or loan programs. Until a few years ago, this was true — F.H.A. would lend to unmarried couples, but would only count the income of the male when making a determination as to whether the family met their income requirements. Since people turn to F.H.A. to start with because they can't qualify for conventional financing, this was a little like saying to a starving person, "I will give you a terrific supper, as soon as you fatten up a little."

F.H.A. now assures us that they no longer discriminate and that unmarried couples are judged by the same criteria that their licensed brothers and sisters are judged by. This means that the agency will count the income of both people when determining financial ability whether people are married or not.

---

* Women who believe that they have been discriminated against should contact the nearest regional Federal Reserve Board office (for bank-related problems) or the nearest regional Federal Trade Commission (for non-bank related problems).

C. TAKING TITLE TO THE HOUSE

When you purchase a house together (or any other property, for that matter), you should both use your correct names. These are the names by which you are generally known and which appear on most of your identification documents, such as your driver's license, passports, credit cards, etc. These need not be the same names that appear on your birth certificates. For example, Keija should take title as Keija Adams if she had adopted Keija as her legal name. This is true even though her birth certificate says Carolyn.

At the time you purchase your home, you will have to decide on how you want to "legally" take title. In most states your choices are in "one person's name", as "joint tenants" or as "tenants in common". Let's pause for a moment to translate these terms into English.

1. In One Person's Name Only

You probably will not be interested in this alternative if you are buying a house together, because unless you have executed a separate agreement (see Section D4, this chapter) it means that the person whose name appears on the deed is the sole owner. Sometimes having only one name on the deed seems momentarily desirable for some reason such as preserving welfare or food stamp eligibility. **Beware!** You may sacrifice a large, long-term gain for a small, short-term one. This is because the person whose name is on the deed is "presumed" to be the sole owner. If you later split up, or the person whose name is on the deed dies, the other person may find that he or she has no rights even though he or she has contributed to the house payments. But shouldn't it be possible for the person whose name isn't on the deed to show that he or she is really part owner from the facts of the relationship? Perhaps — some states allow the presumption that the person who has his or her name on the deed is the sole owner to be rebutted if the facts are strong enough. But even if this is possible it involves the expense and time of going to court.*

2. Joint Tenancy

Taking title to a piece of real property "as joint tenants" means that legally the joint tenants share in property ownership and each has the right to use the entire property.** If one joint tenant dies, the other(s) automatically takes the deceased person's share without the necessity of any probate proceedings. Indeed, when one joint tenant dies, the property can go only to the surviving joint tenant(s), even if there is a will to the contrary. If one joint tenant sells his or her portion to a third party, this ends the joint tenancy. The third party and the original joint tenant become "tenants in common" (see below). Joint tenancy is not appropriate to a situation where a house is owned in unequal shares, only to those where each joint tenant owns the same individed portion as does the other(s).

---

* Those wanting to do more research in this area will want to look at the case of *Antoine v. Thornton*, 81 Wash. 2d 72, 499 P. 2d 864 (1972).

** Sometimes one member of an unmarried couple buys a house and then is tempted to put the house in "joint tenancy" with his or her friend, so that the friend will have it if the purchaser dies. Think before you do this — by putting the house in "joint tenancy", you are probably making a gift of one-half of it to your friend. If you later split up, you will probably be unable to get the half you gave away back. You will probably be better off to keep the house in your name and make a will in favor of your friend. If you wish, the will can always be changed later.

3. Tenants In Common

Tenants in common are also each entitled to equal use of the property, **but if one party dies the other party does not take his share unless this has been specified in the deceased person's will.** If there is no will, the deceased's share in the property goes to the nearest blood relative under the intestate succession laws of the state where the property is located (see Chapter 11).* If this were Aunt Tillie in Omaha, Nebraska, the surviving member of the unmarried couple and Aunt Tillie would now be tenants in common. Therefore, whether you and your partner buy the house as joint tenants or tenants in common will probably depend on who you want to inherit your share of the property.**One word of caution: DO NOT take title to the house as "husband and wife", or as "Felix Finnegan and his wife, Keija". This can only lead to legal problems in the future. Tenancy in common can be used where people own a house together, but in different shares (see D below).

D. CONTRACTS BETWEEN UNMARRIED PEOPLE BUYING HOUSES

It is all very well to list the various common ways of taking title to a house. But how does listing yourself as "tenants in common", or "joint tenants" answer such questions as "who gets to keep the house if we split," or "what do we do if one of us puts in twice as much for the down payment as the other," or "what happens if one of us already owns a house and the other wants to move in and share ownership?" The answer to these questions is that you need to make a written understanding (a contract).

NOTE FOR PEOPLE WHO HATE CONTRACTS: Many people will prefer not to make a contract but rather to fly by the seat of their pants, sure that their love and respect for each other will insure a soft landing. As we discussed in Chapters 3 and 4, this can be dangerous. Where valuable pieces of property such as houses are involved, it is particularly necessary to write something down. If you do split up and you **mutually** agree to a solution different than the one in your written contract, fine. You can tear up the old contract and get on with the new. However, if your relationship ends with more of a bump than you guessed, and you find it hard to communicate, you will still have your written understanding to fall back on.

A house contract can be simple. After reading this section, you may conclude that you can prepare it yourself, either as part of a comprehensive living together contract or as a separate agreement. However, houses are major investments and you don't want to make an agreement that either doesn't solve all your problems or makes them worse. So if your agreement is complicated, you will be wise to have it checked by someone who is familiar with the legal problems encountered by unmarried couples. This doesn't mean that you should take a full wallet and a vague basketful of problems

---

* A surviving tenant in common might argue that he or she should get the deceased person's interest in the property because of the existence of an oral or implied contract under the theory of the *Marvin* case (see Chapters 3 and 11). While this sort of argument will probably work (if the existence of such a contract can be proved), where personal property is involved, it seems to us to be more difficult where real property is concerned. Why? Because a written agreement already exists (the co-tenancy deed), and we believe that courts will be reluctant to change deeds on the basis of oral testimony.

** There are inheritance tax consequences associated with different kinds of ownership. This book does not deal with these tax problems as they are not of major significance to people of average income. If you are very wealthy or are buying property with a high value, you would be wise to discuss these problems with a tax attorney or an accountant.

to a lawyer. It does mean that you should do as much work as possible yourself and only use the lawyer to help you with particular problem areas (see Chapter 13).

Unmarried couples who are jointly buying a house will usually find that the things they want to write down as part of a contract fall into the following subject areas (to make this easier to understand, let's resurrect Felix and Keija):

1. *Who keeps the house if Felix and Keija split up and both want it?*

2. *How do Felix and Keija decide the value of the house if they split up?*

3. *Assuming that Felix and Keija split up and a decision is reached that one of them will keep the house and buy the other out, how is the transfer accomplished?*

4. *If one person invests more money in the house than the other, how can the unequal shares be reflected in a contract?*

5. *If one person moves into a house already owned by the other, what legal steps can be taken to protect both parties?*

We can't give you the answers to every possible variation on all of these subject areas, but we hope at least to give you a structure for thinking about your situation and for dealing with a lawyer if necessary. Before we examine each of these five questions, let's first set out a simple sample contract to give you an idea of what you are aiming at. Under Parts 4 and 5 of this section we will discuss several more complicated agreements.

SAMPLE HOUSE PURCHASE CONTRACT

Keija Adams and Felix Finnegan agree as follows:

1. That they will purchase the house at 1400 Beverly St., San Jose, California for $65,000 and will take title to the home as tenants in common.

2. That Keija and Felix will contribute $10,000 each to the down payment and will each pay one-half of monthly mortgage and insurance costs.

3. Keija and Felix will each be responsible to pay one-half of all property taxes and one-half of any costs for needed repairs.

4. In the event that Keija and Felix decide to separate and both want to keep the house, a friend shall be asked to flip a coin within 30 days of the decision to separate. The winner gets to purchase the house from the loser provided that he (she) pays the loser the fair market value (see paragraph 5) of his or her share within 90 days. When payment is made, the house shall be deeded to the person retaining it.

5. The fair market value of the house shall be determined at any time by either the written agreement of Keija and Felix, or, if this is impossible, by appraisal. The appraisal shall be carried out as follows: Keija and Felix shall each designate one licensed real estate broker or salesperson who is familiar with the neighborhood

where the house is located to make an appraisal. The two appraisers so designated shall jointly agree on a third licensed real estate broker or salesperson to make a third appraisal. The three appraisals shall be averaged to arrive at the fair market value of the house. The fees of the three appraisers shall be paid in equal shares by Keija and Felix.

Date	Date
Keija Adams	Felix Finnegan

Now let's look at variations. This material isn't difficult, but you will want to read it through several times to be sure that you understand it completely.

1. Who Keeps The House If Felix And Keija Split Up?

Let's assume now that Keija and Felix have been living together for three years prior to the time that they decide to buy their house. In the year prior to the house purchase there has been some tension between them — Keija thinks that Felix should be less promiscuous, and Felix gets furious because Keija never cleans the kitchen and squeezes the toothpaste from the wrong end. Both have agreed to work out these problems and plan to continue living together for the indefinite future, but there are just enough clouds on the horizon for both to realize that staying together "until death do us part" is not inevitable. While they are communicating well, both want to write something down so that if they do break up, there will not be a lot of paranoia about who gets the house.

Here are the most common types of contract clauses that would solve this problem. Keija and Felix will have to decide which best suits their circumstances.

a) "In the event that the couple (or one of them) decide(s) to separate, Felix shall keep the house and pay Keija the fair market value of her share within sixty days of the decision to separate." (Of course, this agreement can be reversed by reversing the names.)

or

b) "In the event that the couple (or one of them) decides to separate, the house shall be listed for sale within thirty days of this decision, and the proceeds of the sale equally divided after all costs of sale and mortgage debts are paid."

or

c) "In the event that the couple (or one of them) decides to separate and both want to keep the house, a friend shall be asked to flip a coin within thirty days of the decision to separate. The winner gets to purchase the house from the loser provided that he (she) pays the loser the fair market value of his or her share within ninety days of moving out."

or

d) "In the event that the couple (or one of them) decides to separate and both want to purchase the share of the other, they shall jointly agree in writing on a third person to act as an arbitrator to decide who shall be entitled to purchase the house from the other. The arbitrator shall meet with both Felix and Keija and give each a chance to have his or her say.* The arbitrator shall take the following factors into consideration in arriving at a decision as to who needs the house more:

1) Proximity of the house to Keija and Felix's respective places of employment.
2) The needs of any minor children of the parties.
3) The respective abilities of the parties to find another place to live.
4) (Whatever else you wish to include)

or

e) "In the event that Felix and Keija (or one of them) decide(s) to separate at a time when one of them has physical custody of minor children, the person with physical custody of the children shall have the first choice to stay in the house. The person staying in the house shall pay the other the fair market value of his or her share within ninety days of separation.

2. How Do Felix And Keija Decide The Value Of The House If They Split Up?

When people split up, they often believe that legally they must sever all ties between one another. While at times this may be emotionally desirable, it is not legally required. Keija and Felix may legally continue to own their house or other real property together as long as they wish to, even if they split up fifteen minutes after the house is purchased. However, it is common to find that when people separate and a decision is made for one to stay in the house and the other to leave, the person leaving wishes his or her share of the equity in cash. Sometimes it is possible for the person staying in the home to pay immediately, sometimes not. But before you reach this question, you must determine the value of the house. Here is a contract provision that takes care of this simply and fairly:

a. "If Felix and Keija (or one of them) decide(s) to end the relationship and to divide the equity in the house, the value of the home shall be determined as follows:

1) By mutual written agreement at any time;
2) Or, if agreement is not possible, by appraisal. The appraisal shall be carried out as follows: Keija and Felix shall each designate one licensed real estate broker or salesperson who is familiar with the neighborhood where the house is located to make an appraisal. The two appraisers shall jointly choose a third licensed real estate broker or salesperson to make a third appraisal. The three appraisals shall be averaged to arrive at the fair market value of the house. The fees of the three appraisers shall be paid in equal shares by Keija and Felix.

---

* You will find more information on arbitration at the end of Chapter 4.

3. Assuming That Felix And Keija Split Up And A Decision Is Reached That One Of Them Will Keep The House And Buy The Other Out, How Is The Transfer Accomplished?

Here are some alternatives:

a) *"Within ninety days after Felix and Keija decide to separate, the person staying in the house shall pay to the person leaving his or her share of the equity at which time the person leaving shall deed his or her share of the house to the person staying."* *

b) *"Within ninety days after Keija and Felix (or one of them) decide(s) to separate, the person remaining in the house shall pay to the person leaving one-half (one-third or one-fourth or whatever amount works for you) of his or her share of the equity. The person staying in the house shall also give the person leaving a second mortgage (or deed of trust) for the remainder of his or her share. The mortgage (deed of trust) shall be for a term of five years (three, six or whatever works for you) and shall be payable in equal monthly installments. This mortgage (deed of trust) shall be recorded at the County Recorder's office.*

NOTE FOR PARENTS: If the person staying in the house is going to be primarily responsible for the care of the couple's children, it may be particularly difficult for him or her to raise cash to pay the other off for the house. In this situation it may be wise to establish the value of the respective interests in the house at the time of separation, but not require the person staying (the parent with custody) to pay the other until the children reach the age of majority, or the family moves or the house is sold. This can be done by the person leaving deeding the house to the parent with custody in exchange for a mortgage which doesn't fall due until the appropriate time in the future.

4. If One Person Invests More Money In The House Than The Other, How Can The Unequal Shares Be Reflected In A Contract?

It is common that one person has more money to invest than the other. Suppose, for example, that Jeannie has just inherited $20,000 and can make the entire down payment, while Joe either has no money or only a small amount for the down payment, but does have a steady job and can pay his share (or more than his share) of the monthly payments. In addition, let's assume that the house is an older one in need of lots of repairs and that Joe is a professional carpenter. Here are some ways that this situation could be handled:

a) Jeannie could buy the house as the sole owner and Joe could pay a monthly amount as rent (more about this below under Section D5 of this chapter);

or

b) Jeannie could make a gift of one-half of the down payment to Joe. In this case

---

* Before you know what the equity is you must agree on the fair market value of the home. This is where the appraisal comes in. Once you know the fair market value, you subtract the amount of the mortgages (or deeds of trust) to arrive at the equity. Sometimes it is easier to raise cash on houses than you would first imagine. A financial institution may agree to a new mortgage for a larger amount in the name of the person staying, thereby providing enough money to buy the other person out.

title could be taken under "joint tenancy" or "tenancy in common". See Section C of this chapter for definitions of these terms.

or

c) (This one — or a variation — seems to fit most people's psychological and practical needs.) Jeannie and Joe can take title to the house as "tenants in common" and at the same time can sign a separate contract which makes it clear that they own the house in proportion to the dollar amounts that each has contributed. The contract is then recorded at the County Recorder's office in the county where the property is located. Here is a detailed example of how this sort of agreement might read. Of course, the specifics of your agreement will differ. When houses are owned in unequal shares title should be taken as "tenants in common."

AGREEMENT

Jeannie Parker and Joe Richards agree as follows:

1) That Jeannie and Joe will purchase the house at 1639 Carolina St., Salem, Oregon. Their initial investment (down payment and closing costs) will be $20,000, of which Jeannie will contribute $18,000 and Joe, $2,000. Title to the house will be recorded as "Jeannie Parker and Joe Richards as Tenants in Common."

2) Joe and Jeannie will each make one-half of the monthly mortgage, tax and homeowners insurance payments.

3) Joe will contribute labor and materials to improve the house. His labor will be valued at $12.00 per hour and the materials will be valued at their actual cost.

4) A notebook entitled "Exhibit A - 'Homeowners Record' for 1639 Carolina Street" will be maintained and is hereby incorporated into, and made a part of, this contract as Exhibit A. Joe and Jeannie shall record the following information in their "Homeowners Record".*

    a) The $18,000 initial contribution made to purchase the house by Jeannie;
    b) The $2,000 initial contribution made to purchase the house by Joe;
    c) All money Jeannie contributes for house payments, real property taxes and homeowners insurance;
    d) Joe's labor on home improvements valued at $12.00 per hour;
    e) The dollar amount that Joe pays for supplies and materials necessary for home improvements;
    f) All money that Joe contributes for house payments, real property taxes and homeowners insurance.

5) The proportion of the house owned by Jeannie and Joe respectively as of any particular date shall be computed as follows:

---

* The system we set out here is simple and reasonably fair. It credits both parties with all contributions made (not only those which go to equity). It allocates any natural increase in the value of the home along the lines of total contribution and ignores the fact that Jeannie made a large portion of her contribution before Joe. If you want to work out a more exactly accurate (and complicated) system, see a computer. Several of our friends are using this sort of system and find that it works well.

a) The total dollar amount of the contributions by both Joe and Jeannie as set out in paragraph 4 shall be separately totaled;

b) The total equity interest in the house shall be computed by subtracting the amount of all mortgages and encumbrances from the fair market value of the house as of the date the computation is made. If Joe and Jeannie can't agree on the fair market value, they shall have the house appraised. This shall be done by each of them designating a licensed real estate broker or salesperson who is familiar with the neighborhood to do an appraisal. These two appraisers shall choose a third real estate salesperson or broker who shall also make an appraisal. The average of the three appraisals will be the fair market value of the house;

c) The smaller total arrived at in Section 5a of this contract shall be placed above the total amount invested by both people to form a fraction. This fraction represents the share of the total joint equity interest in the house owned by the person with the smaller share. The remainder of the total joint equity interest belongs to the person with the larger share.

EXAMPLE: If after living together for five years, Joe's contribution totals $20,000 and Jeannie's $40,000, Joe would be entitled to $\frac{20,000}{60,000}$ or 1/3 of the value of the total equity in the house. Assuming that the fair market value of the house was $80,000 and all mortgages and other encumbrances total $40,000, this would mean that Joe would be entitled to 1/3 of $40,000 or $13,333.

6) Either Joe or Jeannie can terminate this agreement at any time. If this occurs, it is understood that the person with the larger equity interest in the house as computed under the terms of paragraph 5 above shall have first choice as to whether he or she wishes to stay living in the house.

7) Should separation occur and a decision made under the terms of paragraph 6 of this contract concerning who is to stay in the house, the person leaving is entitled to receive at least one-half of his or her share as computed under paragraph 5 of this contract in cash within ninety days of the decision to separate. In addition, the person staying shall give the person leaving a three-year mortgage for the remaining portion of his or her share not paid in cash. Said mortgage will be recorded at the County Recorder's office and is payable in 36 equal monthly installments at 9% interest. If the person who wishes to stay in the house is unable to meet the terms of this paragraph, the house shall be sold and the proceeds divided according to the shares established under paragraph 5a of this contract.

_____   _____
Date   Joe Richards

_____   _____
Date   Jeannie Parker

5. If One Person Moves Into A House Already Owned By The Other, What Legal Steps Can Be Taken To Protect Both Parties?

We are commonly asked questions by unmarried couples trying to figure out how to deal with the thicket of legal, practical and emotional problems that can pop up when one person moves into another's house. Sometimes it seems that even the most relaxed people have problems when one invades another's turf. Let's look at a typical situation. A friend (let's call him Alan) calls to say that he has just moved in with his lover (Faye) and that they plan to live in her house. Faye has asked Alan to share equally the monthly house payments, real property taxes, fire insurance, etc. Alan's response to this request is to say, "OK, but only if I somehow get to own part of the house."

As it turns out, the house Faye lives in is worth about $75,000, the existing mortgage is $50,000, and her equity is $25,000. Faye agrees with Alan that if he pays one-half of the payments, he should get some interest in the house, but she raises two good points. The first is that, since she already has a big investment in the house, Alan couldn't hope to get much of a share by paying one-half of the monthly payments. Her second point is in the form of a question. Assuming that it was decided to give Alan an equity (ownership) interest in the house, how could it be fairly done? All of this was getting a little hard to work out over the phone, so we invited Alan and Faye over for a pot of tea and a discussion of possible solutions to their problem. Here are several:

a) The simplest solution would be for Alan to forget buying a share of the house and have him pay Faye a monthly amount for rent. Of course, we pointed out to Faye that this should in fairness be considerably less than the one-half of mortgage, tax and insurance costs that she first requested. Why? Because Faye is buying the house and Alan is not. We suggested that if this approach were adopted, Faye and Alan should check the amounts paid by other people sharing houses in their neighborhood to arrive at a fair rent;

b) Another simple solution would be for Alan to pay Faye an amount equal to one-half of the value of her equity in exchange for her deeding the house to both of them either as "joint tenants" or "tenants in common". In this situation as the equity is $25,000, this would mean that Alan would need to pay Faye $12,500. We explained to Alan and Faye that if they followed this approach, they would probably want to make a contract to deal with questions such as who keeps the house if they break up, etc. (see D1-4 of this chapter). But before we could get too far with this discussion, Alan ended it by standing up and turning his pockets inside out. He had eight dollars and a Swiss army knife with a broken can opener. Even in these days of easy credit this didn't seem to be quite enough for a down payment.

c) A third possible way to resolve Alan and Faye's problem is less simple. Alan and Faye could sign a contract under which Alan agrees to pay one-half (or all or any other fraction) of the monthly expenses in exchange for a percentage of the total equity equal to the proportion his payments bear to the total amount of money invested in the house by both parties.* After we all talked for a while, it became clear that Alan and Faye wished to work out a variation of this approach. As Alan said, "I want to think of myself as more than a boarder, but I don't have the cash to pay for one-half of Faye's share." Here is what they worked out.

---

57 Primrose Path Contract

Alan Martineau and Faye Salinger agree as follows:

1) That Faye owns the house at 57 Primrose Path, Omaha, Nebraska, subject to a mortgage with the Prairie National Bank in the amount of $50,000;

2) That Alan and Faye agree that the house has a fair market value of $75,000 as of the date this contract is signed and that Faye's equity interest is $25,000;

3) That commencing on the date that this contract is signed, Alan shall pay all monthly expenses for property taxes, homeowners insurance, mortgage payments and necessary repairs and shall continue to do so until his total payments equal $50,000 or until the parties separate;

4) When Alan makes payments in the amount of $50,000 as set out in paragraph 3, Faye shall deed the house to "Faye Salinger and Alan Martineau as Tenants in Common".** From this date on, the house shall be owned equally by Alan and Faye and all expenses for taxes, mortgage insurance and repairs shall be shared equally;

5) Should Alan and Faye separate prior to the time that Alan contributes $50,000, the house shall continue to belong to Faye and Alan will be required to leave within thirty days of the decision to separate, but Alan shall be entitled to his share of the equity (see paragraph 7). Alan's share of the total equity value of the house shall be figured at the rate of one-half of one percent for every month that he pays all of the expenses as set out in paragraph 3 above. For example, if Alan pays all the expenses for two years, his interest in the house equity shall be 12%;

6) Once Alan contributes $50,000 and becomes a "tenant in common" with Faye, he shall have an equal opportunity to stay in the house if a separation occurs. If the couple cannot agree amicably who is to stay and who to go after they become "tenants in common", they shall have a friend flip a coin with the winner getting to purchase the share of the other and remain in the house;

7) If a separation occurs either before or after Alan becomes a "tenant in common", the person leaving shall be entitled to receive his or her share of the equity within ninety days of moving out. If there is a dispute about the fair market value of the house, Faye and Alan shall each select a licensed real estate person to make an appraisal. These two people shall themselves select a third licensed real estate person

---

* People who have read this chapter carefully will realize that this is similar to the approach that Keija and Felix chose in slightly different circumstances. See D4 above.
** Alan and Faye could have chosen "joint tenancy", but after talking the situation over, both decided that tenancy in common fit their needs better. See Section C of this chapter.

to make a third appraisal. The three appraisals shall be averaged to determine the fair market value. If it proves impossible for the person who wins the coin flip to pay off the person leaving within ninety days, the other person (the coin flip loser) shall have an additional ninety days to raise the cash to buy out the other person. If neither person is willing or able to buy out the other, the house shall be sold and the proceeds divided under the terms of this agreement.

Date	Faye Salinger
Date	Alan Martineau

NOTE: Several people have asked us how Alan and Faye decided that Alan should pay $50,000 for a one-half interest in the house and how they decided that he should get credit for one-half of one percent of the equity for every month that he paid all of the expenses. As we didn't know for sure, we asked them. Here is Faye's reply:

"We were interested in approximate fairness — not absolute statistical accuracy even if that were possible. We figured that as I already had $25,000 in the house and that the house was likely to go up in value, it would be fair to require that Alan contribute more as his payments would be made gradually. Also, I wanted to give up my full-time job and have more time for painting Japanese miniatures, so I was anxious to have Alan pay all the expenses — taxes, repairs, insurance as well as mortgage payments. $50,000 seemed to be an amount that we could both live with. We gave Alan credit for all of his expenses as part of buying the house — not just his mortgage payments, because we felt that this worked out fairly for us. To arrive at the one-half of one percent per month (or 6% per year) figure, we did some arithmetic and concluded that it would take Alan about eight years (60 months) to contribute his $50,000 and become a one-half owner. If you divide 50% by eight years, you come out to 6% per year or one-half of one percent per month. I am aware that Alan is getting a pretty good deal, but so am I as I don't have to worry about any house expenses for eight years.

nsurance*

We include a chapter on insurance because it is so much a part of our lives — either because we buy and rely on it, or because we consider it a great rip-off and try to avoid it absolutely. Either way, the days when everyone at the job or church or in the small town got together to help each other through times of adversity are gone for most of us. Today, if we want protection, we must buy it from multi-national corporations. Often, the only human contact in the whole process is with that nice, gray-haired man who appears on our T.V. sets to assure us that all the things he has just told us to worry about will be taken care of, if we will only give his company a few pennies a day (hour, minute).

As you may have guessed, we are not great advocates of insurance. The money that many families pay out in premiums is disproportionate to what they receive in return. We have seen too many couples (married and unmarried) who need every penny they can get their hands on to go to the grocery store, laying out large sums to support that gray-haired T.V. actor and the tranquilized deer that wanders around behind him.

We are also frankly worried about what we believe to be the harmful effects of the current "insure everything" mania. The medical malpractice mess (doctors can't afford insurance and can't practice without it) is only the tip of the iceberg. Increasingly we hear tales of people who can't do perfectly sensible things because they can't get insurance. By way of example, here is a story our friend Carole, who lives in Ukiah, California, recently told us.

It seems that there is a day care center in Ukiah which takes care of children from low-income families. In the summer it's like a furnace in Ukiah and the children are at

---

* Parts of this chapter appeared in the *People's Guide To California Marriage Law* by the same authors.

the center all day. But even though there is a good place to swim nearby, the kids can't go in the water. Why not? Well, it's a little complicated, but it boils down to the fact that the non-profit corporation that runs the center has no money to pay the hefty insurance premiums it would take to cover all the kids, and the lawyer for the center has advised that, if there was an accident, a lawsuit could wipe the center out. Thus, no money means no insurance, and no insurance means no swimming. The result is a lot of sweltering kids cooped up in 100 degree heat right next to the water. Pardon us if we think that the kids of 80 or 50 or even 30 years ago hanging out at the local swimming hole weren't better off. Playing it safe makes sense, but not if it means being so safe that you don't play at all.

But aren't there some real needs for insurance? What if your house burns down, or you get in a car wreck, or you die and your children need money to go to school, or you hit someone on the head with a golf ball, or a thief steals your stereo, or you fall in front of a bus, train, trolley, stage coach or riverboat, or you get sick and can't work, or your boat sinks, or a flying saucer falls on your sun porch, etc., etc.? If you are seriously worried about any of these disasters, or the thousands of others that could befall you at any moment, you probably already have insurance. We aren't going to try and talk you out of it either; some types of insurance do make sense. Everyone has to make their own decisions about this sort of thing. A person who believes firmly enough that he needs a million dollars' worth of life insurance and protection from attack by whooping cranes, probably does. Our job here is to outline the more common types of insurance and review with you some of the ins and outs of each. It will be up to you to use your common sense to purchase only the insurance you need.

A. TYPES OF INSURANCE COMPANIES

Broadly speaking, insurance companies are organized in two ways. "Stock companies" (Travellers, Aetna Life and Casualty, Connecticut General, Prudential, etc.) are owned by stockholders and sell most of their insurance through independent agents (often called brokers). These agents have their own businesses and commonly sell the policies of a number of companies. "Mutual companies" (State Farm, Metropolitan Life, Mutual of Omaha, etc.) are owned, at least in theory, by their policy holders and normally sell insurance through their own employees.

Some people believe that "stock" companies and their independent agent system provide better service, on the theory that the independent agent can intervene on your behalf with the company, but that "mutual" companies often offer insurance at lower rates. There may be some truth to these generalizations, but there are many exceptions. After all, professional managers run both types of companies (not the stockholders or policy holders) and they tend to think alike. Most of our friends in the insurance business tell us that the integrity of the individual with whom you are dealing is more important than the type of company for which he works. So while it's interesting to know that there can be differences between "stock" and "mutual" companies, your best bet is probably not to pay too much attention to how a company is organized, but to make your decision on the basis of which company is the most sensitive to the needs of unmarried couples and offers the most coverage at the lowest price.

110

B. DISCRIMINATION AGAINST UNMARRIED COUPLES

Just a few years ago we commonly received calls from unmarried couples who were denied life, car or homeowners insurance because they were not married. These calls have tapered off recently and, although we can't promise you that you won't run into companies which still discriminate, we can tell you that there are now plenty who have changed their rules to accomodate unmarried couples.

On the whole, people in the insurance business tell us that it is easier for unmarried couples to buy insurance on the West Coast than in any other part of the country. More unmarried couples live in California than in any other state and apparently the effect of their numbers has convinced the insurance industry that it is more profitable to go with history than against it. Experienced insurance brokers in New York City have told us that unmarried couples can still face discrimination there. Some companies will only insure them if they have other insurance business, or if they are willing to pay premium rates. But wherever you live, with a little effort you should be able to buy insurance at the same rates married couples get. Shop around.

A few states are enacting laws which state that it is illegal for insurance companies to discriminate on the basis of marital status. Because this area is changing fast, we can't give you a meaningful list. If you want to check out the law in your state, call your State Insurance Commissioner.

C. LIFE INSURANCE

Americans have over 2 trillion dollars of life insurance in force. This seems like way too much to us. If you and your friend are both capable of working and do not plan on children, we can't understand why you would want to send monthly checks to a life insurance company. If you have children and/or a dependent spouse, some life insurance may make sense to tide your family over the immediate hard times that your death and the resultant loss of income would cause. But be careful not to buy more insurance than you can afford. Life insurance salespeople will try to sell you enough insurance to support your family in luxury for the rest of their lives. "Did you ever see children who have lost their Daddy who didn't believe in life insurance?" is one of their favorite sayings. To this you might reply, "Did you ever see kids happy about their Daddy working all day to pay insurance premiums?"

Remember, life insurance companies spend many millions of dollars of your money trying to make you insecure and fearful. The more afraid you are, the more you are likely to believe that you need them. Maybe you do. Certainly many Americans believe that life insurance is necessary. But perhaps you can get along with less insurance than you first thought, or than the insurance companies recommend. Consider that, if one member of an unmarried couple dies, statistics indicate that the other will cope fairly quickly, that needy children can get scholarships or student loans for their educations, and it doesn't hurt people who need money to work. Also, remember that if a wage earner covered by Social Security dies, his or her minor children are entitled to monthly benefits which can extend through college. Sylvia Porter's *Money* book gives a good review of the Social Security system, including tables with benefit amounts. You can also get a great deal of printed information from the Social Security Administration itself. None of us is as essential as that friendly, gray-haired man on the T.V. would have us believe. Consider too that worrying about paying insurance premiums every month may help you to an early grave.

Life insurance companies like to advertise the savings features of their "straight life" insurance policies (you get all your money back and more in twenty years if you don't die, as well as being insured if you do die). This sounds as though you can't lose, but before you get too enthusiastic, remember, the insurance companies aren't in business to do you any favors. The value of a dollar you get back in twenty or thirty years, thanks to inflation, will be worth far less than the dollar you invest now. Also consider that if you put the same money in a savings and loan every month, it would, depending on the amount of interest paid, double and probably redouble in the same time period. If you are curious about this, get an interest chart at the bank and work it out for yourself. Again, this is not to say that unmarried couples shouldn't ever have life insurance, but only that life insurance policies are not a particularly good way to save money. Far from the insurance company giving you a bargain, they are, in fact, getting the use of lots of your money at low rent.

If you decide to buy life insurance, decide first what kind. There are a number of different types, but we have space here to discuss only the commonest.

1. "Term" Life Insurance

This is the cheapest form of insurance and all that many unmarried couples need. You simply pay X dollars for Y amount of insurance for Z years. If you die during the term covered by the insurance, your beneficiaries get paid the face value of the policy; if you live longer than the policy term, no one gets anything. This sort of policy has no savings feature (you get no money if you live to the end of the policy term), so is fairly cheap. A man, age 25, in good health, might expect to pay about $55 per year for a ten-year term policy which would pay off $10,000 if he died during the term. At age 35, the same man would pay about $70 per year. If he were to purchase the same coverage at 45, still assuming good health, the annual premium would be in the neighborhood of $125 to $130.

You should know that insurance salespeople hate "term" insurance and will do all in their power to get you to buy "straight life". They will give you lots of arguments against "term" insurance (most of them phony), but won't tell you the real reason for their preference of "straight life" — that it is far more profitable for them. One of the main arguments they will surely advance against "term" insurance is that your health may change, making it impossible or difficult to buy insurance when you get older and the "term" insurance runs out. There is a simple answer to this question for most people — so what! Life insurance is normally only sensible for people with growing children, and "term" will take care of this need easily and cheaply. As you get older and the children are grown, your need for insurance decreases, and you are better off putting your money in the bank.

2. "Straight Life" Insurance

As mentioned above, "straight life" costs more but, in addition to your beneficiary getting paid off if you die while the policy is in effect, you get a lump sum payment or, in some cases, periodic payments (this is often called an "annuity feature") at the end of the policy period if you are still alive. You also normally have the right to borrow (at a healthy interest rate) against the money that you have paid in on the policy. Insurance companies love you to do this, as they get to lend you back the money which you just gave them for almost nothing at high interest rates. Premiums for a "straight life" policy are much higher than for term insurance since you are buying a savings account in addition to insurance. A man, age 25 and in good health, purchasing a ten-year "straight life" policy which would pay off $10,000 at death, would pay approximately $170 per year. Purchasing the same policy at age 35, his annual premium would be about $235, and at age 45, he could expect to pay about $340 per year.

3. Unmarried Couples And Life Insurance

Life insurance used to be a particular problem area for unmarried couples. Why? Because insurance companies have a rule that, in order to purchase life insurance, the beneficiary of the policy (the person who gets the money if you die) must have an "insurable interest". Boiled down, this means nothing more than that the beneficiary must have a relationship to the insured that makes it unlikely that the beneficiary will

treat the insured to an early trip to the happy hunting ground in order to collect on the policy. To take an extreme example, no insurance company would be enthusiastic about Joe Gunslinger taking out a policy on the life of Harry Sheriff with himself as beneficiary. Children, spouses, parents and other relatives have long been held to have an "insurable interest" in one another, but traditionally insurance companies have refused to write policies for unmarried couples because they felt that there was no "insurable interest". Apparently they believed that people living together were more likely to slip a little arsenic into the rice pudding than were the married. The result of this rule was that many unmarried couples lied — pretended they were married — in order to get insurance that they couldn't get otherwise. This, of course, played right into the insurance companies' sweaty palms. When one member of the couple died, they often refused to pay on the grounds that there had been a serious misstatement of fact on the insurance application. In many instances courts ruled that they could do this.

Enough history. Where are we now? Many insurance companies now rule that people living together do have an "insurable interest" in one another and will write policies for unmarried couples. Some companies still balk, however, and knowledgeable brokers and agents have a few sleight of hand techniques to get policies accepted. One is to write the policy with another relative as the beneficiary, substituting in the member of the unmarried couple later. This is legal as you have a right to change your beneficiary. Another common device is to list your friend as a fiance. This works as the insurance companies never seem to be interested in the length of your engagement. But insurance companies are still sticklers for truth on applications, so don't represent yourself as married it you aren't. If you already have a policy in which you have wrongly claimed to be married, change it.

WARNING! Some companies do try to charge higher rates to unmarried couples. Call a number of companies and compare rates before you buy.

D. INSURANCE ON YOUR HOME

When we think about insuring our home and its possessions, we normally think first about protecting ourselves from fire and theft losses. To do this most people buy a "homeowners policy" (see below for "Renters Insurance"). In addition to fire and theft, this type of policy normally protects you against certain types of personal liability, as well as protecting your home from loss due to other hazards. "Homeowners policies" are often advertised in very general terms as protecting you against most sorts of loss that are likely to befall your home and the things in it. This is not true. These policies have many exclusions and conditions and don't cover some hazards at all. We will mention some of the obvious things to watch out for, but this discussion will be no substitute for your getting out your policy if you have one, or getting several blank ones from different insurance companies if you are thinking about buying, and doing some studying. Policies vary quite a bit from company to company, and you may find that some policies fit your circumstances better than others. Also, it is often possible to buy additional coverage for a risk not provided for in your policy if you pay a little extra.

Homeowners insurance for unmarried couples used to be difficult to buy, but this is changing rapidly. Traditionally, some companies would write fire insurance for an unmarried couple who were jointly buying a house, but would not write a joint homeowners policy containing all of the other provisions discussed below. If the unmarried couple wanted full homeowners coverage, they were each asked to buy separate policies. Of course, this cost considerably more and amounted to a form of discrimination against unmarried couples. But you needn't put up with this sort of nonsense; there are now companies that will write homeowners policies for unmarried couples at the same rates married couples get. To find them, call a younger broker in a part of town where a lot of unmarried couples live. He or she should know which companies to approach.

1. Fire Insurance

Fire insurance is a part of all homeowners policies, or it can be purchased separately. It is always required by banks or other lending institutions such as savings and loans and credit unions as a condition of lending money on a house. The lending institution is interested in protecting their money. They have little interest in yours. This means that they will only require you to have insurance in an amount to cover the amount of money you owe them on the deed of trust (mortgage).

EXAMPLE 1: You buy a house valued at $90,000 (assuming a land value of $20,000 and a structure value of $70,000), making a down payment of $25,000 and getting a first deed of trust for $65,000 from the First National Bank of Condorville. The bank will require that you get at least $65,000 worth of fire insurance to cover their investment. They don't care about your $25,000 in equity, so if you want this covered, it's your decision. As the land is worth $20,000 and doesn't need to be insured, you would only need to insure $5,000 more than the bank requires to be completely covered.

EXAMPLE 2: But what happens if you have a $76,000 house (exclusive of land) and a $48,000 fire insurance policy, and the house suffers major fire damage in the amount of $32,000? Are you fully covered? Perhaps not. Policies are normally written on a percentage of loss basis. Since your house lost one-third of its value, you would in theory collect only one-third of the policy or $16,000. However, we are told by friends in the business that in practice you would stand a good chance of collecting the whole amount.

Some policies are written with an inflation clause so that, as the value of the home increases, the insurance coverage automatically increases too; most are not. In the last few years property values have soared, as measured against our increasingly worthless paper money. This means that many homes are under-insured. You might take a moment to check the amount of your coverage to see if it would cover the loss of your home. In deciding how much insurance is enough, however, remember that your land won't burn, so subtract the value of the land from the total value of your property to determine the insurance you need.

In addition to protecting the dwelling itself, homeowners policies also cover the contents of the home to a stated amount. This amount will cover routine household goods, but will probably not cover particularly valuable items such as jewelry, paintings and furs beyond a minimum limit, often as low as $100. You will find that unusually expensive items must be listed and insured separately at an additional cost. Most policies cover most of your belongings, but again you should read your policy. You may find that something important to you is not covered. For example, many policies exclude goods held for sale. If you are a salesperson or small businessperson

116

and occasionally store merchandise in your home, this could be a problem for you.

Should you be burned out, or otherwise driven from your home by an insured risk (see below), your homeowners policy will pay for temporary substitute lodgings. In many policies the emphasis is definitely on the word "temporary", however.

2. Insurance Against Other Hazards (Windstorm, Hail, Smoke, Falling Trees, Etc.)

In addition to fire, which usually includes lightning, a homeowners policy normally protects you against loss from **certain kinds** of windstorm, hail, explosions, riots, crashing vehicles or aircraft, smoke, vandalism, breakage of windows and falling trees. (Berserk hedgehogs are not covered unless you pay extra.) When we say "certain kinds", this is exactly what we mean, as many types of hazards you might think are covered under these headings are not. For example, under "smoke" many policies exclude smoke from fireplaces, or under "hail" it is common to exclude frost. Read your policy. As with fire insurance, coverage extends to your home and to your personal belongings up to the amounts listed in the policy. When it comes to personal property, there is usually a deductible amount not covered, often $50 to $500 depending on the policy. This means that, should you suffer a loss of $1,000 and have a policy with a $100 deductible clause, the insurance company will reimburse you only for $900.

Several risks are **never** covered in standard homeowners policies. These include flood, earthquake and nuclear explosion or radiation. For many people, flood and earthquake coverage may be important. People who live on flood plains want flood insurance; people who live on active faults want to be protected against earthquakes. For the most part if you need these, you will find that it costs extra and may be hard to get. The reason for this is obvious. Insurance companies make money from charging you for protection against things that almost never happen, not for hazards that are likely. No one wants flood insurance if he lives on a mountain top, slippage insurance if he lives on flat ground, or earthquake insurance if he lives a thousand miles from the nearest fault. Only those who feel themselves threatened by a hazard want to pay for protection.

3. Theft Insurance

Theft insurance is included in homeowners policies and protects you from robberies and burglaries occurring at your home. In some cases it covers personal belongings stolen from other locations. As burglaries have increased, the cost of theft insurance has gone up at the same time that coverage has been cut back.* Most policies now have "deductible" amounts of $100, $200 or even $500, and many don't cover certain items or limit the amount of coverage for a particular item. Thus, some policies exclude cash, credit cards, pets, etc., while others limit the amount of cash covered to $100, the value of manuscripts to $1,000 and jewelry to $500.** Make sure your policy

---

* It is wise to make a list of your valuable possessions before a theft occurs. If you want to be extra careful, put a number on each item and record the numbers on your list. If there is a theft, this will make it easier to collect from your own insurance company which otherwise might question whether some of the items ever existed.
** It is common that expensive jewelry, furs, valuable paintings, etc., must be individually listed and extra premiums paid for coverage.

covers what you think it does. If it doesn't, check out the policies of other companies or think about covering the particular items that you are worried about separately.

We have more than one friend who has met the problem of theft and theft insurance by simply not having a lot of things around that are worth stealing. Often it is easier to have serviceable but older possessions and leave the door unlocked than it is to have a houseful of new trinkets that half the world wants to get away from you.

4. Personal Liability

Homeowners policies also normally provide protection to a certain dollar amount ($50,000 is common) for liability incurred by the insured and his or her family. This means that if you directly injure another person (hit them on the head with a golf ball), they are injured on your property through your negligence (they slip on a broken front step), or you damage their belongings (your garden hose floods the neighbor's cactus garden), you are covered. Here again, there are a lot of things not covered (excluded), the major ones being any damage you do with a motor vehicle, or through your business.

Personal liability coverage is somewhat broader than you might expect,however, as it protects you against injuries occurring off your property. Thus, if you turn quickly on the sidewalk downtown and knock someone over, you are protected up to the dollar amount of the policy if you are found to be negligent.

5. Medical Payments To Others

This covers any medical expenses incurred by people injured on or about your premises. Under most policies it would cover a situation where your dog bites the paperboy.

E. RENTERS INSURANCE

These policies are basically the same as "homeowners" policies, less, of course, the protection for the dwelling itself. While other risks are covered, basically you are buying fire and theft insurance on your personal belongings. There is normally a $200-$300 deductible on the theft portion of the insurance. You also get personal liability coverage as discussed in Section D4 above. In most areas renters insurance is quite reasonably priced. But don't think that you or your belongings are covered because your landlord has insurance. Even if you rent a portion of a duplex from people who also live in the home and have homeowners insurance, you will not be covered under their policy.

Renters insurance is easy for unmarried couples to get separately — that is, one policy for each person. Traditionally there has been some difficulty getting one policy to cover both people, but several brokers tell us that this is changing and it is now possible.

F. AUTOMOBILE INSURANCE

We won't give you a complete review of the ins and outs of automobile insurance because state laws vary a great deal. Many states have adopted some form of no-fault insurance, while others have not. Legislation is pending in Congress to impose federal no-fault standards. When the dust clears and some sort of uniformity occurs, we will include comprehensive information here.

Purchasing automobile insurance can be a problem for unmarried couples, but again not to the extent that it was a few years ago. Before issuing a policy, many companies want a complete list of the people who live in the house with the insured. Do they have cars of their own? What are the license numbers, etc? The insurance company wants to run their own check with the Department of Motor Vehicles to be sure that people with bad driving records are not likely to be driving your car. The more your living situation seems to the company to be communal with a lot of people coming and going, the less likely they are to write insurance.

Unmarried couples who each own their own car should have no trouble getting separate insurance. However, if they own one or more cars jointly, there can be problems. Many companies will not insure both people and cars jointly in the same manner as if they were married, but instead will try to write two separate insurance policies listing each person as the primary driver of one of the cars with the other listed as a secondary driver. This approach sounds OK but it isn't. Why? Because a married couple owning two cars would qualify for a second car discount, but an unmarried couple each listing a car in one name with the other person as a secondary driver would not. One way to get around this is to list both cars in one person's name with the other listed as a secondary driver on both. But again, your best bet is to find a sympathetic insurance salesperson, explore all the the angles and then compare prices. Some companies will give unmarried couples the same privileges and rates as if they were married.

G. SOCIAL SECURITY

The Social Security Program discriminates against unmarried couples. If you are married to a wage earner covered by Social Security, you are eligible to receive retirement benefits. If you are the widow, widower or divorced spouse of a wage earner, you can also get benefits.* However, there are no benefits for people who have been living together unless, of course, they have been individually earned by each wage earner.** Is this unfair? Of course it is, but it is nevertheless the law. If the trend away from marriage continues, changes may be made, but as of now a non-wage earner will come out ahead financially if married to a wage earner rather than living with the same person.

---

* If you have questions concerning what you are or will be entitled to, call Social Security and ask for a pamphlet entitled "Your Social Security".
** Children of deceased or disabled members of unmarried couples are eligible for benefits if paternity can be proven. See Chapter 8, Section J.

COMMON LAW MARRIAGE NOTE: If you have been living with someone covered by Social Security in a state which recognizes common law marriage (see Chapter 1) and your friend has died or become disabled, you may be able to claim that you were, in fact, married and thus qualify for benefits. Common law marriage is just as valid as formal marriage for Social Security purposes.

At the same time that many younger people who live together have been denied Social Security protection because they refuse to marry, older people have been discriminated against if they get married. Sounds crazy doesn't it, but crazy or not, prior to January 1, 1979, Social Security rules were written so that marriage between older people was actively discouraged. This was the result of regulations that stated that, if a widow or widower who received Social Security benefits under the account of a deceased spouse remarried, he/she lost his/her benefits.*   Thus, if Alicia, age 78, who got Social Security because she was Alec's widow, decided to marry Andrew, she would lose her benefits. But if she and Andrew decided to live together, she would still get her Social Security. Not surprisingly, many older couples have had to live together even though they weren't sure that they approved of "such goings on" to save that much-needed Social Security check. In more than one family, this meant that both grandparents and grandchildren were living together, leaving only the middle generation married.**

While living together has been a liberating experience for many older people, it has been an emotional trauma for others. Many people have philosphical or religious beliefs that almost require marriage. Indeed, many older couples have engaged in religious marriage ceremonies, but have not filed the papers with the county clerk, thus satisfying both God and government. But in addition to working out a personal solution to their problem, millions of people have petitioned their legislators to get the unfair Social Security laws changed. Finally, effective January 1, 1979, this has been done.

After January 1, 1979, if you receive widow's or widower's Social Security benefits, your checks will no longer be stopped or reduced if you remarry at age sixty or later. Previously reduced benefits to widows and widowers will be increased. Congress also made another change in Social Security benefits of importance to many older people. Under the new rules, if you are a divorced wife, 62 years of age or older, you can get benefits on your ex-husband's Social Security records if he is getting payments and your marriage lasted at least ten years (instead of 20 years). If you are a surviving divorced wife, survivor's benefits can now start as early as age 60 (50 if you are disabled).

H. PRIVATE DISABILITY INSURANCE

Social Security provides a limited income if you are disabled, either permanently or for a significant period of time (one year or more). States, through Unemployment

---

* Women who were "homemakers" and never themselves worked at jobs covered by Social Security were the largest group of people affected by this rule.
** One grandmother recently told us that when she started living with her lover, her granddaughter said, "Far out", and her daughter, "How could you." To her granddaughter she replied, "Groovy", and to her daughter, "Don't be so square"

Insurance systems, provide some disability insurance for short term disabilities. But no one is going to get rich from the money provided by either of these programs. In fact, these benefits are hardly adequate to keep a modest roof over one's head and a bowl of soup in front of the kids. People who want a T.V. aerial on the roof and a piece of meat in the soup might do well to think about private disability insurance coverage.

With private disability insurance you (or in some cases your employer) pay an insurance company a certain monthly premium. They in turn provide you with a monthly income during months when you are unable to work because of disability or illness. The amount that they pay you is dependent, of course, on the amount that you pay them. Thus, if you have a heart attack and can't work for eight months, the insurance company sends you a check each month, supplementing benefits you get from the government. In addition to sending you money, most policies waive your responsibility to pay premiums while you are ill. Some people find that disability insurance doesn't cost as much as they think it might, because they need only buy enough to supplement available government programs, not to start from scratch.

Rather than go through the details of the various types of disability insurance available, we suggest that you simply take a look at what several insurance companies have to offer. Here are a few questions to ask. Does the policy pay for partial, as well as total, disability? Are there benefits to cover the cost of educational rehabilitation? What happens if there are recurrent disabilities? Can the insurance company cancel the policy, and if so, under what terms?

Disability insurance is often sold through professional, or other trade associations. Sometimes employers will purchase it for their more important employees. If you are interested in purchasing disability insurance, first check whatever business or union group you belong to and find out what is available to the membership.

WARNING: If you are disabled, you might possibly have trouble getting paid. Some insurance companies are miserly to the point of being fraudulent. Call your State Insurance Commissioner if you have trouble. Also beware of any companies which offer to give you a lump sum pay off, or a better policy, once you are disabled. The only reason that business people offer to trade is because they believe that they (not you) will benefit. Never give up a policy on the promise of a better one. Be sure any new policy is completely operational **before** giving up an old one.*

Should you buy disability insurance? Only you can say. Some people who don't buy life insurance get it, because they are more concerned about things that might happen while they are alive, than they are about things that might occur after death. Many consider it an expensive luxury they can do without, while others consider it well worth the money. The authors of this book fall into the former category, but who knows — if we were richer authors, we might change our minds. There is no discrimination against people who are living together as far as purchasing disability insurance is concerned.

---

* Recently lawyers have won some large damage awards for people in this sort of situation. If you think an insurance company cheated you or is trying to, see a lawyer.

I. HEALTH INSURANCE

Many people have called us to complain that the health policy that comes with their job covers a spouse free or at a reduced rate, but does not cover a living together partner. What can we say? It's true, this sort of discrimination is rampant and at this point there is nothing illegal about it.

tarting a Family

One evening you dream about little feet scampering about your house. After satisfying yourself that it's not a dog, cat or hamster that you are hankering for, you and your mate decide that, even though you are not interested in getting married, you would like to have a child. While there are no insurmountable legal problems involved in having children without being married, there are a few things you will want to think about.*

A. DECIDING TO HAVE A CHILD (OR ABORTION)

A father recently came to us and asked if he had to support his child in the following circumstances. He and his mate decided not to have children when they commenced living together. After a couple of years they got married and again rejected the idea of having children. They lived together for two years after the marriage, and both continued to agree that they didn't want children. They then decided to separate. A day or two before they parted, the woman (by her own admission) ceased using her diaphragm without telling the man, in an attempt to get pregnant. She succeeded, although the fact that she was pregnant wasn't known until six weeks after the separation. **Yes,** the father does have a duty to support.

Courts are not interested in why people have children. Whether you decide to have children only after signing a contract, or by throwing the I Ching, or checking the location of the planets, or just letting it happen is legally irrelevant. If a child arrives,

---

* We are talking about having children naturally. The problems unmarried persons encounter adopting children within the United States can be insurmountable. If you wish to adopt, you may well find yourself getting married for this purpose. Although some states such as California now allow single parent adoption in some circumstances, if the single person is living with someone or if both members of an unmarried couple want to adopt, it is unlikely the state would approve such an adoption. Some unmarried couples are able to adopt children in foreign countries, particularly if the country is poor and has a large number of orphans. An exception to this rule occurs when you want to adopt a child who is already living with you. If you have been caring for the child for a long time and the natural parents are out of the picture or approve the adoption, your adoption petition will probably be granted, especially if you are related to the child.

both parents have a duty to support. It makes no difference whatsoever whether the parents are or are not married. But is this fair to the man in the above situation? Perhaps not, but we aren't writing a book about fairness, only about the law the way it is.

What about abortion? That's simple. A woman who is pregnant can get an abortion without the consent of the father, whether or not she is married. According to the United States Supreme Court case *Roe v. Wade*, 410 U.S. 133 (1973), an adult woman's decision can be regulated by the state only in the following manner:*

1. Prior to the end of the first trimester (3 months) of pregnancy, the state may not interfere with or regulate the physician's decision, reached in consultation with his patient, that the pregnancy should be terminated.

2. From the end of the first trimester (3 months) of pregnancy until the fetus becomes viable (is capable of living outside the mother), the state may regulate the abortion procedure only to the extent that such regulation relates to the preservation and protection of the health of the mother.

3. After the fetus becomes viable, the state may prohibit abortion altogether, except in those cases necessary to preserve the life or health of the mother.

4. The state may declare abortions performed by persons other than physicians licensed by the state to be unlawful.

The practical aspects of this case for a woman are that, if you suspect you are pregnant and want an abortion, you should contact a physician as early as possible for verification, and you should compare prices before you select the physician or clinic that will perform the abortion.   The practical aspect for a man is that there is legally nothing he can do to influence a woman's decision to have or not to have a baby. This is true even if they are married and he desperately wants the child.

What about "Right To Life" groups and their fight to pass a constitutional amendment banning abortion? We are against it. While abortion makes us as queasy as the next person, we believe that a woman must have the legal freedom to make the choice. We have seen too many seventeen-year olds, pregnant and miserable, for whom motherhood would be a disaster, to think otherwise. Passage of a constitutional amendment banning abortion will simply drive tens of thousands of women out of hospitals and back to the rusty knives of the side-alley butchers. Of course, no woman should be coerced through the welfare or prison system, or in any other way, to have an abortion that she doesn't want, but at the same time no one should be required to have a child to salve someone else's conscience.

What about the rights of the father? Doesn't it seem somehow unfair to leave all the decision-making to the mother? If she decides to have the child, he has the legal obligation to support it, but if she wants an abortion, he has nothing to say. Yes, this is unfair and for that reason may not last. We expect legislation to be introduced, once

* In the later case of *Belloti v. Bond*, the Supreme Court extended the right to an abortion to minors.

the "Right To Life" people fail to pass their constitutional amendment, giving a father equal rights with the mother in deciding whether or not to get an abortion **if** the couple has agreed in advance by contract to share this decision — unless, of course, the mother's health is threatened, in which case she would have sole power to terminate the pregnancy. If the legal responsibilities of parents to care for and support their children are to survive in anything like the form in which we know them, both parents must have a say in deciding when to, and when not to, have children.

B. NAMING THE BABY

You may give your child any name you like. This includes first, middle and last names. You do not have to give the baby the last name of either father or mother. Thus Mary Jones and Jack Smith could name their child Ephraim Moonbeam if it pleased them.

In most states the normal procedure for naming a baby is substantially as follows:

While in the hospital a representative (frequently a volunteer) of the Health Department or similar agency asks the new mother what the child's name is, plus some other questions regarding the health of the mother and the occupation of the father. This information is then typed on a form that the mother is requested to sign. The mother **does not** have to give the child a name at this time, and she does not have to identify the father, although there may be some pressure to do so. The birth will be registered in any case. In some states a birth certificate reveals whether or not the parents are married. In most states, the birth certificate does not reveal this information.

If the baby was not born in a medical facility, the mother and/or person officiating at the birth are legally obligated to notify state or county health officials of the birth. Again, there is no requirement to name the baby at this time although it is common to do so. If the mother later decides on a name for the child or decides to give the information regarding the father, she should contact the appropriate state agency which usually has a name such as the Department of Vital Statistics, which will furnish her with a form to fill out to amend the birth certificate.

CAUTION: It is a terrible idea to list a person as the natural father if that person is not, in fact, the father. Many women are tempted to do this, especially if they no longer see the natural father and are now involved with someone else. Please be realistic and realize that your new relationship may not last forever, and you may later regret the naming of the wrong person.* We have seen many cases involving complicated questions of paternity and support grow from the seemingly simple act of listing the wrong person as the father of a child. Once a person is listed as a father, it is very difficult, and sometimes impossible, for the mother or the child to get the state to de-list him.

On the other hand, if you feel you have been wrongly named as a father on a birth certificate, this is not proof to a court that you are the father. In a paternity action or a support action you would still be able to contest paternity. The state will not take your name off a birth certificate simply because you state you are not the father, but an attorney may be able to assist you in bringing legal action to have your name removed.

C. PATERNITY

Very simply, paternity means "the state of being a father". For the reasons outlined in Sections C, D, E, F, and G of this chapter, it is essential that the natural father sign a paper stating that he is the father as soon as possible after the baby is born.** This is for the protection of the mother, the baby, and especially the father. Mix-ups over paternity are complicated, humiliating and often expensive. As you will see from reading the rest of this chapter, the law in the legitimacy-illegitimacy-paternity area is so confused that it's hard to be sure what a father's rights are unless he signs a

---

* For further information on naming a baby and changing names and/or amending a birth certificate, see *How To Change Your Name* (California edition) by David Loeb (coupon at end of book).
** What happens if the father doesn't sign the paternity statement when the child is born, but waits and signs it later? This is OK if he signs it before any dispute over custody, adoption, etc. develops. However, if he waits until a custody fight develops and then tries to improve his legal position by legitimating his child, many courts will say that it is too late. If you are in this position, see a lawyer.

paternity statement. You can prepare the necessary form yourself quite easily by reference to the sample shown below. Please do not let your excitement over the baby allow you to forget this simple detail. We include here two sample paternity statements. The first is the traditional type signed only by the father. The second is designed to be signed by both parents. We introduce this second form because we have recently encountered several cases where, after a man has signed the first type statement, the mother, wanting to frustrate his custody and visitation rights, has denied that he, in fact, was the father.

SAMPLE 1

ACKNOWLEDGEMENT OF PATERNITY

Lazarus Sandling hereby acknowledges that he is the natural father of Clementine Conlon Sandling, born January 1, 19   to Rebecca Conlon in New York City, New York.*

Lazarus Sandling further states that he has welcomed Clementine Conlon Sandling into his home and that it is his intention and belief that he has taken all steps necessary to fully legitimate Clementine Conlon Sandling for all purposes, including the right to inherit from, and through him, at the time of his death.

Lazarus Sandling further expressly acknowledges his duty to properly raise and adequately support Clementine Conlon Sandling.

_____   _____
Date   Lazarus Sandling

                    Notarize

SAMPLE 2

ACKNOWLEDGEMENT OF PARENTHOOD

Lazarus Sandling and Rebecca Conlon hereby acknowledge that they are the natural parents of Clementine Conlon Sandling, born January 1, 19   in New York City, New York.

---

* As noted above, there is no legal reason why Clementine's last name must be Sandling for purposes of legitimation. However, as a practical matter our society takes this sort of tradition seriously and it may be easier for everyone in years to come if the child has Lazarus' last name, or a hyphenated version of Lazarus' and Rebecca's names.

Lazarus Sandling and Rebecca Conlon further state that they have welcomed Clementine Conlon Sandling into their home and that it is their intention and belief that Clementine is fully legitimated for all purposes, including the right to inherit from and through Lazarus Sandling.*

Lazarus Sandling and Rebecca Conlon further expressly acknowledge their legal responsibility to properly raise and adequately support Clementine Conlon Sandling.

_____   _____
Date   Rebecca Conlon

_____   _____
Date   Lazarus Sandling

                                          Notarize

_____

(Tear-out Paternity Statements can be found in the Appendix)

FORM PREPARATION NOTE: Your paternity statement should be prepared in triplicate and signed in front of a notary who will then stamp each document. Notarization is not strictly required, but it is a good idea. In the event of the death of the father, the paternity statement will have to be presented to various bureaucracies such as Social Security. The notary stamp proves that the signature is legitimate and that the document wasn't forged after death occurred. The mother and father should each keep one copy and the third copy should be kept safe for the child. Some states are setting up procedures for filing paternity statements with the state Bureau of Vital Statistics. It would be wise for you to do this if possible.

D. LEGITIMACY

Most states and the federal government are moving away from the old concepts of "legitimacy" and "illegitimacy". And about time too — there is something weird about a society that places a higher value on children whose parents happened to get married before doing what comes naturally. A number of states such as California have

---

* There is never a legal problem of a child of unmarried parents inheriting from its mother, but in the past there have been problems inheriting from a father in some states. See Section J of this chapter.

adopted the Uniform Parentage Act*which says that "the parent and child relationship extends equally to every child and to every parent, regardless of the marital status of the parents". **But even in states where concepts of "legitimacy" and "illegitimacy" are mostly out the window, it is still legally important to know who a child's natural parents are. In inheritance, child support, custody, adoption, and many other areas of the law, the rights and duties of parents are clearly marked out. If a father does not voluntarily sign a paternity agreement as discussed above, the state will try to establish that he is the father in other ways.** In states that have adopted the Uniform Parentage Act a man is presumed to be the father if:

Circumstance 1: He is married to the mother at the time the child is born, or was married to her within 300 days of the birth of the child. This means that, if the man dies or there is an annulment or divorce while the mother is pregnant, he is still presumed to be the father.

Circumstance 2: He and the mother, before the birth of the child, attempted to get married in the sense that they got a license, had a ceremony, etc., even though the marriage wasn't valid for some reason such as one of the partners still being married to someone else.

and

The child was born during the attempted marriage or within 300 days after its termination, whether by court order, death or simple separation.

Circumstance 3: After the child's birth he and the natural mother have married (or gone through a ceremony in apparent compliance with law) although the marriage could later be annulled for some reason;

and

a) With his consent, he is named the child's father on the birth certificate, or

b) He is obliged to support the child under a written, voluntary promise, or by court order. (This is the paternity statement situation.)

Circumstance 4: He receives the child into his home and openly holds out the child as his natural child.

You will note if you re-read these rules that we are dealing with presumptions. This normally means in law that a certain fact situation will be presumed to produce a certain legal conclusion unless rebutted by stronger evidence.** As we saw just above, if a man takes a child into his home and says that he is the father even though he was never married to the child's mother, he is legally presumed to be the father. This doesn't mean that he **is** the father — he might still be able to rebut the presumption, that is, prove that, even though he received a child into his home and told his friends

---

* The Uniform Parentage Act has been adopted in California, Colorado, Hawaii, Montana, North Dakota, Washington and Wyoming.
** Many states also have a conclusive presumption (one that can't be rebutted) that says that a child born to a married couple who were living together at the time of conception belongs to the husband unless he was sterile or impotent.

and family that he was the father, in fact, he was not. This is where court fights, blood tests, etc. are common.

Unfortunately, many states have not followed California's example and adopted the Uniform Parentage Act. They still use the terms "legitimate" and "illegitimate". However, in a long line of judicial decisions extending from *Levy v. Louisiana*, 391 U.S. 68 (1968) to *Trimble v. Gordon*, 430 U.S. 762 (1977), the United States Supreme Court has regularly been striking down state laws that give legitimate children more rights than illegitimate children. Thus, even in states that make these distinctions, they mean less than they used to.

In states that still label children, it is normally possible to change the label from illegitimate to legitimate as follows:*

⦿ By the natural parents later marrying each other;
or

⦿ By the father signing a paternity statement — that is, acknowledging that the child is his in writing.

⦿ Some states also would hold that "legitimation" occurs if the father welcomes the child into his home and/or holds himself out to be the father.

⦿ By going to court and having a judge make a ruling. In many states such as New York this can be done by both parents petitioning the court together in a non-adversary proceeding.

If children are born during a marriage that is later annulled, most states have laws that preserve the legitimacy of the children. And remember, the legitimacy of a child is only relevant as to the child's relationship with the father, and the father's family, and the father's benefactors. The mother's relationship with her child is not changed by the child's status.

SUMMARY: If you re-read this section and the previous one, you should conclude that signing a paternity statement is the best (and sometimes the only) way to be sure that your child is legitimate. If you do this, you need not worry about understanding the other legal technicalities.

E. PLANNING FOR SEPARATION

Most parents plan to stay together at least until their children are grown. But somehow the glue that held families together in former generations seems to have lost much of its stick. Whether married or living together, many parents find themselves separating and facing the task ot raising their children while living apart. Doing this in a constructive, humane way is a great challenge. It requires both parents to submerge

---

* You can find out your state law by checking your state legal code. Look in the index under the heading "Children" and the sub-heading "Legitimate". If you have trouble, ask the librarian to help you. In a few states you will find that in theory it is almost impossible to legitimate a child. These laws are no longer constitutional because in *Trimble v. Gordon*, 430 U.S. 762 (1977) the Supreme Court ruled that, while states may set up differing standards as to what proof is necessary to establish paternity, they can't be completely arbitrary. Thus, the court apparently ruled that formal acknowledgment of paternity by the father **or** an adjudication of paternity by a court are always sufficient to establish paternity of a child and allow the child to be treated as if he or she were legitimate. However, in a subsequent decision, *Lalli v. Lalli*, 99 S. Ct. 518 (1978), the Supreme Court ruled that a New York law which only allows legitimation by court action and not by a paternity statement is valid at least as far as inheritance is concerned where there is no will. This is a very confusing case involving five separate opinions by the nine justices. Our conclusion is that a paternity statement is still of some value in New York but that parents may wish to consider formal court action and certainly should prepare a will.

their egos in the best interests of the child(ren). Since unmarried couples don't get divorces, they have no automatic occasion to involve judges and lawyers in their child-raising responsibilities. They are free to make their own child custody, support and visitation arrangements. We believe that, if possible, it is best that they do so.

Here we give you three sample written agreements that you may find helpful. They are quite different, ranging from a joint support-joint custody agreement to a more traditional dad supports-mom takes care of the children arrangement. You may find that no one of these agreements fits your situation perfectly and that you will want to use elements of all three. Remember, no agreement concerning custody, support or visitation can ever be permanently binding, even those ordered by a judge. Because circumstances change, it is necessary that parents approach their agreements with a spirit of openness. What is a fair amount of support today will probably not be enough tomorrow. Custody with one parent may work brilliantly for a period of time and then not so well. Your agreements must be living documents, not museum pieces frozen under glass forever. Think of your first agreement as a mutual statement detailing needs and expectations. You want to lay a solid foundation that will support the changes and additions that will surely come.

NOTE: We assume that by this point you have already both signed a statement acknowledging parenthood, or at least the father has signed such a statement. If this has not been done, turn back to Section C of this chapter. It is essential to everyone's interests (most especially the father's) that a paternity statement be signed.

FIRST SAMPLE SEPARATION AGREEMENT

Rebecca Conlon and Lazarus Sandling, having decided to live together no longer make the following agreement for the purpose of raising their child Clementine in a spirit of compromise and cooperation. Both Rebecca and Lazarus agree that they will be guided by the best interests of Clementine and that:

1) Custody of Clementine shall be joint. This means that all major decisions regarding Clementine's physical location, visitation by the non-custodial parent and any other major decisions such as those relating to Clementine's health, education, etc. shall be made jointly. For the first year after this agreement is signed, Lazarus shall take care of Clementine during the day on all working days and Rebecca shall take care of Clementine nights and weekends.

2) At the time this agreement is made, Lazarus' income as a night disc jockey and Rebecca's income as a day horse jockey are approximately equal and neither person shall pay the other child support. Lazarus shall cover Clementine for health and dental insurance at his job and Rebecca shall contribute an equal amount (about $35 per month) for clothes. Each person shall pay routine costs for food and shelter while Clementine is in their custody.

3) If in the future either Lazarus' or Rebecca's income increases to an amount that is more than 30% over what is earned by the other, the person with the higher income

shall be expected to bear a larger share of the child support with the exact amount to be worked out at that time, based on the income of both parents and Clementine's needs.

4) Lazarus and Rebecca will make an effort to remain in the area of New York City where they presently live at least until Clementine is in junior high school.

5) Should Lazarus and Rebecca have trouble agreeing as to visitation, custody, support or any other problem concerning Clementine, they will jointly agree on a program of counseling to attempt to resolve or compromise their differences. Clementine shall be involved in this process to the maximum amount consistent with her age at the time.

_____   _____
Date   Rebecca Conlon

_____   _____
Date   Lazarus Sandling

NOTE: If communication between Lazarus and Rebecca completely broke down and one or the other filed a formal custody action in court, this agreement would probably be examined by the judge. But considering the fact that the judge has an independent right to make orders for what he or she considers to be in the "best interests of the child", it probably wouldn't count for too much.

SECOND SAMPLE SEPARATION AGREEMENT

Sam Matlock and Chris Woodling make this agreement because they have decided to cease living together, but wish to provide for the upbringing and support of their children, Natasha and Jason. Sam and Chris agree as follows:

1) That until Jason and Natasha are both in school (approximately 3 years) Chris shall have primary responsibility for childcare during the week and Sam shall pay child support in the amount of $200 per month per child;

2) That Jason and Natasha shall spend most weekends and at least one month during the summer with Sam and that Sam shall be available for babysitting at least two weekday nights;

3) That all major decisions regarding physical location, support, visitation, education, etc. affecting Jason and Natasha shall be made jointly by Sam and Chris and that Natasha and Jason shall be involved in the decision-making to an extent consistent with their ages at the time;

4) That when both Natasha and Jason are in school, Chris plans to return to her career as a fashion designer at least part-time and that Sam intends to return to school to finish his Ph.D. It is contemplated that during this period of time Chris will earn enough to support the children and Sam will take on a larger share of the childcare duties;

5) Both Sam and Chris are determined to conduct their affairs without recourse to lawyers and courts. If communication becomes difficult, they pledge themselves to participate in a joint program of counseling. If one issue such as physical custody, or amount of support becomes impossible to compromise, they agree that they will submit the dispute to binding arbitration.

_____   _____
Date   Sam Matlock

_____   _____
Date   Chris Woodling

THIRD SAMPLE SEPARATION AGREEMENT

Joseph Benner and Josephine Clark agree to live separately from this time on, and,

Joseph Benner and Josephine Clark wish to assure that their children, Nancy Benner, born June 1, 19 , and David Clark, both May 20, 19 , have a secure financial future and receive the necessary support that they will need to lead a safe, happy life. Joseph Benner and Josephine Clark agree to the following:

1. Josephine Clark shall have custody of the above minor children reserving to Joseph Benner liberal rights of visitation, including the right to have the children live with him for two months during the summer.

2. For a period of two years beginning February 1, 1980 Joseph Benner shall pay to Josephine Clark the sum of $500 per month for child support for the two minor children.

3. Josephine Clark shall attempt to find employment. Said employment shall not diminish the amount of child support paid.

4. Beginning February 1, 1981, Joseph Benner shall pay to Josephine Clark the sum of $300 per month for child support ot the two minor children. Said support shall continue at the rate of $150 per child until each child has reached the age of majority, marries or is otherwise emancipated.

5. All Payments are due on the first day of each month.

6. The provisions of this agreement may be incorporated into any court order in any court action maintained by either party. if any court action is maintained, this agreement shall be presented to the court.

7. This agreement may be modified only by written agreement of both parties or by order of a court.

_____   _____
Date   Joseph Benner

_____   _____
Date   Josephine Clark

FORM PREPARATION NOTE: These agreements should be prepared in duplicate, each party should sign it in front of a notary public, and each party should keep one copy. It is possible to have these agreements made part of a court order but you will probably need an attorney to do this for you. In that you have already done most of the work, you shouldn't be charged an outrageous fee.

F. CUSTODY

If an unmarried couple breaks up, both parents have an equal right to custody of the child as long as the child has been legitimated. However, if the father has refused to sign a paternity statement or otherwise legitimate his child, he is definitely discriminated against. Why? Because in a series of goofy decisions, the logic of which we can't explain, courts have set up a double standard. A father must support his children, whether legitimate or not, but only has equal rights to custody if he has legitimated them. At the risk of boring you to tears, let us again emphasize the obvious — if a father signs a paternity statement as soon after birth as possible, all this nonsense can be avoided. If he waits until a dispute develops to legitimate his child, it may be too late, but as a general rule even a late legitimation is better than no legitimation as far as a father's rights are concerned.

What do we mean when we say that both parents have equal rights to custody of a legitimate child if they separate? **Just that — unless, or until a judge as part of a custody case makes a different order — neither person has the legal right to deprive the other of the right to have or visit with the children.** If a court does order that one person have custody of the children (say, the mother), if some event such as illness should prevent her from providing care for the child, the other parent (the father) is next in line to exercise custody rights.

EXAMPLE: Rebecca Conlon assumes physical custody of Clementine after a break-up with Lazarus Sandling. A year later Rebecca dies or disappears or is injured to the extent that she cannot care for the child. Lazarus, who has signed a paternity statement legitimating Clementine, has the right to custody of the child and any third party seeking custody would have to petition the court and present evidence as to the inability of Lazarus to care properly for Clementine. Now let's change the example and assume that, instead of dropping out of the picture, Rebecca gets married. What are Lazarus' rights? As long as the child has been legitimated, she cannot be adopted by either Rebecca's new husband, or a third party without the consent of Lazarus, unless he had abandoned the child (failed to support or contact the child for a certain length of time). Abandonment has to be proven to the satisfaction of the court.*

If a child is not legitimate, the father has no legal right to custody if it comes to a fight with the mother, some other relative, or some public agency that wants to place the child in a foster home. A generation ago, an illegitimate father was treated as if he didn't exist. But in a small step toward sanity, the U.S. Supreme Court ruled in the case of *Stanley v. Illinois*, 405 U.S. 645 (1972) that "The state cannot, consistent with due process requirements, merely presume that unmarried fathers in general and petitioner in particular are unsuitable and neglectful parents...The denial to unwed fathers of a hearing of fitness accorded to all other parents whose custody of their children is challenged by the state constitutes a denial of equal protection of the laws". The effect of the *Stanley* case has been that illegitimate fathers are now notified

---

* Before a parent can be judged to have "abandoned" his or her child, he or she must have failed to visit or support the child for a considerable period of time. In most states this is at least two years, although some have shortened it to one year. If you have no money and thus can't support your child, you can't be viewed legally as abandoning the child as long as you visit regularly.

and given a right to be heard whenever some legal proceedings affect their children. In some situations they have been successful in winning custody. BUT — and this is important — fathers of illegitimate children are still discriminated against and still face an uphill battle to win custody. We do not believe that this sort of double standard is consistent with either common sense or the Constitution. Many people believe that eventually the Supreme Court will agree.

G. VISITATION

The unmarried parent of a legitimate child has the same legal right to visitation that a married parent has (see Section C, Chapter 9). This means that the parent who does not have custody has the right to visit with his or her children at reasonable times. Hopefully visitation, like custody, can be voluntarily worked out to the satisfaction of both parents (see Section F of this chapter), but if this is impossible, a judge will spell it out.

As we noted in the previous sections, the unmarried father of an illegitimate child has the duty to support, but few rights. It is unlikely that a court would order visitation for a father of an illegitimate child.

We are often asked what happens if a non-custodial parent who has disappeared, failed to maintain contact with his or her children, and doesn't provide support suddenly shows up and wants to visit his or her children? Many custodial parents who have established new families fear what they regard as "a ghost from the past". The only answer we can give is that it depends on the circumstances. Judges faced with deciding whether or not to approve visitation in this sort of situation usually start by being suspicious of a new-found desire to visit one's children after years of neglect and are usually attentive to the views of the parent who has performed his or her child-rearing responsibilities. However, if the absent parent is willing to provide support and genuinely demonstrates a desire to establish a solid relationship with the child(ren), the judge will probably allow visitation. Most judges believe that it is healthy for children to have a relationship with both natural parents even if they are less than perfect.

H. ADOPTIONS

The legitimated child of an unmarried couple cannot be adopted by a third person without the consent of both parents, unless one of the parents has abandoned the child. This means that fathers who sign a paternity statement, support (if they have the ability to do so) and maintain a relationship with their children are in no danger of seeing the children adopted by someone else. Mothers who don't have custody needn't sign a paternity statement, but must help with support if they are able, and visit their children.

The law of most states provides that when a child is "illegitimate", the consent of the natural father is not necessary for his (her) adoption, although the mother and the child depending on its age must consent. Either a state agency or a state-licensed

adoption agency must submit a report and recommendation in all non-stepparent adoption cases. These agencies have become very cautious recently, and if there is any question as to whether a child has been legitimated, they will withhold their recommendation that an adoption be granted until a court has determined that the father's consent is not necessary, either because the father has forfeited his parental right by abandonment (his failure to support or contact the child during a specified period of time), or because there has been no legitimation. As noted above, recent law changes require that even the father of an illegitimate child be given notice of the adoption court hearing and a chance to be heard.

Stepparent adoption cases are those where one of the natural parents has married someone else, and the new spouse wishes to adopt the children. There is a tendency for these adoptions to be approved more readily than other kinds of adoption, probably because the child is already in the home and will stay there even if the adoption is not approved. However, reports from a governmental (state or county) agency are also required in these cases. This means that the home is visited and a background study is made of the natural parents, the adopting parent and the child. Just as in other kinds of adoptions, whether the child is legitimate or illegitimate will determine whether the natural father must consent to the adoption. The natural mother must always consent unless the court terminates her parental rights by finding she has abandoned the child either through her failure to contact the child or her failure to support the child for a certain length of time.

Now let's look at what might happen given several different fact situations:

EXAMPLE: Linda and Frank are not married to each other. Linda has Frank's baby, but Frank takes off before the baby is born and does not contact Linda or the baby and does not send any support. Linda contacts an adoption agency which agrees to arrange for an adoption of the child. Linda must consent to the adoption. Frank's consent is not necessary but an effort must be made to notify him of the proposed adoption. If he shows an interest in the proceedings, he must be given a hearing, but his opposition probably won't be counted for much.

EXAMPLE: Same as above, except Linda keeps the baby and later marries Herman. Herman wants to adopt the baby. Linda's consent is necessary but Frank's consent is not. Frank will be notified of the action and is entitled to a hearing if he opposes the adoption.

EXAMPLE: Linda and Frank are unmarried. Linda has Frank's baby and they live together several years, then split up and Linda keeps the child. Frank always says that the child is his and continues to visit the child and pay support after he and Linda separate, but never signs a paternity statement. Whether the child can be adopted by either another couple or by Linda's new spouse without the consent of Frank depends on state law. In some states such as California, Frank has legitimated the child by welcoming it into his home and acknowledging that he is the father. This means that in California, if Frank opposes the adoption, he would be able to stop it. However, in other states such as New York, simply living with a child and saying that it is yours is not enough to legitimate it and Frank might be unable to stop an adoption.

EXAMPLE: Same as above, except when the baby is born, Frank signs a paternity statement. Linda keeps the child after the split up and later marries Herman, who wishes to adopt the baby. In the meantime, Frank has continued to see and support the child. There is no way that the adoption would be approved in any state without Frank's consent.

EXAMPLE: Same as above, except before Linda and Frank split up, Frank has signed a paternity statement legitimating the child. Linda keeps the child, and Frank is never heard from again (or else he visits very seldom and sends no support or very little support for the child). Is Frank's consent to an adoption necessary? Probably. If Frank refuses to consent or can't be found, a court hearing will have to be held to determine whether he has forfeited his parental rights by abandoning the child. Frank will have to be given notice of the hearing and a chance to present his views. If the court finds he has so abandoned the child, the adoption will be allowed.

EXAMPLE: Same as above, except when they split up, Frank keeps the child. Linda and Frank must consent to any adoption action and must be notified of any hearing to terminate their parental rights. Of course, if Linda does not support or contact the child for a certain length of time, a court can find that she has abandoned the child and declare that their consent is not necessary.

NOTE: Most states provide that a child can be declared "freed for adoption" for reasons other than abandonment. Some of these reasons are imprisonment for a felony, mental retardation, or unfitness of the natural parents. We do not deal specifically with these situations since contested adoption actions are not common in these areas.

I. SUPPORT OF AN ILLEGITIMATE CHILD

As we noted in Section F, a father has a duty to support even in cases where the child is illegitimate and he has no right to custody. Both parents have a legal duty to support all their children, although some states put the primary duty on the father. There is no reason for a court to get involved in support questions if the parents can work it out to their mutual satisfaction. In Section D of Chapter 9 we discuss support of legitimate children in detail.

The mother of the child or a person acting on behalf of the child can sue the father in a court action and obtain a court order setting an amount of child support the father will have to pay. If the father does not support the child, the District Attorney may prosecute the father in a criminal action which will result, if he has the ability to support but continues to withhold payment, in his going to jail. The county jails are full of people who failed to take their support obligation seriously.

Of course, if the child is subsequently adopted by another person or persons, all parental rights of the natural parents are terminated and their duty to support the child is also ended. Likewise, if one of the parents should later marry and the new spouse should adopt the child (stepparent adoption), the parent whose parental rights are terminated no longer has a duty to support the child.

J. BENEFITS FOR THE CHILD OF UNMARRIED PARENTS (SOCIAL SECURITY, ETC.)

There are many benefits that a child can become entitled to through his or her parents. To name a few: Social Security if a parent becomes disabled or dies; union benefits; insurance benefits. Until recently these programs discriminated against illegitimate children — particularly benefits derived through the father. For example, until recently Social Security regulations provided for unequal sharing of benefits among the legitimate and illegitimate children of a deceased or retired or disabled father with a preference for legitimate children. The United States Supreme Court held in the case of *Jimenez v. Weinberger*, 417 U.S. 628 (1974) that this was unconstitutional. Similar discriminating provisions in other government programs have likewise been held to be unconstitutional and now it makes no difference whether a child is legitimate or illegitimate for purposes of receiving Social Security and similar benefits.

As noted earlier in this chapter, we believe strongly in the father signing a paternity statement. If a father dies, benefits under Social Security or other federal, state or private insurance programs may be denied, not because the child is illegitimate, but because there is no proof that the deceased was actually the father. A paternity statement solves this problem.

K. INHERITANCE RIGHTS OF AN ILLEGITIMATE CHILD

Inheritance laws can be complicated. Most states have provisions that diminish the rights of illegitimate children if a parent dies without leaving a will. Many states provide that an illegitimate child inherits as if he were legitimate from his mother but not from his father, unless, of course, the father has legitimated the child by signing a paternity statement or in some other way sufficient under the law of the state in which the parent lives. In *Trimble v. Gordon*, 430 U. S. 762 (1977) the Supreme Court made it clear that a paternity statement is normally adequate to guarantee the inheritance rights of children born out of wedlock. However, in *Lalli v. Lalli,* 99 S. Ct. 518 (1978) the Court also upheld a New York statute which requires a court decree of paternity (not just a paternity statement) for a child to inherit without a will. We recommend that if you live in a state that has not adopted the Uniform Parentage Act you should play it safe and execute both a will and a paternity statement.

Of course, you can leave your property to anyone you want to in a will, or by other simple trust or joint ownership devices. See Chapter 11.

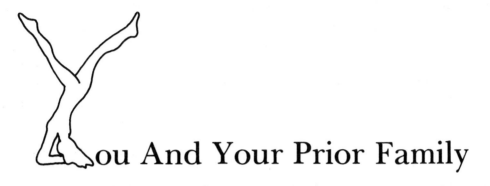

CHAPTER NINE

You And Your Prior Family

If you have been married previously or are still married to someone other than the person with whom you are living, you might encounter special problems.* This is particularly true when you and a former spouse have left each other in anger and bitterness. Fortunately, more and more people are finding it possible to split up without nasty court battles. We apparently aren't the only ones who have learned that lawyers benefit from domestic strife, and court fights normally last only as long as the money holds out. So try and talk your problems out with your former mate. Remember, you got yourself into the relationship and in the last analysis, you are the only ones who can get yourselves out. It's never too late to try getting along, if not in a loving fashion, at least in a civilized one. Paranoia is almost always a part of separating. If there is nothing major to get upset about, people will manage to worry about who gets the teaspoons or the ten-speed bike. To get on top of this kind of situation, an excellent place to start is with yourself.

A. GETTING A DIVORCE WHILE LIVING WITH SOMEONE ELSE

1. Divorce Based On Fault

A few states still have a divorce system based on "fault". This means that in order to get a divorce one party must prove that the other in some way mistreated him or her. And not only is the person proving fault entitled to a divorce — he or she may also be entitled to a greater share of the couple's property, alimony and custody of the children.

---

* If you live in California, you will find much specific information about custody, visitation, adoption and children of former marriages in the *People's Guide To California Marriage Law*, by Warner and Ihara. (See order information at the back of this book.)

How do you prove fault? One sure way is to show that a spouse is committing adultery. This means that if you are living with someone and you and your spouse are fighting over kids, alimony, amount of child support or the division of property, you can bet your bottom dollar (if you still have a dollar left) that your living arrangement (adultery) will be dragged into court. How much it will influence a judge's decision is not certain. As the twentieth century marches on, living with someone is not as shocking (even to judges) as it once was, and many will minimize it even in "fault divorce" states. But one thing is sure — it won't count in your favor. If you are employing an attorney to help you with your divorce, it would be wise to discuss your living arrangement with him or her.

CHART 1

IS DIVORCE ALLOWED ON NO FAULT GROUNDS?

(This chart is a shorthand guide only. The laws of many states are complicated. Check yours out in detail.)

Some states allow no fault divorce on the petition of either party with no requirement that the parties have lived apart for any particular period of time prior to filing. They include:

Alabama, Alaska, Arizona, California, Colorado, Delaware, Florida, Georgia, Hawaii, Indiana, Iowa, Kansas, Kentucky, Maine, Michigan, Minnesota, Missouri, Nebraska, New Hampshire, New Mexico, North Dakota, Oklahoma, Oregon, Washington and Wyoming.

Other states allow no fault divorce only after a certain period of time has passed since separation. In a few of these states, the divorce can go through immediately if both parties agree.

6 months' wait — Montana and Vermont
1 year's wait — Maryland, Nevada, North Carolina, Virginia, Wisconsin, and Washington, D.C.
18 months' wait — Connecticut
2 years' wait — Ohio and West Virginia
3 years' wait — South Carolina and Texas
5 years' wait — Idaho and Rhode Island

Some states which have passed so-called "no fault" divorce laws have retained fault divorce too with adultery as one of the "fault" grounds. People who don't want to wait (six months to 5 years) to qualify for a "no fault" divorce or who don't qualify for a "no fault" divorce for some other reason must still allege fault to get an immediate divorce. These states include:

Alabama, Arkansas, Georgia, Idaho, Kansas, Louisiana, Maine, Maryland, Massachusetts, Mississippi, Missouri, New Hampshire, New Mexico, New York, North Carolina, North Dakota, Ohio, Oklahoma, Pennsylvania, Rhode Island, South Carolina, Tennessee, Texas, Utah, Vermont, Virginia, West Virginia, Wisconsin and Wyoming.

Some states don't allow no fault divorce as a matter of right although Mississippi, Massachusetts and Tennessee allow it if both parties agree, and Arkansas, New Jersey and New York allow divorce on grounds of desertion. State where "no fault" is difficult or impossible include:

Arkansas, Illinois, Louisiana, New York, South Dakota, Pennsylvania, and Utah.

REMEMBER: Many people get sensible, civilized divorces even in states where there is "fault divorce". They do this by going through the motions of pretending one person is in the wrong when they fill out their court papers, but make their decisions about children, support, and property in a spirit of common sense and compromise rather than "who is more right". If you and your spouse are separating in this spirit (or if you have no property or children to fight about), you need not worry about the effect of living with someone else. But just in case memories grow short, it might make sense to make a written note as to your understanding. Of course, you will have to modify this to fit your circumstances.

CO-OPERATIVE SEPARATION AGREEMENT*

Sean and Barbara Washington agree to the following:

1. That they have decided to go their separate ways and no longer plan to live together.

2. That John Washington, age 5, and Richard Washington, age 3, will reside with Barbara Washington, and Sean will spend as much time as possible with the children.

3. That Sean will provide a reasonable amount of support to Barbara each month, taking into consideration his salary and the needs of the children. Initially, this will be $350 per month.

4. That as neither Sean nor Barbara plan to marry again immediately, it is understood that both will have friendships that may involve sex and may decide to live with someone of the same or the opposite sex.

---

* This sort of agreement is not technically enforceable in court, especially as it relates to the custody of children. As we learn later in this chapter, a court may look at all factors when considering "the best interests of the child". Still, amicable agreement between yourselves is desirable and many judges would give it considerable weight. If one spouse suddenly starts dragging the other's lifestyle into court, a judge might well ask "How come you didn't object to his (her) living with someone the day you signed the 'Separation Agreement', but now suddenly do?"

5. That Sean and Barbara will proceed to get a divorce as amicably as possible and that neither will try to influence the decision of the court by referring to the fact that the other is having a relationship with, or living with, a third person.

Date	Barbara Washington
Date	Sean Washington

---

2. "No-Fault Divorce"

Many states (see Chart) have adopted a "no-fault divorce" law. In some of these states such as California even the word "divorce" has been replaced by "dissolution of marriage". The idea behind "no-fault divorce" is simple — a court should not be a place where couples are encouraged to drag each other through a morass of petty wrongs and broken expectations. States that have adopted "no-fault divorce" laws commonly provide that the only grounds for ending a marriage are for such vague reasons as "irretrievable breakdown", "incompatibility of temperament" or "irreconcilable differences". In these states the reasons for the incompatibility are not admissible in court to decide issues of property division, alimony (spousal support), etc. Thus, *whether or not one spouse is living with someone else has no relevancy to the divorce.* However, as we will see in Section B of this chapter, it may be brought up in court in a child custody dispute.

B. CHILD CUSTODY

If you and your spouse agree on child custody, the court will normally ratify your agreement (to award custody according to your joint desire) without looking at the details of your life. Remember, the judge won't know whether one of you is living with a third person unless it is brought to his or her attention. However, if you and your spouse are seriously fighting over the question of who shall have custody of your children, the best conservative legal advice has been not to live with a person of the opposite sex and to be very discreet in all your sexual activity, at least until the court has made a decision regarding custody. This advice has applied to both "fault" and "no fault" divorce states as the living arrangements of both parties are always admissible in custody disputes under the theory that a court needs as much information as possible to determine "the best interests of the child".

Perhaps you noted that we used the word "has" in the last paragraph to describe the kind of "no sex no living with anyone" conduct that should be followed by parents engaged in a custody fight. We did this because there has been a considerable relaxation of uptight legal attitudes toward living together in the past few years. While we can't say that most judges are enthusiastic about granting custody to a parent who is living with someone, there is a definite trend away from denying custody for this reason and we feel that a decision as to whether it is wise to live with someone while fighting over child custody must be decided on a situation-by-situation, state-by-state basis.

In all states child custody is decided according to "the best interests of the child". What does this mean? It seems to mean that the judge who hears a disputed custody fight can take into account all the evidence and allegations before him, then decide which party can provide the "best home" for the child. In practice our historical societal prejudice in favor of a mother raising children usually prevails. However, the almost automatic preference for the mother is not nearly as strong as it once was, and many men are winning custody of their children. In some states the law specifically provides that the mother will get custody of young children, unless she is shown to be "unfit" or unless the circumstances show that the children would be better off with the father. But most states now provide that both parents have an equal right to custody with the award made on a "best interests of the child" approach.* In any state, under any test, the trial judge has almost complete discretion in awarding custody where two parents are fighting over the issue.

People frequently ask:

"If I live with a man, can my children be taken from me?"

"If my husband is an alcoholic, will he be able to have the children?"

"I have an arrest for possession of marijuana; does this mean I cannot get the children?"

"My husband does not pay his child support; can he take the children from me?"

"My son is nine years old and wants to live with me; will the court do what he wants?"

"I only earn $5,000 a year and my spouse earns $25,000; does this mean he will get the children?"

Is it actually possible for a father to get custody of young children?"

---

* In California and in many states "joint custody" is possible. We recommend this when parents have a record of good communication and an equal dedication to raising the children. "Joint custody" is advantageous because it equalizes the balance of power among the parents and gives each an equal say in raising the children. In our experience fathers are much more likely to support and maintain close relationships with their children when they are truly involved in decision-making. "Joint custody" means that the parents (and hopefully the children) continue to plan jointly for their children's future just as they did before divorce. Actual physical custody of the children is worked out between the parents, taking into consideration schools, neighborhoods, the children's wishes, etc. "Joint custody" does not mean that the children must spend six months of each year with each parent. A common criticism of joint custody is that since neither parent has the final say, arguments can go on forever even though both parents feel that they are highly motivated to be good parents. This point has some validity and we feel that "joint custody" often works best where parents and children commit themselves to a program of family counseling (sometimes called "divorce" or "separation" counseling) to help them over the rough spots. We haven't seen a whole lot of marriages "saved" by counseling, but have seen many families saved much anguish by separation counseling. Remember, a good divorce can be as precious as a good marriage.

The answer to all these questions is, "It depends". In spite of what your next-door neighbor, your best friend, or your brother-in-law has told you, the law does not say that adultery, smoking pot, drinking, etc. will necessarily result in the loss of custody (in fact, it often does not). It is up to each individual judge to determine who shall get custody, and he or she will necessarily apply his or her own standards (prejudices). Some judges do not like dope; some do not like arrest records; some do not like political activity; some do not like poor people; and some, in spite of prevailing attitudes, do not like unmarried persons living together, although as we noted above, this isn't nearly the no-no it used to be.* Each judge is an individual, each case is unique, and the judge has a lot of latitude in deciding each case. People worried about custody sometimes ask if it is better to have their friend live with them and help raise the children, or to have the friend live elsewhere and visit. If you are not fighting over custody, neither is a problem. If you are fighting over custody, neither will do you any good, but we feel that in **most** communities, in **most** fact situations, neither dating nor living with someone in a stable relationship will be cause to deny custody.

In reaching the conclusion that cohabitation is not usually viewed as a reason to deny custody, we have carefully researched the recent case law. While we don't have the space to do a state-by-state breakdown, here are some typical holdings: "We have long passed the point where sexual misconduct automatically disqualifies a mother from obtaining custody of her minor children." *Greenfield v. Greenfield*, 260 N.W.2d 493 (Nebraska 1977). "The fact of the mother's adulterous relationship is of importance in a child custody case only as it may affect the best interests of the child." *Bonjour v. Bonjour* 566 P.2d 667 (Alaska 1977). If you want to research other recent cases in this area, see the Family Law Reporter which you will find in all law libraries. It is still possible to find cases from conservative states where a court held cohabitation to be a reason to deny custody, but they are few and getting fewer.**

1. Deciding The Contested Custody Case

In most states judges do not decide custody cases simply by inviting the parents to present their rival arguments. Long before the parents even get to court, other governmental agencies are involved. In many states the agency with primary responsibility is the County Juvenile Probation Department. Other states use names such as "Social Services Department" or "Department of Child Welfare", but the functions carried out are similar everywhere.

What normally happens is something like this. The lawyers (or the parties themselves if they are in pro per) notify the court that, as part of a divorce proceeding, there is a fight over custody. The judge then asks the relevant county department to make an investigation. The case is assigned to a case worker (almost always trained as a social worker) who investigates the entire situation and presents a written report and recommendation to the court. In the process of investigating, the social worker inter-

---

* Problems of gay people living together and wanting to raise the children of one or both are discussed in Chapter 12.
** Louisiana in *Beck v. Beck*, 341 So. 2d 580 (1977) and Missouri in *In Re Marriage of J-H-M*, 544 S.W. 582 (1976) are two states that still find that cohabitation is a reason to deny custody. Illinois has ruled that custody should be denied when a parent with custody lives with someone who is married, *De Franco v. De Franco*, 384 N.E. 2d 997, but that living with someone who is not married is O.K., *Jarrett v. Jarrett*, 382 N.E. 2d 12 (1978).

views the parties, assembles background information, collects arrest and health records, checks with references provided by the parties, sometimes talks with the children and sometimes requests psychological testing or psychiatric reports.

Individual social workers have different degrees of skill in interviewing and assessing personalities, and some are more energetic than others. Like judges, social workers have their own biases and a recommendation will reflect the prejudice of the worker as well as what may be considered the "facts" of the situation. While as a whole these investigative personnel are younger and more tolerant than most judges, a social worker will probably feel compelled to mention your living situation in the report. Even though the particular person who did the investigation might not think it important that you are living with a person of the opposite sex, the judge may feel differently.

What happens once a judge receives a child custody report? Your attorney will have the opportunity to read the report before court proceedings and discuss it with you. The judge is not compelled to go along with the report, but he or she usually does. If the investigative officer has recommended that you have custody, you have won more than half the battle. If the report recommends that you not have custody of your children, you are at a serious disadvantage, but you are still entitled to a trial on the issue, and you may request that the social worker come to court so that he can be cross-examined about the contents of the report. If, after the report is received, you and your spouse still cannot agree as to who shall have custody of the children, the next step is to have such a trial. At the trial your children may be asked where they want to live. Judges vary on this procedure, with some always asking the children if they feel that they are old enough to answer, and others never talking with the children. As a very general guide, most judges will pay little attention to the opinions of a child under 7, will probably respect the wishes of teen-age children if the chosen parent is otherwise suitable, and will listen to children between 7 and 12, but not necessarily give them what they ask for. There is also a strong tendency for judges to keep brothers and sisters together, although this is not always done.

CAUTION: In a custody proceeding held in the context of a divorce or dissolution of marriage, a judge need not award custody of the children to either the husband or the wife; he can award custody to a relative, a friend or even the local juvenile court. This law is noted here to warn hostile parents that too much mud-slinging may, and frequently does, convince the judge that neither parent is fit.

C. VISITATION OF CHILDREN

Let's say it is agreed that your spouse is to have custody of the children. Unless your physical presence can be shown to be actually detrimental to the welfare of the children, you will be given the right to visit.* If you and your spouse are still friendly

---

* Section 4601 of the California Civil Code is a typical state statute. It reads: "Reasonable visitation rights shall be awarded to a parent unless it is shown that such visitation would be detrimental to the best interests of the child. In the discretion of the court, reasonable visitation rights may be granted to any other person having an interest in the welfare of the child."

enough to agree on how the visitation rights are to be exercised, the court will probably say that you have "reasonable visitation rights", and leave it to you to work out times and places. If, however, you and your spouse are at such a bad place that you cannot agree on such simple things as when, where and how the visitation will take place, the court will define visitation rights more or less rigidly. For example, the court may say, "Barbara Washington shall have the right to visit with the children every Saturday from 10:00 a.m. to 5:00 p.m. plus one week during·the summer months, said week to be agreed upon by the parties"; or "Sean Washington shall have the right to visit with the children on the first weekend of every month from 6:00 p.m. on Friday to 6:00 p.m. on Sunday provided that he pick up and deliver the children to the home of Barbara Washington", etc.

Occasionally, a court will impose further restrictions on visitation such as a requirement that the visiting parent tell the other parent of his or her intention to visit 24 hours before the time of visitation, a requirement that the visiting parent not remove the child from the county or the state or, in rare cases, the child's own home or the house of a third party, or a requirement that the visiting parent not drink alcoholic beverages while he is visiting with the children. But, can the court impose a restraint on Sean Washington that he not visit with his children in the presence of Doris Williams (the woman with whom he is living)? Or that his children may not spend the night with him if Ms. Williams is also present in the house? There is little in the way of case law from appeals courts that declare this legal or not; likewise, there are no statutes in this area. However, even today, some judges occasionally make such orders, supposedly to "protect the children". If you are faced with such an order, you should speak with your attorney as to your obligations and rights and the possibility of appeal. It is rarely wise to violate a court order.

D. CHILD SUPPORT

What happens if you have custody of the children and you are living with someone else? Is your spouse or former spouse still required to support the children? YES, but read on.*

In theory, child support depends on two factors:

1. The ability to pay of the parent who does not have custody. You cannot get out of child support by quitting your job or refusing to look for work. Court orders are made and enforced on the basis of ability to work, not inclination to work.

Here is a rough guide used by judges in Marin County, California in deciding how much child support to order in an individual case. Judges rarely follow this schedule exactly, or the similar ones in use in other counties, since the facts (human needs and responsibilities) of each situation vary. Please note that these figures don't include spousal support. This is because spousal support is awarded much less frequently

---

* Failure to support your children if you have the ability to do so is a crime in all states. Many people who don't take their obligation seriously end up with a free education at a county school with high grey walls and bars on the windows.

than it used to be, as most younger women are wage earners.

SCHEDULE FOR CHILD SUPPORT PAYMENTS WHERE NO SPOUSAL SUPPORT IS ORDERED

Non-custodial Parent's NET Monthly Income*	One Child	Two Children	Three or More Children
$ 400.00	$ 100.00	$ 100.00	$ 100.00
500.00	125.00	150.00	175.00
600.00	150.00	200.00	225.00
700.00	150.00	250.00	275.00
800.00	150.00	250.00	300.00
900.00	175.00	275.00	350.00
1000.00	175.00	300.00	375.00
1200.00	200.00	350.00	450.00
1400.00	250.00	400.00	525.00
1600.00	250.00	450.00	600.00
1800.00	275.00	500.00	675.00
2000.00	300.00	550.00	750.00
Above 2000.00	Court's discretion		

This schedule is prepared on the assumption that the custodial parent's net earnings are at least 25% less than that of the non-custodial parent, and that there is no award of spousal support.

The rule for support is intended to be the same whether the custodial parent is the father or the mother. If the non-custodial parent carries hospital, medical or dental insurance covering the children, the cost attributable to the children's coverage may be deducted from the support payments.

2. The needs of the children. The person with whom you are living has no obligation to support your children. Logically, the amount of child support the father (or mother, if the father has custody) is ordered to pay should not be affected by the fact that you are living with someone else. However, if such person is actually providing shelter or buying food or clothing or other items for your children, this might possibly be taken into consideration by the court when it decides how much money the non-custodial parent will have to pay.

EXAMPLE: Barbara Washington and Sean Washington get a divorce and the custody of the two children is awarded to Barbara with reasonable rights of visitation awarded to Sean. Sean is ordered to pay Barbara $200 per month per child for child support. A year later Barbara starts living with (or marries, it makes no difference)

---

* Income after compulsory deductions such as income tax, FICA, SDI and compulsory retirement.

Harold, who owns his own business and nets $100,000 per year. Harold takes an interest in the children and spends money on them freely. Barbara continues working at her job as a librarian. Sean petitions the court and asks that the amount of his support obligation be reduced to $125 per month. Will he succeed? Perhaps, because Barbara is now living in a situation where there is more than adequate money. While the judge will not require Harold to support Sean's children and is not supposed to look at the money that he actually contributes (in fact he or she probably will), the court is required to look at Barbara's total financial picture. As Harold and all of his money are part of Barbara's life, a judge might well rule that Barbara could now spend more of her own income to support the children.

What if you are the parent without custody and you are living with someone? How does this affect the amount of child support you will be ordered to pay? Perhaps you are actually supporting the person with whom you are living and maybe even that person's children, in whole or in part. Legally, you have no obligation to support these persons and few judges will allow the fact of such support to in any way reduce the support you will be ordered to pay for your natural children. The law clearly states that your primary duty is to support your own children and not someone else or their children. Likewise, if your own living expenses are reduced by the fact that you share rent, etc. with another person, this will be taken into account in determining your ability to pay.

NOTE: We have seen this area of the law work great hardship on people who were honestly trying to be decent and caring. For example, this situation often occurs when a man gets a divorce and lives with another woman and her children whom he helps to support in the absence of their father who has skipped. This, of course, does not free him of his legal duty to support his original family even if his former wife has remarried. He will be hauled into court if he fails to do so. Thus, one man trying to do right finds himself with an impossible burden while others avoid doing even part of their share. We don't have any magic answers to this problem, but we do feel that laws causing so much hardship should be re-examined in the light of what life is really like these days. We are particularly concerned that present laws result in a massive, but uneven and often unfair, shifting of money from one family to another, with a great deal of the money sticking to the fingers of the shifters — lawyers, social workers, court personnel and all sorts of other bureaucrats.

IMPORTANT: Most states are tightening requirements regarding child support. For example, in 1974, California enacted a law which states that, if an absent parent falls behind two months in his child support payments, the judge **must** make an order assigning his wages. This means that the absent parent's employer will be required to pay the amount of the child support directly to the custodial parent or some official agency. The absent parent will never see this money in his paycheck. Also, cooperation between states in collecting child support from persons who move to another part of the country is becoming more efficient. This involves the use of federal government computers to trace people through social security numbers, etc.*

E. SPOUSAL SUPPORT (ALIMONY)

Alimony, a necessary concept a generation ago when papa went to the office and mama stayed home to tend the babies and the spaghetti, is dying as lifestyles change. Among younger people especially, alimony is no longer routinely granted and is not even requested in a large number of cases. Any alimony (spousal support) that you do receive will terminate upon your remarriage, in the absence of a specific agreement or

---

* The best (and only) book on collecting child support and alimony is *How To Collect Your Child Support And Alimony*, by Luboff and Posner. This book is written specifically for people in California, but has skip-tracing information of value everywhere (order information at back of this book).

court order to the contrary. What happens if you do not remarry but just move in with someone else? The rules vary state-to-state. In New York, living with someone is not grounds to end alimony **unless the living together relationship has lasted six months and the woman receiving alimony holds herself out as being the wife of the person she is living with.** However, in California a recent law change (Civil Code 4801.51) states: "Except as otherwise agreed to by the parties in writing, there shall be a rebuttable presumption...of decreased need for support if the supported party is cohabiting with a person of the opposite sex. Upon such a finding of changed circumstances, the court may modify the payment of support..." *

RESEARCH NOTE: If receiving alimony is important to you, don't live with someone unless you thoroughly check out the current law in your state. The trend of state law is probably to follow the lead of California and restrict or eliminate alimony when the person receiving the alimony lives with someone, but many states agree with New York and impose no restrictions. Go to a public law library (in the county courthouse) and get a copy of your state's laws. These come in many volumes, and you will want to start with the index. Look at the headings under Alimony and Spousal Support. Be sure to check the back of the index to see if there are any staple-bound pages (called pocket parts) which contain recent law changes. Check with the librarian to be sure that you are looking at up-to-date material. Also, ask the law librarian if there are any books on the domestic relations law of your state. All of the big states will have them. For example, in California, they are published by Continuing Education of the Bar (CEB). Also ask the librarian to refer you to the Family Law Reporter which contains a digest of case law decisions. If you are in doubt, check your conclusions with a lawyer (see Chapter 13).

F. DIVIDING THE PROPERTY

If you were married for more than a few minutes, you and your spouse probably accumulated both property and debts. Property includes houses, other real property such as improved land, furniture, cars, motorcycles, savings accounts, checking accounts, stocks, bonds, income tax refunds, money owed you by other persons, interests in retirement funds or pensions, some kinds of disability benefits, vacation pay earned during the marriage, businesses you or your spouse may have operated, etc. Whether the property will be divided by the court depends on when it was acquired, whether your state recognizes community property, the interests of other persons in the property, etc. In states with "no fault divorce" laws, property and debts are almost always divided equally between the husband and the wife. In "fault" states, one of the primary reasons for proving to the court the "wrong-doing" (adultery, drunkenness, violence, mental cruelty, desertion, etc.) of the other party is to obtain all or a majority of the property as the "innocent party" may be awarded the property in compensation for the "wrongs" he or she has suffered.

If you live in one of these states and you have a large amount of property which you and your spouse cannot agree on how to divide, you should settle yourself in for a long, tedious battle and start saving money for your lawyer's fees. Of course, if you and

---

* As this book goes to press Alabama is the only other state to adopt legislation to provide for termination of alimony when the person receiving it lives with someone. However, the question has also been considered by a number of state courts, some of which have cut-off alimony, some of which have refused to do so and some of which have made different rulings depending on the circumstances.

your spouse have already agreed on a reasonable division of the property in view of the needs and earning capabilities of each person, then you should not allow lawyers or others to talk you into a needless fight. Remember, divorce lawyers, like gunfighters, often get more money and power when they fight than when they show you how to arrive at an early compromise.

If you are already divorced when you start living with another person, it is almost certain that your property from your marriage is already divided. In this case, you do not have to worry about the court changing its decision if someone tells the judge you are living with someone. The decision has been made, and the matter cannot be reopened. However, if you are not yet divorced, and the state you live in does not have a no fault divorce system, and you and your spouse are fighting over the division of the property, then you can be sure your living situation will be brought to the attention of the judge. Your adultery, desertion, abandonment and infliction of mental cruelty will be taken into consideration with the other facts of the case and may influence the court's decision.

G. AFTER THE DIVORCE

Your marriage is now legally finished; you are settling down to a new life with your new partner. Can you forget about all the above because now the court has made its orders regarding child custody, visitation, child support, and spousal support? NO. All orders regarding the above matters except those pertaining to the division of the property may be changed by the court if it finds that the circumstances have changed since the making of the original order.

EXAMPLE: At the time you were awarded custody of the children, you were a Sunday School teacher whose only recreation was to attend Sunday afternoon piccolo concerts. Now you and your children are living in a commune for ex-alcoholic slide trombone players. Can your former spouse ask the court to change custody and does the court have the power to do so? Yes. Will the court change custody? Perhaps, depending on what the judge thinks of your current lifestyle. You will have less trouble if you can show that the children are secure, well taken care of, and doing OK in school; but you have a serious problem if it looks as though you are trying to raise kids in an unstructured zoo.

EXAMPLE: At the time of the dissolution you were a medical student with no income but now you are a doctor earning $50,000 per year. Can your ex-spouse ask the court to raise the amount of child support and/or alimony and does the court have the power to do so? Yes. Will it do so? Almost certainly.

EXAMPLE: At the time of the divorce you earned $15,000 per year as a bricklayer and you lost your job a couple of months ago. Can you ask the court to lower the amount of child support you were ordered to pay? Yes. Will the court grant what you want? Perhaps, depending on why you lost your job, your chances of getting another job, your current sources of income, etc.

What can you do to keep your former spouse from taking you back to court? Very little. Your ex-spouse has the right to petition the court to change its order on child custody, support and visitation at any time. You have the same right. Your best course of action is to maintain amicable relations with your ex-spouse. For example, if you are extremely cooperative about visitation, your ex-spouse will probably be less likely to petition the court to change custody if your lifestyle changes. Likewise, if you are prompt and reasonably generous with your child support and alimony payments, your ex-spouse is much less likely to hassle you about visitation. If your income goes up (or down) you and your spouse should try to work out a voluntary change of the support amount. If you do, you should make a note of it.

SAMPLE SUPPORT CHANGE AGREEMENT*

Sean Washington of 100 South Street, El Monte, California, and Barbara Washington of 57 San Pablo Avenue, Redding, California, make the following agreement regarding the support of their two minor children, John Washington and Richard Washington:

1. That because Sean Washington has suffered a serious illness which has reduced his income by 50%, it is agreed that the $500 per month child support ordered in the divorce action between the parties is too high.

2. In order to avoid an expensive court proceeding to lower child support, and because Sean Washington's health problems should improve in the next six months, it is agreed that Sean Washington will pay to Barbara Washington the sum of $225 per month for the support of John and Richard commencing May 1, 19   and terminating with the payment of November 1, 19   and that all additional amounts of support for this time are forever given up by Barbara Washington.

3. It is further agreed that the full amount of support ordered as part of the divorce proceedings ($500) will be paid commencing December 1, 19

Date	Sean Washington
Date	Barbara Washington

---

* It is not necessary to notarize this sort of agreement, but it would be a good idea to do so. If one or the other person fails to live up to it, it may be necessary to present it in court in which case it may carry more weight if notarized.

SAMPLE SUPPORT CHANGE AGREEMENT

Hermione Brown of 6 Briar Close, Larchmont, New York and Cecil Brown of 11 Brookside Drive, Mamaroneck, New York agree as follows:

1. That because Cecil Brown has received a promotion and is now receiving $4,000 per year more than was received at the time of the original court child support order entered on_____ ;

and

2. That in order to avoid the expense of a court appearance to modify child support to an amount that is fair, taking into consideration Cecil's increase in income;

3. The parties hereby agree that Cecil shall pay Hermione the amount of $175 per month for the support of each child commencing May 1, 19____ and continuing indefinitely or until the parties jointly agree on a modification.

_____   _____
Date   Cecil Brown

_____   _____
Date   Hermione Brown

NOTE: If you and your former spouse are planning to agree on a permanent change in support and you have had problems with misunderstandings in the past, you will probably wish to take your agreement to a lawyer and have him or her present it to the court in the form of a "stipulated" or agreed upon modification. As long as you are in agreement, this shouldn't take the attorney more than three or four hours total and shouldn't cost a great deal.

Every year many attorneys get rich because two people cannot sit down and work out their domestic problems. When problems first arise, try to talk them out with your ex-spouse, maybe giving a little more than you had planned. Try not to let your pride or ego get in the way of making an agreement. Only if this fails should you contact an attorney and pay him many hundreds (often thousands) of dollars to fight for you. In our experience attorneys don't normally arrive at better solutions — just solutions that take longer and cost more.

oving On— Dividing Things

A. ON BEING HUMAN

Even the nicest relationships come to an end. Whether you leave one another with good or bad feelings is probably largely dependent on how you feel about yourselves at the time. Still, no matter how sensitive, caring and giving each of you is, there are likely to be some sticky moments. The loss of an important part of your life can't help but affect you in powerful ways. It is easy to allow this feeling of loss (anger, hostility, guilt, resentment) to manifest itself in bitter arguments over who will get the coffee pot, dessert forks, children or house. Take a moment now if you are in this situation and think of how you would advise your closest friends, should they be breaking up. Now, see if you are applying this advice to yourself.

It used to be that many people were pressured by door-to-door salesmen into signing expensive contracts for things that they didn't really want. A signature on a contract at a moment of emotional overeagerness, and the unlucky buyer found himself faced with many months (or years) of payments. Eventually, Congress dealt with this kind of injustice with a law that provided a person signing one of these contracts a three-day "cooling-off period" during which he could cancel the contract without the necessity of giving a reason. The idea was that folks should not be stuck permanently with their own hasty actions committed in an emotion-charged atmosphere. We think this is a good plan to follow in breaking off a relationship. You have had an argument, you are both tired of each other, and you have both very likely said things to hurt the other. Don't stomp out with your back scratcher and the check books and announce you will never return. Give yourself three days (at least) to "cool off", either in the apartment or house or somewhere else. If, after this time, you are still convinced that you want to split and you are both able to discuss matters rationally, sit down and

divide. But, if one of you still cannot talk without fighting or crying, wait another week or so before you again try to settle the financial matters. Of course, division of property, etc. is not important compared to what is really going on, but, a year from now, **you** will feel better if you think you got your fair share of the material items. Also, more importantly, you will not be able to complain bitterly about your financial losses and fool yourself that this is what really concerns you.

One of the authors was once contacted by a man in his forties who was being sued for divorce by his wife of twenty years. The wife had asked for custody of the minor children and, from the information volunteered by the husband, it seemed likely that the court would follow her wishes. There were many bills, but few assets other than the furniture and an automobile. The man bitterly complained, "What have I got to show for 20 years of marriage?" The author suggested that he had lived twenty years in a close relationship. Some of these years were good, and many of them were enjoyable, and he had children who continued to love him even though they preferred living with their mother. Living together, whether married or not, is not an investment, it is a shared experience. The question is not what you have at the end of the relationship, but what happiness you enjoyed and were able to give while it lasted. If you were together for some time, you did it because that was what you wanted.

Every attorney who does any domestic work is all too familiar with the client who files for a divorce announcing he or she wants everything he or she can get, refuses to accept any reasonable offer of settlement, obtains a judgment and continues to be dissatisfied, no matter how favorable the court's decision was. This kind of person travels from lawyer to lawyer, seeking to have the case re-opened, castigating the spouse, the previous attorneys, and the judge for their share in the "humiliation". This sort of person never lets go, continues to make himself (or herself) knowledgeable as to the whereabouts and actions of the other spouse and never lets an opportunity for a little gratuitous harrassment pass. Commonly this type of bitterness leads to fights over support until the children have become adults and the spouse remarries or dies. Payments are not made on time or in full, and the spouse is continually going to court to attempt to change the support order.

The sight is not pretty. It takes only a minimal knowledge of psychology for the outsider to evaluate what is really happening. Don't let yourself get involved in this sort of bitter craziness. It is so easy to become a prisoner of your own bad feelings and not always so easy to stay in touch with your humanity. **It is not worth** engaging in marathon battles particularly if the other person is as bad as you say he (she) is.

B. PROPERTY

If you have paid attention to Chapters 2, 4 and 6 of this book and have been careful to order your economic affairs along the lines of any one of the sample property agreements we have given you, you're in good shape — maybe not emotionally, but at least materially. Dividing things up according to the guidelines you yourselves have set up should not be difficult. If you do run into problems due to a conflicting interpretation of one or more contract clauses, consider getting a neutral third person to help you make a compromise. Going to court to fight over property almost always costs more than the property is worth, so you have every incentive to compromise even if you end up with less than you believe to be reasonable.

But what happens if you and your partner never wrote down anything **and** you have accumulated assets and debts? If, after discussing property division with your friend and making every effort to divide things fairly you are unable to reach complete agreement, you should do one of the following:

1. Consider simply forgetting about the whole thing and letting your friend take what he (she) wants. We strongly advise this course if the disputed items are not valuable. We have seen thousands of cases where the objects of dispute were not worth a fight. Also, a little generosity often works wonders in getting your friend to be more reasonable.

2. Consult a third party, together if possible (an attorney may be helpful if you are unclear as to the law), with the idea of working out a compromise.

3. Engage in an all-out war, each with an attorney, involving court fights, etc. We recommend this last course of action if there is a great deal at stake **or** if you feel sorry for lawyers and want to give them all your money. However, if you decide to go this route, you will want to know what law exists governing the property rights and obligations of unmarried couples. Here is where the *Marvin v. Marvin* case comes in again. Re-read Chapter 3 carefully and decide if your situation resembles any of those that would qualify you to claim an implied agreement or partnership or any of the other equitable remedies that are discussed. If you feel you have a worthwhile case, see an attorney. As you must understand by now, this is a highly complex, changing area of the law. Most lawyers know little about it, so if you do wish to go to court you will have to investigate carefully to find someone knowledgeable. Finding a clever, resourceful attorney named Marvin Mitchelson didn't hurt Michelle Marvin.

But remember, lawsuits take a lot of time and cost a lot of money. Michelle Marvin first filed her lawsuit on February 22, 1972. The California Supreme Court handed down its decision on December 26, 1976, and the Superior Court finally entered its judgment giving Michelle $104,000 in April of 1979. The wheels of justice do not spin quickly — indeed, they barely move. Fundamental court reform giving people reasonable access to their own dispute resolution process is way overdue.

C. PATERNITY

Before reaching the question of custody some people will first have to cope with a father who refuses to acknowledge that he is the father. Yes, this is a nasty situation as well as being a serious legal problem if you do not have an acknowledgment of paternity such as the one in Chapter 8. If you are faced with this problem, or if you will need financial support to raise the children properly and the other parent refuses to pay such support, you should see an attorney, or if you have little money, the district attorney. Paternity actions are unpleasant, but children should not have to suffer because their father is an idiot.

D. SUPPORT FOR DEPENDENTS

If you and your partner have had children together, and if you are to have custody, you will want to be sure that you have enough money to support them. Many parents regularly contribute to the support of their children even if they do not have custody,

without the necessity of a court order. You are fortunate people if you have the good sense to work out a voluntary support, visitation and custody agreement (see Chapter 8). However, please remember that a "promise" cannot be enforced legally if the paying parent decides differently in the future. If you believe that there is any possibility that support will not be provided voluntarily, you will need a court order.

Hopefully, when the child was born, the father signed an acknowledgment of paternity statement as described in Chapter 8. If he did not do so, it is extremely important that he do this before you two say good-bye. Even if your break-up is bitter, you must take care to protect the rights of your children. Assuming the father has signed the statement, and that while you were living together the question of support never arose, you are now going to have to deal with some hard facts of life. First try to work out an appropriate amount for the child support contribution. To do this both parents should sit down together. The parent who will have custody of the children should list her (his) monthly income and monthly expenses of the children. Be realistic. Your children need adequate food, clothing, shelter, education including entertainment, and a feeling of security. You are not out to get the other parent and you are not out to be a martyr; you are trying to deal seriously with the future of your children. The parent who will not have custody should also list his monthly income from all sources and his monthly expenses. It may be that your estimates are fairly close and the parent without custody will agree to pay the difference between the income and the expenses of the parent with custody. Re-read Chapters 8 and 9 which contain considerable information on children, support, visitation, etc. If you are not able to arrive at a mutually agreeable solution, the parent with custody may be forced to hire an attorney to get adequate support. This is silly since your children need the money more than the lawyer does. Try again to work out a settlement. There are three alternative custody and support agreements included in Section E of Chapter 8. Read them through thoroughly before writing out your own agreement.

REMEMBER: Most low and middle income families cannot realistically expect to support two households on one income. This means that if there is only one wage earner, no one is going to have enough money to be comfortable. We have seen thousands of cases where, with all the good faith in the world, there simply is not enough money to go around. What can we say to help? Not much, except to urge you to pay attention to your friend's needs as well as your own, to try to avoid being paranoid or vindictive, and to remember that in addition to a decent place to live, good food and a feeling of being loved, there is something in the soul of a child that needs a lollipop once in a while.

E. SUPPORT FOR ONE ANOTHER

It is not uncommon that when people separate there is a mutual understanding that in fairness one owes the other some support. This commonly occurs when one person has been paying the other's school expenses and the breakup happens before the money is repaid. We discuss making an agreement to cover this possibility in advance in Chapter 4. Often, however, people don't plan ahead and must do the best they can in the here and now.

If you have decided that one person will continue to support the other person for a period of time, you should sign an agreement to this effect. Here are two samples:

SAMPLE SEPARATION AGREEMENT

Roger Bane and Mildred Perkins have decided to live separately from this time on. For the past five years they have lived together and Mildred has provided many household services for Roger and has foregone any paid employment.

It is hereby agreed between the parties that commencing March 1, 19   and continuing for a period of one year Roger shall pay to Mildred the sum of $150 a month for a total of $1,800. Said payments shall be made on the first of every month.

Date	Roger Bane
Date	Mildred Perkins

SAMPLE SEPARATION AGREEMENT

Sue Jessup and Eric Smallwood agree as follows:

1. That for most of the last three years Eric has supported Sue while she got her Doctor of Divinity degree and that the amount of support provided was approximately $8,000.

2. That commencing July 1, 19___ Sue will pay Eric $200 per month. Payments shall be made on the first of each month and shall continue for a total of forty months.

_____   _____
Date   Sue Jessup

_____   _____
Date   Eric Smallwood

Like other agreements, these should be prepared in duplicate. Notarization is optional unless the contracts involve real property, but it never hurts. This sort of support agreement is in the form of a contract and can be enforced in court. If your friend (perhaps we should say former friend) will not sign this kind of agreement and you believe that in fairness he or she should, there remains the possibility of a quantum meruit recovery as discussed by the California Supreme Court in the *Marvin* case (see Chapter 3).

F. CUSTODY OF CHILDREN

If you can't even get to the question of child support because you and your partner cannot agree who should have custody of the children, re-read Chapters 8 and 9 on child custody and starting a family. If you still can't work out a custody agreement, try to get a third party to help. A family counselor may be of great assistance in working out a sensible compromise, fair to all. Only if all else fails, see an attorney. It is very difficult to represent yourself in a contested custody situation (see Chapter 13).

CONCLUSION

When you have taken care of the property, debts, custody and support of children, you have come through one of the most important and toughest periods of your life. Probably you have had to call on more maturity, patience, intelligence and plain courage than you thought you had. Now, whatever your experience, let the recriminations of the past drop away, stay in touch with your strength and centeredness and make sure you haven't lost your sense of humor. If you have, try looking for it next to your sense of optimism, right behind wonder and delight.

eath

A. INHERITANCE RIGHTS OF UNMARRIED COUPLES

Many of us turn off when the subject of death is raised, no matter what the context. We act as though, by ignoring death's inevitability, we can somehow get death to ignore our mortality. This reaction to death is so prevalent that our society has passed laws to cope with it. They are called "intestate succession" laws and are designed to pass the property (less a healthy chunk for the tax man, of course) of those who themselves make no provision to do so, to their relatives.

It is particularly important for unmarried couples to understand that, according to the "intestate succession" laws of all fifty states, they (i.e., the relationship) do not exist and that, unless they take sensible steps to protect themselves, are extremely likely to be screwed. In all states, in the absence of a will, one member of a married couple will inherit at least part of the estate of the other spouse if there is no divorce decree. Likewise, the spouse will enjoy considerable protections even if the other spouse attempts to give away all the property to some other person or organization in a will. In no state does a person who has been living with another have a right to any property of that person if he (or she) dies without leaving a will.* Children born to unmarried couples who have been legitimated (a paternity statement does this in most states, but in New York and some other states a court proceeding is necessary) will inherit absent a will or other estate planning devices, but here too it is wise to be on the safe side and specifically provide for the children by use of a will or trust or joint ownership or insurance plan such as those mentioned in this chapter.

EXAMPLE: Keija and Felix live together for ten years. Each accumulates $50,000 in their own separate bank accounts. They are saving this money for their joint future, but have made no contracts or wills. A brick falls on Felix's head killing him instantly.

---

* A surviving member of an unmarried couple may be able to claim that an oral contract like those discussed in Chapters 2 and 3 existed by which they claim ownership of some of what otherwise would be the deceased's property. We discuss this possibility in Section G of this chapter.

His only blood relative is Aunt Tillie in Omaha, Nebraska whom he hasn't seen in fifteen years and whom he doesn't like. Who inherits, Keija or Tillie? You guessed it — Tillie.

B. DEFINITIONS

Now that we have established the idea that unmarried couples must do some planning if they wish to leave property to each other, let's learn the meaning of a few terms. Please pay attention (try putting your head under a cold shower half-way through) as the legal gobbledygook relating to death and dying is both specialized and necessary to an understanding of what we are talking about.

ADMINISTRATION (OF AN ESTATE)—the distribution of the estate of a deceased person. The person who manages the distribution is an ADMINISTRATOR (male) or ADMINISTRATRIX (female).

BENEFICIARY—the person or organization who is entitled to receive benefits. Often used in trusts.

CODOCIL—a supplement to a will containing a modification, amendment, explanation, etc.

COMMUNITY PROPERTY—exists in Arizona, California, Idaho, New Mexico, Louisiana, Texas and Washington only; consists of that property which is acquired by either party during marriage unless the property is inherited or given to one's spouse as a gift.

ESTATE—all the property of a person who has died.

HEIR—a person who inherits.

HOLOGRAPHIC WILL—a will that is completely handwritten. Such a will is valid in 21 states. (See Section D, below).

INHERIT—to receive from someone who has died.

ISSUE—the children and descendants of a person.

INTESTATE—without a will. To die intestate means to die without having a will. INTESTATE SUCCESSION is the way property of a deceased person is distributed if the deceased did not leave a valid will.

LIFE ESTATE—the right to use property, most often real property, during one's lifetime. This is a valuable property interest short of absolute ownership.

PERSONAL PROPERTY—all property which is not real property.

PER CAPITA—a method of dividing an estate between relatives in use in many states. You will see it used in this chapter in the chart outlining the laws of the various states if you die without a will. For example: if a deceased person died intestate leaving five grandchildren, three of whom were the children of a deceased child and two of whom were the children of another deceased child and the grandparent died in a "per capita" state, each grandchild would receive one-fifth of the estate.

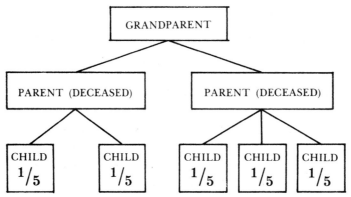

PER STIRPES—a method of dividing an estate between relatives in use in many states. It is somewhat different from the "per capita" system. As with "per capita" above, it is important in this chapter in understanding the laws of the various states if you die without a will. For example: if a deceased person died intestate leaving five grandchildren, three of whom were the children of a deceased child, and two of whom were the children of another deceased child, and the grandparent died in a "per stirpes" state, the three children of the one deceased child would divide one-half of the estate and the two children of the other deceased child would divide the other one-half.

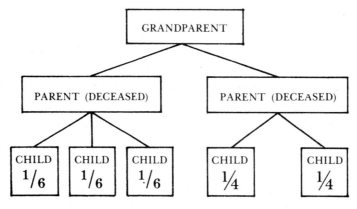

PROBATE—the name for the court procedure designed to prove a will authentic and distribute the property according to the will.

REAL PROPERTY—land and those items attached to the land such as buildings, etc.

RESIDUE—that which is left when something is taken out.

SEPARATE PROPERTY—in states which have community property laws, that property which is not community property.

SIBLINGS—brothers and sisters.

SUCCESSION—who gets what when someone dies. THE LAWS OF SUCCESSION are the laws which regulate who will share in the estate.

SURVIVE—to be living when someone dies.

TRUST—a relationship in which one person (the trustee) holds title (often subject to a number of conditions) to property for the benefit of another person (the beneficiary). A trust is commonly used when money is left to people inexperienced in its management such as children or as a tax saving device.

WILL—a legal document in which a person states who he wants to inherit his property.

C. INTESTATE SUCCESSION: WHAT HAPPENS TO YOUR PROPERTY IF YOU DIE WITHOUT A WILL?

Before discussing the various ways that you can leave your property, let's first understand what happens if you don't leave a will or adopt some other device to pass property such as "joint tenancy". What happens depends a good deal on the state you and your property are located in. All states have systems of "intestate succession"that will pass your property to your relatives if you have any, and to the state if you don't. The systems in use in the various states are similar to one another but do differ in detail. It may be that your state provides for a system of intestate succession that is exactly what you want. If so, a will would be redundant.* The following chart outlines intestate succession in the fifty states. It is only an outline and does not deal with certain spousal rights that may be provided by your state. If you have any questions, you should be sure to contact an attorney since this area can be very complicated. This is especially true if you have a lot of property. A simple consultation with a probate attorney should not cost too much.

IMPORTANT: Before you can make an intelligent will or some other arrangement to pass on your property at death, you have to know what property is yours. Don't laugh. This can sometimes be a tough one. If you have lived with a person for a long time, your property may have gotten so mixed up with your friend's that it is difficult to tell who owns what. If you find yourselves in this situation and have a reasonably small amount of property, it would be a good idea to sit down with your friend and make an agreement as to who owns what. Have the agreement notarized. If large amounts of property are involved, you may want to get professional help.

---

* Both leaving property under a will or by intestate succession ends up requiring that your property go through probate in most states. Many people wish to avoid the time and expense of probate and thus pass their property in other ways. See Section E of this chapter.

SAMPLE PROPERTY OWNERSHIP AGREEMENT

Felix Finnegan and Keija Adams agree as follows:

1. That they have been living together for ten years and that during that time much of their real and personal property has become mixed together so that it is not completely clear who owns what;*

2. That the purpose of this agreement is to divide all of Keija's and Felix's real and personal property into two categories as set out below;**

3. That it is agreed that, from the date this agreement is signed by both parties, all property listed in category 1 belongs solely and absolutely to Felix and that all property listed in category 2 belongs solely and absolutely to Keija;

Category 1 (Felix)

1. 1980 Ford
2. G.E. Washer & Dryer
3. 100 Shares of stock in Melt-
      in-Your-Mouth Popcorn, Inc.
4. Etc.
5. Etc.

Category 2 (Keija)

1. 1980 Yamaha Cycle
2. BMX Stereo & related stereo equipment
3. $12,000 in the Restaurant Worker
      Credit Union
4. Etc.
5. Etc.

_____   _____
Date   Keija Adams

_____   _____
Date   Felix Finnegan

Notarize

* Where real property is involved, you will want to be sure that ownership of the property on the title slip conforms with this agreement.
** It would also be possible to set up a third category for property owned jointly. If you do this, each piece of property and how it is owned should be listed. For example, "House at 1547 Jones St. in joint tenancy".

Intestate Succession:
What Happens to Your Property If You Die Without A Will?

KEY

The numbered sections listed under each state refer to the following situations:

1. If your **spouse and children** or their descendants are still living: How the *real property* is divided.
2. If your **spouse and children** or their descendants are still living: How the *personal property* is divided.
3. If your **spouse** is still living, but no children or their descendants are living. NOTE: In every state, if only your children or their issue survive, your estate is divided per capita among your children and per stirpes among the issue of any deceased children.
4. If your **parents** are still living, but no spouse or children or their descendants are still living.
5. If your **siblings** are living, but no spouse or children or their descendants or your parents are still living.

ALABAMA
1. Life estate in one third to spouse, residue to children.
2. If husband survives: half to husband, half to children. If wife survives with one child: half to wife, half to child; with 2-4 children: wife and children share equally per capita; with more than four children: one-fifth to wife, four-fifths to children.
3. All to spouse.
4. If both parents survive: half to each. If one parent survives: half to parent, half to brothers and sisters or their issue per stirpes. If one parent and no brothers and sisters or their issue: all to parent.
5. Equal shares to brothers and sisters or their issue per stirpes.

ALASKA
1. Half to spouse, half to children.
2. Same.
3. All to spouse.

4. Half to each parent or all to surviving parent.
5. Equal shares to siblings or their issue per stirpes.

ARIZONA
1. **Separate property:** life estate in one third to spouse; residue to children. **Community property:** half to spouse, half to children.
2. **Separate property:** one third to spouse, two thirds to children. **Community property:** half to spouse, half to children.
3. If parents still living: half of separately owned real property to them, all other separate property and all community property to spouse.
4. If both parents survive, half to each. If one parent survives: half to parent, half to brothers and sisters or their issue. If one parent and no brothers and sisters or their issue survive, all to parent.
5. Equal shares to brothers and sisters or their issue per stirpes.

169

ARKANSAS

1. Life estate in one-third to spouse, residue to children.
2. One-third to spouse, two-thirds to children.
3. If married to you at least three years, spouse takes all; if married to you less than three years, half to spouse and half to parents unless parents are deceased in which case spouse takes half and siblings or their issue take half. If neither parents nor siblings, nor their issue, are living, all to spouse.
4. Half to each parent or all to surviving parent.
5. Equal shares to the heirs (determined at the time of your death) of a spouse who died earlier and who was married to you at the time of his or her death; siblings do not take anything.

CALIFORNIA

1. **Separate property:** With one child, half to spouse and half to child. With more than one child: one-third to spouse, two-thirds to children. **Community property:** all to spouse.
2. Same.
3. If parents survive: half of separate property to them, half to spouse and all community property to spouse. If parents not living: half of separate property to siblings or their issue, half of separate property and all community property to spouse. If neither parents, siblings, nor their issue survive, all to spouse.
4. Half to each parent or all to surviving parent.
5. Equal shares to siblings or their issue per stirpes.

COLORADO

1. Half to spouse, half to children.
2. Same.
3. All to spouse.
4. Half to each parent or all to surviving parent.
5. Equal shares to siblings or their issue per stirpes.

CONNECTICUT

1. One-third to spouse, two-thirds to children.

2. Same.
3. Spouse takes $50,000 and three-quarters of residue, remainder to parents.
4. Half to each parent or all to surviving parent.
5. (1) equal shares to brothers and sisters or their issue per stirpes. (2) if no siblings survive, equal shares to half brothers and half sisters or their issue per stirpes.

DELAWARE

1. Life estate in one-third to spouse, residue to children.
2. One-third to spouse, two-thirds to children.
3. All to spouse.
4. Half to each parent or all to surviving parent.
5. Equal shares to siblings or their issue per stirpes.

DISTRICT OF COLUMBIA

1. Life estate in one-third to spouse, residue to children.
2. One-third to spouse, two-thirds to children.
3. If parents living, half to them and half to spouse. If parents not living, half to siblings or their issue, half to spouse. If neither parents nor siblings nor their issue living, all to spouse.
4. Half to each parent or all to surviving parent.
5. Equal shares to siblings or their issue per stirpes.

FLORIDA

1. Each receives an equal share.
2. Same.
3. All to spouse.
4. Half to each parent or all to surviving parent.
5. Equal shares to siblings or their issue per stirpes.

GEORGIA

1. Half to spouse, half to children.
2. Same.
3. All to spouse.
4. Equal share to parents and siblings, whether whole or half blood, or their issue per stirpes.
5. Same.

See KEY on first page of chart for explanation of numbered paragraphs.

HAWAII
1. Life estate to spouse, residue to children.
2. One-third to spouse, two-thirds to children.
3. All to spouse.
4. Half to each parent or all to surviving parent.
5. Equal shares to siblings or their issue per stirpes.

IDAHO
1. **Separate property:** With one child or issue: half to spouse, half to child. With more than one child or issue: one-third to spouse, two-thirds to children. **Community property:** all to spouse.
2. Same.
3. If parents are living: they take half of separate property, wife takes residue and all of community property. If parents are not living, spouse takes all.
4. Half to each parent or all to surviving parent.
5. Equal shares to siblings or their issue per stirpes.

ILLINOIS
1. Life estate in one-third to spouse, residue to children.
2. One-third to spouse, two-thirds to children.
3. All to spouse.
4. Equal shares to parents and siblings or their issue, but if one parent is dead, surviving parent takes a double share.
5. Equal shares to siblings or their issue per stirpes.

INDIANA
1. With one child or issue: half to spouse, half to child. With more than one child or issue: one-third to spouse, two-thirds to children.
2. Same.
3. If parents are living, one-quarter to them and three-quarters to spouse. If not, all to spouse.
4. One-quarter to each surviving parent, the rest equally to brothers and sisters or their issue per stirpes.

5. Equal shares to siblings or their issue per stirpes.

IOWA
1. One-third to spouse, two-thirds to children.
2. Same.
3. Spouse takes first $25,000 of nonexempt property plus half of residue; parent(s), if living, take(s) other half of residue. If parents are not living, spouse takes all.
4. Half to each parent or all to surviving parent.
5. To brothers and sisters and their issue per stirpes as though through the estates of the parents.

KANSAS
1. Half to spouse, half to children.
2. Same.
3. All to spouse.
4. Half to each parent or all to surviving parent.
5. To brothers and sisters and their issue per stirpes as though through the estate of the parents.

KENTUCKY
1. Half to spouse, half to children.
2. Same.
3. All to spouse.
4. Half to each parent or all to surviving parent.
5. Equal shares to siblings or their issue per stirpes.

LOUISIANA
1. Life estate to spouse, residue to children.
2. Same.
3. If parents are living, half to them and half to spouse. If parents are not living, all to spouse.
4. One-quarter to each parent and remainder in equal shares to siblings or their issue per stirpes.
5. Same.

MAINE
1. One-third to spouse, two-thirds to children.

See KEY on first page of chart for explanation of numbered paragraphs.

2. Same.
3. If parents are living: spouse takes $10,000 plus half of remaining personal property and two-thirds of remaining real property, parents take residue. If parents are not living: spouse takes $10,000 plus half of remaining personal property and two-thirds of remaining real property, siblings and their issue take residue. If neither parents nor siblings nor their issue are living, spouse takes all.
4. Half to each parent or all to surviving parent.
5. Equal shares to siblings or their issue per stirpes.

MARYLAND
1. One-half to spouse, one-half to children.
2. Same.
3. If parents are living: half to them and half to spouse. If neither parents nor issue are living, spouse takes all.
4. Half to each parent or all to surviving parent.
5. Equal shares to siblings or their issue per stirpes.

MASSACHUSETTS
1. One-third to spouse, two-thirds to children.
2. Same.
3. If parents are living, spouse takes $50,000 plus half of residue and parents take other half of residue. If parents are not living, spouse takes all.
4. Half to each parent or all to surviving parent.
5. Equal shares to siblings or their issue per stirpes.

MICHIGAN
1. First $60,000 plus one-half residue to spouse, one-half to children.
2. Same.
3. First $60,000 plus one-half residue to spouse, one-half to parent(s).

4. Half to each parent or all to surviving parent.
5. Equal shares to siblings or their issue per stirpes.

MINNESOTA
1. With one child or issue: half to spouse, half to child. With more than one child or issue: one-third to spouse, two-thirds to children.
2. Same.
3. All to spouse.
4. Half to each parent or all to surviving parent.
5. Equal shares to siblings or their issue per stirpes.

MISSISSIPPI
1. Equal shares to spouse and children or their issue per stirpes.
2. Same.
3. All to spouse.
4. Equal shares to parents and siblings or sibling's issue per stirpes.
5. Same.

MISSOURI
1. Half to spouse, half to children.
2. Same.
3. Half to spouse, half to surviving parent(s), sibling(s), and siblings' issue per capita.
4. Equal shares to parents and siblings or sibling's issue per stirpes.
5. Same.

MONTANA
1. With one child or issue: half to spouse, half to child. With more than one child or issue: one-third to spouse, two-thirds to children.

See KEY on first page of chart for explanation of numbered paragraphs.

2. Same.
3. All to spouse.
4. Half to each parent or all to surviving parent.
5. Equal shares to siblings or their issue per stirpes.

NEBRASKA
1. With one child or issue: half to spouse, half to child. With more than one child or issue: one-third to spouse, two-thirds to children.
2. Same.
3. If parents are living, parents take half and spouse takes half. If parents are not living, siblings or their issue take half and spouse takes half. If neither parents nor siblings nor their issue are living, all to spouse.
4. Half to each parent or all to surviving parent.
5. Equal shares to siblings or their issue per stirpes.

NEVADA
1. **Separate property:** With one child or issue: half to spouse, half to child. With more than one child or issue: one-third to spouse, two-thirds to children. **Community property:** All to spouse.
2. Same.
3. If parents are living, parents take half of separate property and spouse takes other half and all of community property. If parents are not living, siblings or their issue take half of separate property and spouse takes other half and all of community property. If neither spouse nor siblings nor their issue are living, spouse takes all.
4. Half to each parent or all to surviving parent.
5. Equal shares to siblings or their issue per stirpes.

NEW HAMPSHIRE
1. One-third to spouse, two-thirds to children, with the exception that husband takes only for life if no issue by him and he has no estate.
2. Same.
3. If parents are living, spouse takes $10,000 plus

half of residue and parents take other half of residue. If parents are not living, spouse takes $10,000 plus half of residue and siblings or their issue take other half of residue. If neither parents nor siblings nor their issue are living, spouse takes all.
4. Half to each parent or all to surviving parent.
5. Equal shares to siblings or their issue per stirpes.

NEW JERSEY
1. Life estate in half to spouse, residue to children.
2. One-third to spouse, residue to children.
3. All to spouse.
4. Equal shares to parents and siblings (whether whole or half blood) or their issue per stirpes.
5. Same.

NEW MEXICO
1. **Separate property:** one-quarter to spouse, three-quarters to children. **Community property:** all to spouse.
2. Same.
3. All to spouse.
4. Half to each parent or all to surviving parent.
5. To siblings and their issue per stirpes as though through the estates of the parents.

NEW YORK
1. With one child or issue: spouse takes $4,000 plus half of residue, child takes other half of residue. With more than one child or issue: spouse takes $4,000 plus one-third of residue, children take other two-thirds of residue.
2. Same.
3. If parents are living, spouse takes $25,000 plus half of residue and parents take other half. If parents are not living, spouse takes all.
4. Half to each parent or all to surviving parent.
5. Equal shares to siblings or their issue per stirpes.

NORTH CAROLINA
1. With one child or issue: half to spouse, half to

See KEY on first page of chart for explanation of numbered paragraphs.

173

child or issue. With more than one child or issue: one-third to spouse, two-thirds to children or issue.
2. Same.
3. If parents are living: spouse takes half of real property and $10,000 of personal property plus half of excess, and parents take residue. If parents are not living, spouse takes all.
4. All to parents or surviving parent.
5. Equal shares to siblings or their issue per stirpes.

NORTH DAKOTA
1. With one child or issue: half to spouse, half to child. With more than one child or issue: one-third to spouse, two-thirds to children or issue.
2. Same.
3. If parents are living, spouse takes $50,000 plus half of residue and parents take other half of residue. If parents are not living, spouse takes $100,000 plus half of residue and siblings or their issue take other half of residue. If neither parents nor siblings nor their issue are living, spouse takes all.
4. Half to each parent or all to surviving parent.
5. Equal shares to siblings or their issue per stirpes.

OHIO
1. With one child or issue: half to spouse, half to child. With more than one child or issue: one-third to spouse, two-thirds to children or issue.
2. Same.
3. If parents are living, spouse takes three-quarters and parents take one-quarter. If parents are not living, spouse takes all.
4. Half to each parent or all to surviving parent.
5. Equal shares to siblings or their issue per stirpes.

OKLAHOMA
1. With one child or issue: half to spouse, half to child. With more than one child or issue:

one-third to spouse, two-thirds to children or issue.
2. Same.
3. If parents are living: parents take half and spouse takes half. If parents are not living: spouse takes half and siblings or their issue take half. If neither parents nor siblings nor their issue are living, all to spouse.
4. Half to each parent or all to surviving parent.
5. Equal shares to siblings and their issue per stirpes.

OREGON
1. Half to spouse, half to children.
2. Same.
3. All to spouse.
4. Half to each parent or all to surviving parent.
5. Equal shares to siblings or their issue per stirpes.

PENNSYLVANIA
1. With one child or issue: half to spouse, half to child. With more than one child or issue: one-third to spouse, two-thirds to children or issue.
2. Same.
3. If parents are living, spouse takes $20,000 plus half of residue and parents take other half of residue. If parents are not living, spouse takes $20,000 plus half of residue and siblings or their issue take half of residue. If neither parents nor siblings nor their issue are living, spouse takes all.
4. Half to each parent or all to surviving parent.
5. Equal shares to siblings or their issue per stirpes.

RHODE ISLAND
1. Husband takes life estate in all; wife takes life estate in one-third; remainder to children.
2. Half to spouse, half to children.
3. If parents are living: spouse takes life estate in all real property and first $50,000 of personal property plus half of residue; parents take remaining personal property. If parents are not

See KEY on first page of chart for explanation of numbered paragraphs.

living: spouse takes life estate in all real property and first $50,000 of personal property plus half of residue; siblings or their issue take remaining personal property.
4. Half to each parent or all to surviving parent.
5. Equal shares to siblings or their issue per stirpes.

SOUTH CAROLINA
1. With one child or issue: half to spouse, half to child. With more than one child or issue: one-third to spouse, two-thirds to children or issue.
2. Same.
3. Spouse takes half and other half goes in equal shares to parents and siblings or sibling' issue. If neither parents nor siblings nor their issue survive, spouse takes all.
4. Equal shares to parents and siblings or sibling' issue per stirpes, descendants of the whole blood preferred.
5. Same.

SOUTH DAKOTA
1. With one child or issue: half to spouse, half to child. With more than one child or issue: one-third to spouse, two-thirds to children or issue.
2. Same.
3. If parents are living: spouse takes $100,000 plus half of residue and parents take other half of residue. If parents are not living: spouse takes $100,000 plus half of residue and siblings or their issue take other half of residue. If neither parents nor siblings nor their issue are living, spouse takes all.
4. Half to each parent or all to surviving parent.
5. Equal shares to siblings or their issue per stirpes.

TENNESSEE
1. Life estate in all to husband; life estate in one-third to wife; residue to children.
2. Equal shares to spouse and children or their issue per stirpes.

3. Spouse takes all the personal property; wife has a right of dower in one-third of the real property, the remaining real property is shared first by siblings or their issue and second by the parents.
4. Real property descends first to siblings or their issue and then to the parents (if no siblings or issue survive). Personal property descends first to parents and then to siblings or their issue per stirpes (if parents do not survive).
5. Same.

TEXAS
1. **Separate property:** life estate in one-third to spouse, residue to children. **Community property:** half to spouse, half to children.
2. **Separate property:** one-third to spouse, two-thirds to children. **Community property:** half to spouse, half to children.
3. Spouse takes all community property and all separate personal property plus half of separate real property, parents and siblings or their issue take half of residue.
4. If both parents survive, half to each. If one parent survives, half to parent and half to brothers and sisters or their issue.
5. Equal shares to siblings or their issue per stirpes.

UTAH
1. With one child or issue: half to spouse, half to child. With more than one child or issue: one-third to spouse, two-thirds to children or issue.
2. Same.
3. If parents are living: spouse takes $100,000 plus half of residue, parents take other half of residue. If parents are not living: spouse takes $100,000 plus half of residue, siblings or their issue take other half of residue. If neither parents nor siblings nor their issue are living, spouse takes all.
4. Half to each parent or all to surviving parent.
5. Equal shares to siblings or their issue per stirpes.

See KEY on first page of chart for explanation of numbered paragraphs.

175

VERMONT

1. With one child or issue: half to spouse, half to child. With more than one child or issue: one-third to spouse, two-thirds to children.
2. Spouse takes all clothing and ornaments and one-third other property, residue to children.
3. If parents are living: spouse takes $8,000 plus half of residue, parents share remainder equally. If parents are not living: spouse takes $8,000 plus half of residue and siblings or their issue take remainder per stirpes. If neither parents nor siblings nor their issue are living, spouse takes all.
4. Half to each parent or all to surviving parent.
5. Equal shares to siblings or their issue per stirpes.

VIRGINIA

1. Life estate in one-third to spouse, residue to children.
2. One-third to spouse, two-thirds to children.
3. All to spouse.
4. Half to each parent or all to surviving parent.
5. Equal shares to siblings or their issue per stirpes.

WASHINGTON

1. Half to spouse, half to children.
2. Same.
3. If parents are living: spouse takes half community property plus three-quarters of other, parents take residue. If parents are not living, spouse takes all community property plus three-quarters of other and siblings or their issue take residue. If neither parents nor siblings nor their issue are living, spouse takes all.
4. Half to each parent or all to surviving parent.
5. Equal shares to siblings or their issue per stirpes.

WEST VIRGINIA

1. Life estate in one-third to spouse, residue to children.
2. One-third to spouse, two-thirds to children.

3. All to spouse.
4. Half to each parent or all to surviving parent.
5. Equal shares to siblings or their issue per stirpes.

WISCONSIN

1. First $25,000 to spouse plus one-half of residue if there is one child or issue, remainder to child. With more than one child, one-third of residue to spouse, two-thirds to children or issue.
2. Same.
3. All to spouse.
4. Half to each parent or all to surviving parent.
5. Equal shares to siblings or their issue per stirpes.

WYOMING

1. Half to spouse, half to children.
2. Same.
3. Spouse takes $20,000 and three-quarters of residue, parents and siblings or their issue share one-quarter of residue.
4. Equal shares to parents and siblings or their issue per stirpes.
5. Same.

See KEY on first page of chart for explanation of numbered paragraphs.

D. MAKING A WILL

If you are not happy with the intestate succession scheme in your state (and most unmarried couples will not be) you will want to consider alternative ways to dispose of your property. One common method is by making a will. Wills work well to pass small amounts of property, but like intestate succession, wills result in property going through probate. In Section E below, we will briefly discuss some ways to leave property that avoid probate.

There are commonly two kinds of wills: "witnessed wills" and "holographic wills". A witnessed will is usually prepared by an attorney who knows the proper procedures and forms. Most states are quite fussy about the number of witnesses who must be present and the language that must be used. If you have a large estate, you need to do some homework especially on the tax consequences of your acts.* Once you know what the rules are, you may wish to have a lawyer help you with the paperwork.

A holographic will is one that is dated, written and signed entirely in your own handwriting. It must not be typewritten, nor may any typewriting appear on the will. No other writing or printing other than your own may appear on the will. Holographic wills are valid only in the following states: Alaska, Arizona, Arkansas, California, Idaho, Kentucky, Louisiana, Mississippi, Montana, Nevada, North Carolina, North Dakota, Oklahoma, Pennsylvania, South Dakota, Tennessee, Texas, Utah, Virginia, West Virginia and Wyoming. In these states a holographic will is just as valid as the kind the attorney prepares. You do not have to use any formal language and only need to be careful that you write what you intend.** An example of a holographic will follows.

WARNING: Let us repeat: Holographic wills are fine for small estates; however for large ones, especially where someone may contest the will, there can be problems proving that the signature on the will is really that of the deceased. For these and other reasons, it is not wise to use a holographic will if you are leaving a big estate.

IMPORTANT: You may change your will at any time. The simplest way of doing this is to physically destroy the original will and all copies when you make your new will. If this can't be done, you may revoke a former will by specifically stating that you are doing so in a later will. Your will should be kept in a safe deposit box or other safe place. Be careful that no one who benefits from the will has physical possession of it as this can create nasty legal problems. It is fine to give a beneficiary a summary of the will so that he or she may know where he or she stands at your death.

---

* We don't have the space here to deal with estate taxes and ways to avoid them. Basically, you are exempt from federal estate tax liability after 1981 if your total estate is less than $175,625. We recommend *Federal Estate and Gift Taxes Explained*, New York, Commerce Clearing House, for a detailed discussion of federal tax law. For state tax information, contact your state tax collector. Californians have an even better source of information: *Planning Your Estate*, Clifford, Nolo Press.
** The French philosopher Rabelais left a will of admirable simplicity. It reads in its entirety: "I have nothing. I owe a great deal. The rest I give to the poor."

Last Will and Testament

I, Felix Finnegan, declare this to be my Last Will and Testament. I revoke all prior wills, and codocils:

First: I leave no property to my children or my wife [former wife].*

Second: I leave my collection of bumper stickers to the Berkeley Public Library.

Third: I leave my dog Beagle, to Delilah Kimura, who resides at 1137 Penn Street, Oakland, California.

Fourth: I leave my 350 cc Honda motorcycle to Ruth More, who resides at 1143 Penn Street, Oakland, California.**

Fifth: I leave the remainder of my estate to my companion of many years, Keija Adams. If she is not then living, I leave the remainder of my property to my parents, Herbert Finnegan and Mary Finnegan, in equal shares. If my parents do not survive me, I leave the remainder of my property to the American Civil Liberties Union of Northern California.

Sixth: I nominate Keija Adams as executrix of my will. If she is not then living, I nominate Delilah Kimura to act in her place. I direct that no bond be required of my executrix.

Executed at Berkeley, California, on February 23, 1980.

Felix Finnegan

* In some states if you fail to mention children or spouses in your will, there is a presumption that you left them out inadvertently and that they should receive a share anyway (this is especially true for children and spouses who came along after the will was written). So keep your will up-to-date and specifically state that you don't want to leave them anything if that is your plan.

** In this will we assume that you are leaving only small amounts of property, having taken care of more major items in other ways so as to avoid probate. As long as you are only willing a dog, or teacups, or a motorcycle or a little furniture, your will won't be probated. However, if you are using a will to leave property worth **more** than $10,000- $20,000, your will is likely to result in a probate proceeding and you will want to guard against the danger that a person who inherits under the will may die before your probate is completed. If this happens, your property will go to that person's heirs and will have to go through probate twice. To avoid this, you can include the following clause: "To inherit under the terms of this will, a person must survive me by 180 days. If he/she does not, the property left that person shall pass under the terms of the remainder clause of this will which is paragraph_____."

E. AVOIDING PROBATE

As mentioned above, passing property by will won't avoid probate in most states except where small amounts of property are concerned ($10,000-$50,000 depending on the state). To avoid the time, expense and court appearances involved in probating a will, more and more people are transferring assets at death by other means. We don't have space for a comprehensive discussion of all probate-avoiding devices here, but the following are some of the commonest.

1. Joint Tenancy

This has been discussed in Chapter 6; briefly, not only real property, but bank accounts, automobiles, savings bonds, stocks and other items may be owned jointly so that when one "joint tenant" dies, the other joint tenant owns the whole asset without the necessity of disposing of it in a will. As a matter of fact, if two persons own an asset in joint tenancy, one person will own the whole asset upon the other person's death, even if the deceased person tried to dispose of his share in a will.

2. Life Insurance

You should name a living individual as your beneficiary and a contingent beneficiary who will take the proceeds if the primary beneficiary is not living at the time of your death. You do not want the benefits paid into your estate, which is what will happen if there is no living beneficiary. Paying money into your estate will necessitate court action, whereas proceeds of a life insurance policy will ordinarily be paid to the beneficiary without regard to the terms of the deceased person's will, and without court probate proceedings. There are often substantial tax savings if you give the policy to the beneficiary. See *Planning Your Estate*, Clifford, Nolo Press.

3. Trusts

Most kinds of trusts are cumbersome and involve administrative costs. However, if you have a large estate, you may wish to consider this method. It is possible to set up an "inter vivos" (living) trust, whereby you keep control of your assets while you live, but at death they pass to your friends and relatives without the necessity of going through probate. You should definitely do some of your own research and check with an attorney or tax accountant on this, since the tax consequences of different types of trusts are very different.

There is one kind of trust that may suit your needs even if you are not wealthy. This is the informal bank trust account which is held as follows: "Keija Adams, Trustee for Felix Finnegan". On the death of Keija, Felix owns the entire account. However, while both parties are living, only Keija has access to the account. Your local bank can help you set up this kind of trust account.

4. United States Savings Bonds

If you own such bonds (which are **not** a very good investment if you are concerned with the rate of return on your money), you can register them in your name with the further designation "P.O.D. (Pay on Death) to name of beneficiary". You can change the beneficiary at any time without the beneficiary's permission and, at your death, the bonds will then be payable to the designated bereficiary without the need for any court proceedings.

5. Miscellaneous Benefits

Many people are covered by Social Security, Veterans Benefits, Railroad Pensions and various other pension and/or retirement plans. Under most of these plans you have no right to any benefits if the person with whom you have been living dies. This is true of the government plans and many private plans. You should check to see if your private plan allows you to name a beneficiary. If this is the case, you should immediately do so. You can always change your beneficiary, but if you do not have one, it may end up that no one gets your benefits and they will go back into the company. No matter how many promises you and your partner made to each other, and no matter how much you were dependent on his or her income to exist, if you want to partake in any of these plans, you must be named in writing. Otherwise, you have no rights in the event of the death of your partner.

REVIEW NOTE: How to dispose of your estate depends mainly upon how much (and what) you have and your relations with the persons close to you. However, one word of caution: **If you have been living with someone for a long time, do not assume that you have been provided for. Ask** your partner if he or she has a will, and check how your assets are owned. If you and your friend do not make preparations ahead of time, one of you may find himself/herself left with nothing, even though this is not what was intended. There is no reason to let mean old Tillie in Omaha have a cent if you do even a little planning.

F. PROVIDING FOR YOUR KIDS BY WILL

There isn't a whole lot we can do to protect our children even if we are model parents. In the last analysis, they are responsible for making their own destiny. Still, we worry that if we die, things will be hard for them and we hope that we can make plans now that will ease their way if we are no longer here. It is particularly necessary that we do this for children born outside of marriage as these children may not be included under the intestate succession laws of some states. Legal problems tend to fall into two broad areas: support and custody.

If property is being left to a child, it is very common to name a "guardian of the estate" in the will.* The guardian of the estate manages and controls the property inherited by or otherwise owned by the minor, but has no right to custody. Guardians of the estate are quite common and are frequently used even if the other parent is living. This is especially true if you have a trusted friend or relative who is knowledgeable about money matters, and the other parent is not. To appoint a guardian of the estate of a minor, you can use language like this in your will:

"At my death, if any of my children are minors, I appoint __(name of guardian)__ of_____(address)_____as guardian of the estate of my minor child or children. If he/she shall for any reason fail to qualify or cease to act as such guardian, I appoint _____(name)_____ as such guardian in his/her place."

People are often more concerned about the custody of their children if they suddenly die than they are with financial matters. It is common, for example, that a divorced parent who is living with someone will want that person rather than the other parent to have custody. Indeed, it is a common misconception that people can "will" their children to someone other than the natural parent. This cannot be done if the natural parent has been visiting and supporting his or her child unless the parent is obviously unfit. The law of every state strongly favors the interests of natural parents over everyone else (see Chapters 8 and 9). However, if the other parent is not living or his (her) whereabouts are not known, or he (she) has no interest in the child and will not attempt to obtain custody, it is possible to designate in a will the person whom you wish to be the guardian of the child should you die. In legal jargon this is known as a "testamentary guardianship" and the person who is named as the guardian is known as "guardian of the person" of the minor. Here is language which you can use in your will:

"If at my death any of my children are minors, I appoint_____(name)_____ of _____(address)_____as guardian of the person of my minor child or children. If he/she shall for any reason fail to qualify or cease to act as such guardian, I appoint _____(name of successor)_____ of _____(address)_____to serve in his/her place."

If a parent does name a testamentary guardian in his or her will, the court is not required to actually appoint this person as the guardian. However, the wishes of the parent are accorded great respect, and the court will usually appoint the person named in the will unless there is evidence showing that person is unfit.

---

* In thinking about providing for your children's financial future, don't forget that, if a wage earner dies, his dependent children are entitled to Social Security survivor's benefits.

** If any substantial amount of property is to be given to a minor it is important to do this under the terms of the Uniform Gifts to Minors Act. This can be done as follows, "To _____, an adult ____Californian or whatever_____, or appropriate _____(STATE)_____ financial institution as custodian for _____(NAME OF MINOR)_____ under the _____(STATE)_____Uniform Gift to Minors Act."

NOTE: Be realistic if you name someone as a guardian. Check to make sure the person is willing and able to assume custody of the child. Also be sure to keep this provision up-to-date. In an era of changing lifestyles and mobility, it is very difficult to predict the behavior and whereabouts of your friends throughout the minority of your child. Your sister and her husband may be very nice people, but ten years from now they may be divorced or living on a mountain top in Tibet. In most states a child of a certain age (typically 14) may nominate his own guardian and it may be better to give the choice to your child if he or she is of a suitable age.

G. DEATH AND THE MARVIN CASE

What does the *Marvin* case have to do with death? Nothing directly, but its implications are considerable. You will remember that in Chapters 3 and 4 we discussed the fact that *Marvin v. Marvin* not only made it clear that written contracts between married couples are enforceable, but also approved oral and implied contracts as well as several other equitable remedies. How does this relate to death, you say? Just be patient — we are getting to the point. Let's go back to the example at the beginning of this chapter involving the brick that falls on Felix's head and Aunt Tillie from Omaha who is as mean as a wounded rattlesnake and wants the $50,000 that Keija feels should rightly go to her. Remember, we told you that things didn't look good for Keija because Felix left no will, and under the "intestate succession" law, Tillie as the nearest relative inherits. This didn't seem to be fair (did it?) and you may have wondered if there isn't something that Keija can do.

Perhaps there is. Remember Keija and Felix were each saving money for their "joint future". Keija might claim that under the theory of the *Marvin* case she and Felix had an oral contract to share all of their earnings. If this were the case, then the money would belong to Keija. Of course, Keija would very likely have a hard time proving that an oral contract existed unless she had witnesses or some other documentation. Tillie would clearly claim that the fact that Keija and Felix kept their money in separate accounts was some evidence that they didn't mean to combine it.

We can't give you any hard and fast rules as to when the surviving member of an unmarried couple might be able to claim that a contract existed in order to get some of the deceased's estate if the deceased dies without a will. The courts have not yet made enough rulings in this area to have established guidelines. But if you are the survivor, you may have a case if any one of the following situations exist:

■ You have been working in the home and your friend has been making the money. You might be able to claim under an oral contract (if one existed) or under an implied contract, or perhaps that you were entitled to money under an equitable theory (see Chapter 3);

■ You and your partner had been buying things and saving jointly and had agreed that all property belonged to both. Of course, you would have absolutely no trouble if you had followed our advice and written your agreement down, but even if your agreements were only oral, you may be able to prove them (see Chapter 3);

■ You and your partner jointly contribute to the purchase of real property, but for some reason the property was not put in "tenancy in common" or "joint tenancy", but only in the deceased's name. It is not easy to rebut the presumption that the person whose name is on the deed is the legal owner, but sometimes a "resulting trust" can be established (see Chapter 3).

NOTE: If your friend has died leaving no will or joint ownership provisions and you believe that you are entitled to inherit some or all of his or her property, see a lawyer immediately. There are a series of legal decisions in several states which have given relief to people in this situation.

H. WHAT ABOUT MY BODY?

Most of us have no great attachment to our bodies once we take leave of them. Those of you who are into cryogenics (body freezing) and related body-saving techniques will have to look elsewhere for information. Here we are concerned only with those who are done with their bodies at death, not those who want to put them on the bedpost overnight for future use.

Many people make burial or cremation plans informally, trusting their families or friends to take care of the details after death. This works fine as long as you have confidence that your plans will be carried out. Often, however, there is a justifiable fear that your family will ignore your wishes after death, substituting their own. This is especially true if your blood relatives dislike the person you are living with.

If you are concerned about funeral arrangements, we suggest you do the following:

☯ Make practical arrangements for your funeral yourself. Get your burial plot or arrange for cremation, plan whatever ceremony you want and pay for it in advance;

☯ Leave instructions as part of your will. This can be done and is legal. You might include a provision in the will as follows: "*Upon my death I wish to be buried in the Little White Chapel Cemetary in Lancastershire, Massachusetts in plot number_____which is reserved and paid for (which will be paid for by my burial insurance through Carpenters Union 18). I wish no elaborate ceremony and wish my remains to be prepared for burial by the Fraternal Brothers Burial Society under the contract that I have signed with them. Any decisions not already made, or necessitated by circumstances that I cannot now foresee, I entrust to my friend of many years, Lucinda Whitehorse .*"

☯ Leave a letter of instructions in a place or with a person where it will be available immediately at your death. This letter should contain the same information about burial plans that is contained in your will. If your will is in a safe deposit box at your death, it may take several days to get it and a letter of instructions will be a great aid to family and friends.

ay Couples

Why Americans engage in a national pastime of categorizing people according to whom they crawl into the sack with is a mystery to us. Most real things (kindness, sensitivity, imagination, a sense of humor, a spirit of adventure) have little to do with how we rub our bodies together. But sensible or not, our society does shape many of its attitudes and laws around whether people get off on folks of the same or different sex. This being so, it is necessary to make a few comments on the special legal problems of gay couples.

Most of the material in this book applies equally to gay and straight couples. A contract to share a rental apartment or to buy real or personal property will be no different for gay couples than for anybody else. But because gay people are subject to special forms of discrimination, intimidation and harassment by legal authorities, several areas present particular problems. In this chapter we will discuss some of these problems: If you have not already done so, you should first read the material on the subject areas that interest you in the first eleven chapters and then check here to see whether it is an area in which gay couples need to be extra careful.

A. SEX LAWS

We titled Chapter 1, Section I, "If It Feels Good, It May Be Illegal". This heading, which sums up the legal situation applicable to unmarried straight couples in many states is even more true for gays. The majority of states still have laws against sodomy and oral copulation (see list in Chapter 1). Law changes which do away with government regulation of private sexual activities of consenting adults have been proposed in every state. We expect that in many, these long overdue reforms will soon be enacted. There has also been a move to get the U.S. Supreme Court to declare laws banning sodomy and oral copulation between consenting adults unconstitutional as an infringement of fundamental first amendment rights. But it seems unlikely that this sort of constitutional theory will be adopted until the present composition of the Supreme Court changes radically.

In many urban areas of the country there is little harassment of gays who are discreet. After all, you can't convict people of holding hands or kissing. The District Attorney has to produce hard evidence that the technical language of the sodomy or oral copulation statutes has been violated. Proof in these areas is very difficult to get if gay couples are being even minimally careful. To be sure, any possibility of harassment by the legal system is serious, but things are improving. For a discussion of people facing criminal proceedings, we suggest *The Rights of Suspects*, by Rosengart (Discus/Avon).

What about blatant police harassment, especially common in rural middle America, but possible anywhere? What can you do about the cop who pays no attention to the law and simply goes after gay people? The answer is very little, except to organize politically and develop sufficient clout to cause local authorities to make sure that you are treated with respect. The lesson for all discriminated-against groups in this country, whether blacks, browns, workers, women, asians or gays, has been, and continues to be, organize.

B. CONTRACTS

In Chapters 3 and 4, we discuss the fact that people living together can legally contract with one another and that it is sensible for them to do so. The information and the contracts in these chapters can easily be adapted for use by gay couples. We have been asked if we believe courts will enforce contracts between gays? Our answer is a qualified "yes".

In the states that have done away with sodomy laws (see Chapter 1), it seems clear that contracts between partners of a gay couple are legal as long as sexual conduct is not the basis of the contract. Thus, it would be fine to write an agreement to share a house, or a car, or earnings as long as it wasn't tied directly to how many times the couple was going to sleep with each other, etc. As we have never seen a contract between either homosexual or heterosexual couples based on sex, this hardly seems to be a real problem, but it is one that is raised by judges so, at the risk of sounding a little silly, we are doing our conscientious duty by mentioning it.

Now to the "qualified" part of the "yes". Suppose a contract between a gay couple ended up in court in a conservative state with laws against sodomy? Would a court enforce it? Probably, as all mentally competent adults have the right to execute contracts. But suppose one member of the couple (presumably the person who wanted it voided) claimed that, even though the written document didn't mention it, homosexual conduct formed the basis of the contract? Some judges might refuse to enforce the contract.

NOTE: Very few living together contracts between either homosexual or heterosexual couples will ever end up in court. Their purpose, after all, is to allow people of good faith to make a record of their understandings so as to avoid court proceedings. You are much more likely to get into court hassles if you fail to make a contract than if you write your understandings down.

C. FINDING AND RENTING A HOME

Often gay couples have an easier time renting a place than unmarried straight couples. This is true if the landlord doesn't know you are gay. It would be almost funny (if it weren't so crazy) that roommates of the same sex are often more desirable

to a landlord than an unmarried couple if they sleep in different beds, but less desirable if they sleep in the same one. Whether you decide to be candid with the landlord or decide that what he (she) doesn't know won't hurt him (her) is up to you. In most places a landlord can refuse to rent to you simply because you are gay. This is beginning to change and a number of cities and counties have recently enacted laws which prohibit discrimination in rental housing on the basis of "sexual orientation". These are listed in the chart at the end of this chapter.

One problem which occurs when there are prohibitions against gay discrimination concerns your rights if a landlord discovers that you are gay after you move in, then tries to evict you. If you are renting under a month-to-month rental agreement he or she can simply give you a 30-day notice to get out. This can be done for any reason, or no reason at all, and you have no protection. You are in better shape if you have a lease. In this situation a landlord would have to rely on one of the fine print lease clauses to get you out before the end of the lease term. Most leases prohibit illegal activity on the premises and the landlord might threaten to bring an eviction action under this provision — particularly in some conservative sections of the country since the local judges and sheriffs may be hostile to gays, therefore not require much in the way of hard evidence. This sort of eviction would be very difficult in most urban areas, however, as the landlord would have to **prove** that illegal activities were going on on his or her property, and in most cases such proof would be impossible to get.

If you are faced with an eviction or other landlord harassment because you are gay, and you wish to fight back, we strongly urge you to get a lawyer who is sympathetic to, and knowledgeable about, your situation. Most gay political organizations should be able to give you a referral and may, if your case is of sufficient political significance, help with expenses.

D. TRAVEL

Many gay friends tell us that they have no difficulty getting hotel or motel rooms together as long as they are minimally discreet. Of course, it would be nice if discretion was not necessary and gays could openly and honestly show their affection for one another without fear of reprisal. Unfortunately, however, it is legal for a hotel or motel to refuse accomodations to people because they are gay except in a few cities which have passed ordinances banning discrimination against gay people in public accommodations. See chart at the end of this chapter.

E. CREDIT AND INSURANCE

As we suggest in Chapter 4, we feel it is a bad idea for couples (whether gay or straight, married or single) to have joint bank accounts, credit cards, etc. Gays will find it impossible to open joint credit accounts at many stores although it is not difficult to get a second credit card issued under one person's account (see Chapter 2 for dangers of doing this). Joint bank accounts should not be a problem. On the whole, credit discrimination against gays is not a major problem, although it would be a positive thing to ban it on the national level. Several cities have done it at the local level. See chart at the end of this chapter.

Gay people living together may have a very difficult time getting renters insurance or car insurance if they admit that they are gay. However, most insurance companies won't ask and we see no particular reason to raise the issue. If you are buying a house together, you should be able to get comprehensive (including fire) insurance fairly easily. There are no laws saying that insurance companies can't discriminate against homosexuals, however, and if you do have trouble, we suggest that you check with friends and find a gay insurance broker, or at least someone sympathetic to gay concerns.

F. PROPERTY AND DEBTS

If both people are working and supporting themselves, there isn't much reason to worry about financial entanglements as long as your property and debts have been kept separate. The contracts discussed in Chapters 3 and 4 can be adapted to fit your concerns. But is it necessary to make a contract if everything is already kept separate? Does the reasoning of the *Marvin* case (that if an unmarried couple has no written contract, they still might be held to have an oral or implied contract) also apply to gay couples? There are no judicial decisions in this area, but logically there is no reason why a gay couple can't form non-written contracts just as easily as a straight couple. This also means that to play it safe a gay couple may want to write a brief contract even if they plan to keep all of their property separate. It might look like this:

SAMPLE CONTRACT

Shelly Kaufman and Iris Porter agree as follows:

1. That they are living together and plan to continue to do so;

2. That the earnings of each and any accumulations of property traceable to that income belong absolutely to the person who earns the money;

3. That they will maintain separate checking and credit accounts and that neither is in any way responsible for the debts of the other;

4. That if they make any joint purchases they will be covered by a separate, written agreement;

5. That in the event of separation, neither person shall have any claim against the other for money or property.

_____   _____
Date   Shelly Kaufman

_____   _____
Date   Iris Porter

NOTE: Some couples also like to make a list of the property that belongs to each at the time that they get together and make it a part of the contract. This seems a little excessive to us, but then we don't own much that's valuable.

If the relationship you contemplate is one where one person is going to make a majority of the money while the other performs most of the domestic tasks, a written contract is almost essential. The person who is not earning the money has no right to it, or any of the accumulations that result from it, without a contract. The issues you must deal with are the same as those faced by heterosexual couples in the same situation and you will be able to adapt the agreements discussed in Chapter 4 to your needs.

REMINDER: It is always a good idea to make a written agreement when two (or more) people jointly purchase any major item, or jointly plan to build something such as a house, hot tub, boat or whatever. The agreements in Chapters 4 and 6 will work as well for gays as straights.

G. SPOUSAL SUPPORT (ALIMONY)

Does a person who has married and who, as part of a divorce, received an order of spousal support, face the possibility of losing this support by living as part of a gay couple? The answer is yes — there is a small chance that this could happen. If a judge were convinced that the person's role as part of the gay couple is similar to the traditional economic role of a woman in marriage (economically dependent), he might terminate spousal support. In one such case alimony was terminated when a woman commenced living in a lesbian relationship on the theory that this relationship precluded the possibility of remarriage which would have been a change of circumstances sufficient to end alimony, *Anonymous v. Anonymous*, Minnesota District Court, 2nd District, 5 Family Law Reporter 2127. Generally, however, sharing a living arrangement with a person of the same sex has not been found to be grounds for terminating alimony from a previous relationship.

Part of the reason that we can't answer this question definitively is again that there are few judicial decisions in the area. If you did end up arguing about this kind of case in court, the judge's decision might well turn on the facts of your situation. Questions having to do with the length of the marriage, amount and duration of support, ability of the person receiving support to be self-sufficient would be important. If you are seriously worried about this type of problem, see a lawyer (see Chapter 13).

H. CHILD CUSTODY

Recently a number of lesbian mothers have tried to keep their children while living with their lovers.* When objections have been raised (often by a former spouse, grandparent, neighbor, school official, etc.), courts have generally found that such living arrangements are harmful to the child. Some courts have ruled that the mother could retain custody as long as the lover lived outside of the house; others have simply denied custody to all lesbian mothers.** A few years ago there were no cases where mothers living with a lover of the same sex won the right to custody. This has changed somewhat. A few courts have awakened to the realities of the last quarter of the twentieth century and have found that lesbian mothers can be fit parents. But most judges still have their heads in the sand and almost automatically deny a homosexual custody.*** Often this is done sneakily, by stating reasons other than homosexuality as grounds for denial of custody. As we learned in Chapter 9, a judge has a great deal of discretion in deciding child custody based on the vague "best interests of the child test" and there is every reason to believe that homosexuals (usually lesbian mothers) are commonly discriminated against without even the courtesy of being told why.****

In an encouraging recent case (*In Re Hatzopoulos*) a Denver, Colorado Juvenile Court judge awarded child custody to the lesbian lover of a deceased mother where the child's father was unknown. The friend prevailed over a maternal aunt who also wanted custody after proving both a strong commitment to raising the child and a

---

* We know of some gay men jointly raising the children of one member of the couple but are unaware of any court cases in this area. We suspect that, because of the usual court prejudice in favor of women raising children, gay men will have an even harder time keeping their children while living with their lovers than will gay women.
** How about this gem..."I don't say that a mother cannot be fit to rear her children even if she is a lesbian, but I wonder if she is fit when she boldly and brazenly sets up in the home where the children are to be reared, lesbian practices..." *Townsend v. Townsend*, 1 Family Law Reporter, 2830 (1975).
*** For an excellent (but slightly dated) discussion of the few reported cases in this area, see *The Law of Lesbian Mother Cases*, Buffalo Law Review, Vol. 25, P. 693 (1976).
**** The law in the lesbian mother area is changing quickly. For up-to-date information check the Family Law Reporter and the SexuaLaw Reporter available at your local law library or contact the Women's Litigation Unit, San Francisco Legal Assistance, 1093 Market St., San Francisco, Calif. or The National Gay Task Force, 80 Fifth Ave., Room 903: New York, New York 10011.

190

stable home life. This 1977 case is reported in Volume 4 of the Family Law Reporter on page 1021. A California trial court judge has ruled that a mother's lesbianism has no bearing on whether she should be granted custody (*Jullion v. Jullion*, Alameda County Superior Court, April 1978).

Homosexual parents also have problems when they already have custody of a child, but the other parent or perhaps a relative tries to get custody changed because of the custodial parent's sexual preferences. However, lesbian mothers have been more successful in keeping custody than in winning it in the first instance. In a landmark case (*Shuster-Isacson* reported in 1 Family Law Reporter, 2004 (1974), a Seattle, Washington judge allowed two lesbian mothers to continue to live together and to keep custody of their children. Unfortunately the case of *In Re Jane B*. 380 N.Y.S.2d 848 (Sup. Ct. 1976) is more typical. Here a judge changed custody of a ten-year old from a lesbian mother to the father stating: "The home environment with her (the mother's) homosexual partner in residence is not a proper atmosphere in which to bring up this child or in the best interest of this child".

NOTE: Many thousands of children are living in homes with parents whose sexual preferences are for people of the same sex with no problem because no one has made an issue of the parents' homosexuality. Given the present state of the law, many people find that discretion makes more sense than heroism.

I. EMPLOYMENT

Traditionally it has been legal to fire homosexuals because of their sexual preference. The fact that gay people live together is only relevant to employment in that it may call an employer's attention to (or make them acknowledge) their sexual preferences.

As societal attitudes toward gays have mellowed, protections against employment discrimination have grown. It is too soon to say that all, or even most, employers are prohibited from firing homosexuals because of their private sexual preferences, but the trend is in that direction. Here we give you a brief summary of the state of the law as this book goes to press. Court decisions and legislation are happening fast in this area, however, and before relying on information presented here, you will want to be sure that it is up-to-date. One good source is the SexuaLaw Reporter available at your law library or from 1800 North Highland Ave., Suite 106, Los Angeles, Calif. 90028.

1. Private Employment

In most parts of the country, an employer may still fire a person because he or she is a homosexual. This is true even though Title VII of the Civil Rights Act of 1964 bans discrimination in employment on the basis of sex. Why? Because the Civil Rights Act has been interpreted by a predominantly straight, predominantly elderly male judiciary to apply only to traditional discrimination against women because they are women, not to homosexuals. Some enlightened employers (Harvard University and the University of California) have voluntarily adopted policies protecting gay employees from employment discrimination. Where such policies exist, employees may legally rely on them. Of more importance is the fact that many cities and counties have adopted ordinances banning discrimination against gays in private employment. Hopefully, states and perhaps even the federal government will follow suit. A California judicial decision may be interpreted to ban discrimination against gays by both public and private employers. *Gay Law Students Assoc. v. Pacific Telephone & Telegraph,* See the chart at the end of this chapter for a list.

2. Federal Government Employment

Due to a number of court decisions and changes in civil service rules, gays have won considerable protection in federal jobs outside the military and not involving national security. Homosexuals may now only be dismissed if their conduct adversely affects their job fitness. Since it is hard to see how the private conduct of consenting adults can affect job fitness, it is fair to say that gays are in pretty good shape as far as legal rights in civil federal employment are concerned. Even where civilians are working in national security areas, there is some protection in that the government must establish a rational business justification for discharging or refusing to hire a homosexual.

a) Uniformed Military Service: The Army, Navy, Air Force and Marines all expressly discriminate against homosexuals. If you admit you are gay, you are discharged. While there have been a number of cases extending the rights of homosexuals to fair hearings, honorable discharges, etc., it is too soon to say that homosexuals may openly and honestly serve in our military without fear of reprisal.

3. State And Local Government Employment

In some states courts have given homosexuals a measure of protection in stating that there must be some relationship between a person's homosexuality and impaired job performance before a person can be fired. However, many state courts still discriminate. To find out how your state stands, check your state Civil Service Rules and then see if any legal decisions have been made interpreting these rules. Local gay activist organizations should have this information.

Pennsylvania, by executive order of the governor, has banned discrimination against gays in state governmental employment, and California has done the same by court decision which also includes employees of private and public utilities.* Similar rules are in force in a number of cities including the ones listed in Section J of this chapter.

NOTE: Federal courts are also starting to get involved in cases involving employment discrimination against gays by states and localities and it is fair to say that, although gays don't yet have the sort of tough protections won by traditional minority groups in the areas of race, religion, national origin, etc., they are moving in that direction.

One area where discrimination against gays is both rampant and uncontrolled is in the teaching profession, especially in the lower grades. Somehow our society assumes that heterosexuals will not act out their sexual fantasies, but that homosexuals can't be trusted not to molest children in the coatroom. There are numerous court decisions which approve the firing of gay teachers for no reason other than that they are gay. For the latest information, see the SexuaLaw Reporter.

J. GAY RIGHT LAW CHART

DATE ENACTED	MUNICIPALITY	CONDITIONS
1972	Atlanta, Ga.	Municipal employment/Exec. order
2/72 & 1/78	New York City, N.Y.	Municipal employment/Exec. order
5/72	Washington, D.C.	Employment, by Board of Education

* *Gay Law Students Assoc. v. Pacific Telephone* — may be interpreted to prohibit all employment discrimination against homosexuals in private as well as public employment.

DATE ENACTED	MUNICIPALITY	CONDITIONS
11/73	Washington, D.C.	Employment, housing, credit, public accommodations, education
7/72	Ann Arbor, Mi.	Housing, employment, public accommodations
8/72 & 7/78	San Francisco, Ca.	All encompassing
5/73	East Lansing, Mi.	Employment, public accommodations
11/73	Seattle, Wa.	Municipal & private employment
11/73	Toronto, Ont.	Municipal employment
11/73; 10/78	Berkeley, Ca.	Municipal employment, employment with private employer under city contract; all encompassing
11/73	Detroit, Mi.	Municipal employment
1/74	Columbus, Oh.	Employment, housing, public accommodations
3/74	Minneapolis, Mn.	All encompassing
5/74	Alfred, N.Y.	All encompassing
8/74	Palo Alto, Ca.	Inclusion in jurisdiction of human rights commission
11/75	Palo Alto, Ca.	Employment by Board of Education
9/74	Ithaca, N.Y.	Municipal employment
12/74	Sunnyvale, Ca.	Municipal employment
12/74	Portland, Or.	Municipal employment
2/75	Cupertino, Ca.	Municipal employment
3/75	Mountain View, Ca.	Municipal employment
3/75	Madison, Wi.	Employment, housing, credit, public accommodations
7/75	Austin, Tx.	Municipal employment, labor union membership, employment agency referrals
8/75	Santa Barbara, Ca.	Municipal employment
9/75	Chapel Hill, N.C.	Municipal employment
11/75	Urbana, Il.	Employment, credit, public accommodations
4/76	Ottawa, Ont.	Municipal employment
4/76	Boston, Ma.	Municipal employment (exec. order)
4/76	Pullman, Wa.	Municipal employment
5/76	Amherst, Ma.	All encompassing
1/77	Tuscon, Az.	Employment, housing, public accommodations

DATE ENACTED	MUNICIPALITY	CONDITIONS
3/77	Windsor, Ont.	Municipal employment
5/77	Iowa City, Ia.	Employment, credit, public accommodations
7/77	Champaign, Il.	Employment, housing, public accommodations
12/77	Aspen, Co.	All encompassing
1/79	Troy, N.Y.	All encompassing
1/79	Detroit, Mi.	All encompassing
5-7/89	Los Angeles, Ca.	All encompassing

DATE ENACTED	COUNTY	CONDITIONS
7/75	Santa Cruz County, Ca.	Affirmative Action Policy
11/75	Howard County, Md.	All encompassing
6/78	Ingham County, Mi.	All encompassing

DATE ENACTED	STATE	CONDITIONS
4/76	Pennsylvania	State employment (exec. order)
12/77	Quebec, Canada	Employment, public accommodations, housing
5/79	California (by court decision)	State employment & employment with public utilities

awyers

St. Yves is from Brittany
A lawyer but not a thief.
Such a thing is beyond belief!*

Professionals of all sorts are in bad repute these days. There is a strong and often justifiable feeling that they hide behind knowing looks, mumbo jumbo and monopoly powers to charge high prices for what are often simple services. Lawyers are particularly guilty of this practice, for a great deal of what they do at $50 to $100 per hour amounts to little more than paper shuffling — paper shuffling that you can do simply and safely for yourself if you have the necessary information. Of course, keeping information hidden or obscured by funny sounding Latin and old-fashioned English terms is one way that lawyers protect their monopoly.

Does this mean that we don't think you should ever go near a lawyer? No. The fact that the legal system is riddled with abuse doesn't mean that you can completely avoid it. This book necessarily covers a lot of ground and may not be sufficiently detailed for all your purposes. You may need the information a lawyer has on some specific point or you may simply want an expert to check your work. What you want to do is use lawyers for your purposes, not theirs. Don't put yourself in the role of a passive "client".**Approach lawyers with a thorough knowledge of how they can help you and how much it will cost.

---

* Even in the middle ages lawyers allied themselves with the rich and powerful. This is part of a French poem about a lawyer who served the poor, which was such an unusual thing that he was made a saint. We discovered the quote in an excellent history of our legal system entitled *Law And The Rise Of Capitalism*, by Tigar and Levy: Monthly Review Press.

** In an interesting article entitled "Valuable Deficiencies, A Service Economy Needs People In Need," in the Fall 1977 Co-Evolution Quarterly, John McKnight Points out that "The Latin root of the word 'client' is a verb which translates 'to hear', 'to obey'."

A. LAW LIBRARIES

Lawyers are experts at recycling information and charging enormous amounts for this limited service. We say limited because lawyers (or their para-legal assistants or secretaries) are often doing no more than opening a book of legal forms or information and copying out the answers. For example, if you want to form a corporation or process an adoption, name change, divorce or almost anything else, the lawyer will do little more than fill in the boxes on pre-printed forms. Why can't you do this for yourself? Often you can if you know which book to look in. They are all in your county law library which is free and open to the public (it ought to be as in most states your court filing fees pay for it).

The most important tool in your county law library is the annotated state codes. "Annotated" means that after each law is set out, there is a digest of excerpts from relevant judicial decisions and cross references to related articles and laws. The judicial decisions are kept in books that are arranged according to a simple code which your law librarian can quickly explain. Also, ask your librarian to show you any legal encyclopedia which explains your state laws. These are indexed by subject (you could look up cohabitation, child support, etc.) and are much like any other encyclopedia. You will want to check out the "Form" books. These are collections (often in many volumes) of sample legal forms designed to accomplish many thousands of legal tasks. Finally ask the law librarian if your state has a set of books designed to keep lawyers up-to-date. In California these are called CEB books and there is one covering every common area of law. There are also several national services in areas such as tax law, labor law, etc. As noted several times in this book, the one most relevant to you will probably be the Family Law Reporter and the SexuaLaw Reporter. The best general guide to using the law library is *Cluing Into Legal Research*, Honigsberg, Golden Rain Press.

B. WHEN DO YOU NEED A LAWYER?

There is no simple answer to this question, but we can give you some suggestions:

1. Information

If after reading this book you feel you need more detailed information on a particular subject, a lawyer may be able to help you. Talking your problems over with a knowledgeable person may be all you need. You might, for example, want to know more about common law marriage rules or the tax consequences of setting up a trust. Because a great deal of this information is virtually inaccessible to the non-lawyer (hopefully this will change), lawyers may be your only resource. When making an appointment to get information from a lawyer, always observe rule one: find out in **advance** how much a consultation will cost.

2. Double-checking

You may feel that you have an excellent grasp on the legal aspects of a problem, but still feel that you want, and are willing to pay for, an expert opinion. A contract between you and your friend to buy a house is a good example of a situation where you might wish to have an attorney double-check your work. A will that involves considerable property is another. Where a lot is at stake, it never hurts to be a little extra careful. But be sure that the lawyer you approach is supportive of the idea that you intend to do most of the work yourself and that his or her role is that of a helper. Many lawyers resent people making their own decisions, so be wary.

3. Fighting In Court

The American judicial system is so slow, cumbersome, expensive, time-consuming and divorced from everyday reality, that we strongly urge you to avoid it if possible, even if this involves giving up some property or principles that are important to you. However, if you find yourself in court, whether in a property division or custody case or some other serious action, you should consult a lawyer. This doesn't mean that you should hire a lawyer to represent you. Most disputes that you are likely to become involved in are not difficult and representing yourself in court is not as hard as lawyers would like to pretend. Did you ever think that the old saying "a person who represents himself has a fool for a client" is such an old saying because lawyers have been brain-washing the public with it for generations. You want to find a lawyer who will help you to understand the procedures and issues involved. This can often be arranged for a fraction of the cost of turning the whole dispute over to a lawyer. Be sure your lawyer is willing to tell you how much he or she will charge in advance, what the charge is for. Remember, it's your case and your life, and you should be the one making the decisions.

C. FINDING A LAWYER

Finding a lawyer who charges reasonable prices and who you feel can be trusted is not always an easy task. There is always the fear that by just picking a name out of the telephone book you may get someone unsympathetic, or perhaps an attorney who will charge too much. Certainly you have better things to do than talk to a lawyer who thinks that living together is a sleazy, sinful practice. You should realize that you are not the only one who feels a little scared and intimidated. Here are some suggestions:

1. Legal Aid

If you are poor, you may qualify for free help from your legal aid office (often called legal services or legal assistance). Check your yellow pages under Attorneys for their location or ask your county clerk.

2. Group Legal Practices

A new but rapidly growing aspect of law practice in many states is the Group Legal Practice program. Many groups, including unions, employers and consumer action groups, are offering plans to their members whereby they can get legal assistance for rates which are substantially lower than those offered by most private practitioners. Some of these plans are good, but most are mediocre or worse. Before getting involved in a group practice plan, ask whether the plan has a legal clinic approach aimed at allowing you to do at least some of your own work and involving you in decision-making. For example, a good plan will offer do-your-own-divorce, bankruptcy, name change, adoption, etc. clinics. Watch out for so-called group practice plans that consist of no more than traditional private practice lawyers offering a slight discount off their regular fees.

3. Private Attorneys

If you don't know an attorney who can be trusted and can't get a reliable recommendation from a friend, you have a problem. While you might be lucky and randomly pick an attorney who matches your needs perfectly, you might just as easily wind up paying too much for too little. Here are some suggestions that should make your search a little easier:

Avoid referral panels set up by local bar associations. Any lawyer can get on these panels by paying a fee. You would do as well, and often better, to stick a pin in the Attorneys section of the phone book. Also, sticking a pin in the phone book is free whereas some of the reference panel systems will charge you as much as $25 for the referral;

◑ Check with a local consumer organization to see if they can recommend someone;

◑ Check the ads in the paper usually listed under "Business Personals" in the classified section. Often younger attorneys just starting out advertise low rates to build up a practice. Also, we know several semi-retired attorneys who advertise very reasonable rates for consultations with the understanding that they will not take cases to court. This could be just what you need.

◑ Shop around by calling different law offices and stating your problem. Ask them how much it would cost for a visit. Try to talk to a lawyer personally so you can get an idea of how friendly and sympathetic he is to your concerns. If you want advice on a specific area as opposed to turning your whole legal life over to the lawyer, make this clear from the beginning. Don't be afraid to fire a lawyer if you feel your problems are not getting sufficient attention. There is a growing surplus of lawyers (one out of every 400 Americans will be one by 1980. If we just look at white males, the figure is one out of 100).

EXAMPLE: Let's think back to Chapter 6. Remember Keija and Felix and the contract they wrote when buying a house. This is the sort of agreement that they might want checked by a lawyer. As they have already done their homework, they should pay less than $100 for this service. But, if instead of doing most of the work themselves, Keija and Felix simply call up the first lawyer someone suggests and show up at his or her office with a confused mish-mash of facts and hopes, they can expect to pay the lawyer a big chunk of cash (say $500-$1,000) to sort it out. This is assuming, of course, that the lawyer is sympathetic to start with. One couple called us recently and said that, after listening to their problems (which weren't difficult), a lawyer who was a friend of their parents made a pyramid of his fingers, cleared his throat, looked wise and told them "get married". Two days later a bill arrived for $100.

Younger attorneys are probably going to be more sympathetic and knowledgeable about the problems of people living together than are their older colleagues. Remember, lawyers whose offices and lifestyles are reasonably simple are more likely to help you for less money than lawyers who feel naked unless wearing a $400 outfit. You should be able to find someone to help you for $25-$40 per hour. **Anything more is excessive.**

When talking to the lawyer on the phone, or at the first conference, ask some specific questions. If the lawyer answers them clearly and concisely — explaining, but not talking down to you — fine. If he or she acts wise, but says little except to ask that the problem be placed in his or her hands (with the appropriate fee, of course), watch out. You are either talking with someone who doesn't know the answer and won't admit it (common), or someone who finds it impossible to let go of the "me expert, you peasant" way of looking at the world (even more common).

Appendix

LIVING TOGETHER CONTRACT

BETWEEN _____

AND _____

    We, _____

and _____,

make this agreement to set out the rights and obligations of our joint living arrangement. It is our intention to follow this agreement in a spirit of good faith and cooperation. We agree as follows:

ARTICLE I

We choose to live together outside the formal state regulations governing marriage and divorce. This is our free choice and desire and we specifically state that we do not intend our relationship to be interpreted as a common law marriage. We further state that we each make this agreement in consideration of the agreement of the other, and that the provision of sexual services by either of us is not the basis of this contract. We further state that this agreement will remain in full force and effect until such time as we separate, or change it with a subsequent written, signed agreement.

ARTICLE II

We are each equal and independent people, willing and able to support ourselves. We will share our love and good energy, but we reject the idea that one of us should be dependent upon the other for support.

ARTICLE III

We agree that all income, however derived, and any accumulations of property traceable to that income, belongs absolutely to the person who earns or otherwise acquires the income. At the time of signing this contract, we have each prepared a list of major items of property that each of us owns. This list is marked as Exhibit 1 and is attached to this contract and by this reference made a part of this contract. We shall update this list as it becomes necessary. Any and all joint purchases shall be made under the terms of Article VI below.

ARTICLE IV

We agree that any gifts or inheritances that either of us receives shall be the separate property of that person. Should a gift or inheritance be made to us jointly, we shall consider that we own it in equal shares unless otherwise specified by the donor.

ARTICLE V

We agree that each of us will keep our own money in our own separate bank accounts and that we shall not open joint bank or credit accounts. We each further agree to return any credit cards that are issued to both of us, and, in addition, not to make any purchases using the credit or credit cards of the other.

ARTICLE VI

As set forth in Article III above, we will each individually own all property purchased with the money we individually earn or otherwise accumulate. However, from time to time it may be necessary or desirable for us to pool our money to buy some item. If this is done, we will make a separate written agreement to cover each particular item of property that we acquire jointly. These agreements shall be marked Exhibit 2 and shall be attached to and incorporated in this agreement. As part of each joint agreement, we shall include a clause providing for what happens to the property if we separate. If for some reason we fail to provide for the contingency of our separation, we agree to divide all jointly-owned property equally. If we can't agree as to an equal division we shall sell the jointly-owned property and equally divide all proceeds of the sale.

ARTICLE VII

We agree to share equally all monthly household expenses. This includes food, incidental supplies necessary to home maintenance, rent and utilities, not including long distance phone charges which shall be paid by the person making the call.

ARTICLE VIII

We each agree to own, insure and pay for the maintenance of our own motor vehicles. If at any time we wish to share ownership of a motor vehicle, we shall make a separate written agreement as to ownership under the terms of Article VI and shall have the fact of joint ownership recorded on the motor vehicle title slip.

ARTICLE IX

We do not at present jointly own any real property. Should we jointly buy a house, land in the country, investment property or any other real property, we agree that a copy of a deed to the property and any and all supplementary contracts or agreements covering the property shall be marked as Exhibit 3 and attached to this contract and that when this is done they shall be incorporated into this contract. We further agree that neither of us shall have any rights to, or financial interest in, any separate real property of the other, whether acquired before or after the signing of this contract, unless such interest is set forth in a written agreement signed by both parties to this contract.

ARTICLE X

We realize that our power to contract as far as children are concerned is limited by state law. With this knowledge, and in a spirit of cooperation and mutual respect, we wish to state the following as our agreement should we have children.

1) The father shall sign a written statement acknowledging that he is the father of our child(ren) within ten days after birth;

2) Our child(ren) shall be given the following last name _____;

3) We reject the idea that one of us should do most of the child care tasks while the other provides the income. We will do our best to jointly share in the many responsibilities involved in feeding, clothing, loving and disciplining our child(ren);

4) Because of the possible trauma our separation might cause our child(ren), we shall each make a good faith effort to participate in a jointly-agreed upon program of counseling before separation;

5) If we separate, we shall do our best to see that our child(ren) has/have a good and healthful environment in which to grow up. Specifically we agree to the following:

a) We will do our best to see that our child(ren) maintain a close and loving relationship with each of us;

b) We will share in the upbringing of our child(ren) and, on the basis of our respective abilities to pay and the needs of the child(ren), in his/her or their support;

c) We will make a good faith effort to make all major decisions affecting the health and welfare of our child(ren) jointly;

d) Should circumstances dictate that our child(ren) should spend a greater portion of the year living with one of us than the other, the person who has actual physical custody shall be sensitive to the needs of the other to have generous rights of

visitation and shall cooperate in all practical steps necessary to make visitation as easy as possible;

e) If after separation we have problems communicating as to the best interest or interests of our child(ren), we shall seek out help in the form of a jointly-agreed upon program of counseling with the hope that we can work out our differences without having to take our problems to court;

f) At the death of either of us, our child(ren) shall be cared for and raised by the other whether or not we are living together at the time of the death.

ARTICLE XI

We agree that either of us can end our agreement to live together at any time by simply ceasing to live with the other. If this is done, neither of us shall make claim upon the other for money or support, except as provided for by the terms of this agreement pertaining to the division of jointly-owned property (Article VI).

ARTICLE XII

We agree that from time to time this contract may be amended. All amendments shall be in writing and shall be signed by both of us.

ARTICLE XIII

We further agree that if any courts finds any portion of this contract to be illegal or otherwise unenforceable, that the rest of the contract is still valid and in full force.

Executed at _____

_____   _____
Date   Signature

_____   _____
Date   Signature

APPENDIX 1

The following personal property is the separate property of _____

_____

The following personal property is the separate property of _____

_____

APPENDIX 2

The following property is jointly-owned by both of us under the terms and in the proportions set forth:

LIVING TOGETHER CONTRACT

BETWEEN _____

AND _____

We, _____

and _____,

make this agreement to set out the rights and obligations of our joint living arrangement. It is our intention to follow this agreement in a spirit of good faith and cooperation. We agree as follows:

ARTICLE I

We choose to live together outside the formal state regulations governing marriage and divorce. This is our free choice and desire and we specifically state that we do not intend our relationship to be interpreted as a common law marriage. We further state that we each make this agreement in consideration of the agreement of the other, and that the provision of sexual services by either of us is not the basis of this contract. We further state that this agreement will remain in full force and effect until such time as we separate, or change it with a subsequent written, signed agreement.

ARTICLE II

From the date this contract is signed, we will share all of our income and property accumulated with that income without regard to which of us earns or otherwise receives it. This does not include inheritances or gifts made to one of us. These shall remain the separate property of the person receiving the gift or inheritance under the terms of Article IV.

ARTICLE III

At the time of signing this contract, we have each prepared a list of major items of property that each of us owns as separate property. This list is marked as Exhibit 1 and is attached to this contract and by reference made a part of this contract. We shall update this list as it becomes necessary.

ARTICLE IV

We agree that any gifts or inheritances that either of us receives shall be the separate property of that person. Should a gift or inheritance be made to us jointly, we shall consider that we own it in equal shares unless otherwise specified by the donor.

ARTICLE V

We agree to maintain such joint and separate bank accounts and joint-owned separate credit accounts as appear to be reasonable from time to time. We agree to consult one another on all purchases whether for cash or credit which exceed $200 and to make a good faith effort not to overspend our account.

ARTICLE VI

We each agree to own, insure and pay for the maintenance of our own motor vehicles. If at any time we wish to share ownership of a motor vehicle, we shall make a separate written agreement as to ownership under and shall have the fact of joint ownership recorded on the motor vehicle title slip.

ARTICLE VII

We do not at present jointly own any real property. Should we jointly buy a house, land in the country, investment property or any other real property, we agree that a copy of a deed to the property and any and all supplementary contracts or agreements covering the property shall be marked as Exhibit 3 and attached to this contract and that when this is done they shall be incorporated into this contract. We further agree that neither of us shall have any rights to, or financial interest in, any separate real property of the other, whether acquired before or after the signing of this contract, unless such interest is set forth in a written agreement signed by both parties to this contract.

ARTICLE VIII

We realize that our power to contract as far as children are concerned is limited by state law. With this knowledge, and in a spirit of cooperation and mutual respect, we wish to state the following as our agreement should we have children.

1) The father shall sign a written statement acknowledging that he is the father of our child(ren) within ten days after birth;

2) Our child(ren) shall be given the following last name _____ ;

3) We reject the idea that one of us should do most of the child care tasks while the other provides the income. We will do our best to jointly share in the many responsibilities involved in feeding, clothing, loving and disciplining our child(ren);

4) Because of the possible trauma our separation might cause our child(ren), we shall each make a good faith effort to participate in a jointly-agreed upon program of counseling before separation;

5) If we separate, we shall do our best to see that our child(ren) has/have a good and healthful environment in which to grow up. Specifically we agree to the following:

a) We will do our best to see that our child(ren) maintain a close and loving relationship with each of us;

b) We will share in the upbringing of our child(ren) and, on the basis of our respective abilities to pay and the needs of the child(ren), in his/her or their support;

c) We will make a good faith effort to make all major decisions affecting the health and welfare of our child(ren) jointly;

d) Should circumstances dictate that our child(ren) should spend a greater portion of the year living with one of us than the other, the person who has actual physical custody shall be sensitive to the needs of the other to have generous rights of visitation and shall cooperate in all practical steps necessary to make visitation as easy as possible;

e) If after separation we have problems communicating as to the best interest or interests of our child(ren), we shall seek out help in the form of a jointly-agreed upon program of counseling with the hope that we can work out our differences without having to take our problems to court;

f) At the death of either of us, our child(ren) shall be cared for and raised by the other whether or not we are living together at the time of the death.

ARTICLE IX

We agree that either of us can terminate this agreement by simply choosing not to live with the other. Should this be done, all jointly-owned property shall be equally divided at the time of the separation. Neither of us will have any obligation to support the other after separation.

ARTICLE X

We agree that from time to time this contract may be amended. All amendments shall be in writing and shall be signed by both of us.

ARTICLE XI

We further agree that if any court finds any portion of this contract to be illegal or otherwise unenforceable, that the rest of the contract is still valid and in full force.

Executed at _____

_____   _____
Date   Signature

_____   _____
Date   Signature

APPENDIX 1

The following personal property is the separate property of _____

_____

The following personal property is the separate property of _____

_____

ACKNOWLEDGEMENT OF PATERNITY

_____ hereby acknowledges that he is the
natural father of _____, born _____
to _____ in _____ .
_____ further states that he has welcomed
_____ into his home and that it is his intention and belief
that he has taken all steps necessary to fully legitimate _____
for all purposes, including the right to inherit from, and through him, at the time of
his death.

_____ further expressly acknowledges his duty
to properly raise and adequately support _____ .

_____   _____

DATE

STATE OF

COUNTY OF _____ } SS

On _____ , 19___, before me, the
undersigned, a Notary Public in and for said State, personally appeared _____

_____
and _____

_____,
known to me to be the persons whose names are sub-
scribed to the within instrument, and severally acknowl-
edged to me that they executed the same.

Witness my hand and official seal.

_____
Notary Public in and for said State

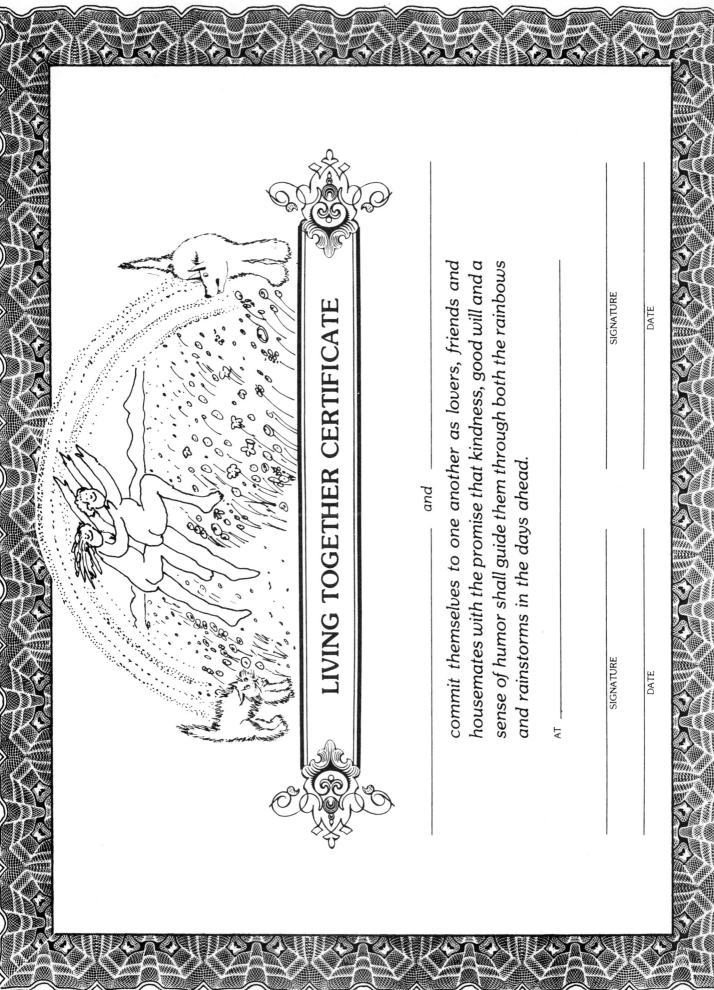

LIVING TOGETHER CERTIFICATE

_____

and

_____

commit themselves to one another as lovers, friends and
housemates with the promise that kindness, good will and a
sense of humor shall guide them through both the rainbows
and rainstorms in the days ahead.

AT _____

_____
SIGNATURE

_____
DATE

_____
SIGNATURE

_____
DATE

ABOUT RALPH

Ralph is the leader of the "do your own law" movement on the West Coast. As a co-founder of Nolo Press and the author of numerous books and articles aimed at giving the non-lawyer so-called "legal information" to deal with their own life decisions, he has constantly tried to expand the areas in which people can help themselves.

Ralph has a license to practice law. He doesn't use it. Instead, he gives lectures and workshops on such subjects as "Law For Unmarried Couples", "Tenants' Rights", and "How To Use Small Claims Court". Recently, Ralph has taught a series of all-day workshops for unmarried couples under the auspices of University of California Extension.

Ralph lives in Berkeley with Toni, a somewhat nutty black hound named Clem and Annie, a pinchy-faced orange cat.

ABOUT TONI

Toni is an anthropologist turned lawyer who is totally at a loss for a response when anyone asks "why did you go to law school?" She is the co-author and illustrator of *Ups And Downs, The Treasure Of Lost Dragon Castle*, as well as several "do your own law" books including *The People's Guide To California Marriage Law*.

Toni is an original member of the Nolo Press family and has been involved in the people's law movement since its inception. Her articles have appeared in New West and Ms. Magazine.

Other Books Published by Nolo

HOW TO FORM YOUR OWN CALIFORNIA CORPORATION (Second Edition): This extremely popular book, by California attorney Anthony Mancuso, includes tear-out Articles, Bylaws, minutes and stock certificates and all the instructions necessary to set up your own small California corporation. The tax consequences of incorporating are thoroughly discussed. Takes advantage of the 1977 Corporation law. For profit corporations only.
$12.00

THE CALIFORNIA NON-PROFIT CORPORATION HANDBOOK: Attorney Anthony Mancuso provides step-by-step instructions and all the forms necessary to choose a name, draft Articles and Bylaws, attain favorable tax status and get your non-profit corporation started. Applicable for all groups who qualify for Section 501(c)(3) non-profit status under the Internal Revenue Code.
$12.00

HOW TO CHANGE YOUR NAME (California Edition): Changing your name is cheap and easy. This book comes complete with all the forms you need to do it yourself. Full information on women's name problems with special attention to women who want to retain, or return to, their own name after marriage or divorce. This book is primarily valuable to Californians.
$7.95

EVERYBODY'S GUIDE TO SMALL CLAIMS COURT (Second Edition): Attorney Ralph Warner takes you step-by-step through the Small Claims procedure, providing practical information on how to evaluate your case, file and serve papers, prepare and present a case, and, most important, how to collect when you win. New 50 state Appendix contains information on Small Claims procedures in all states. Separate chapters on common situations such as automobile sales and repair, landlord-tenant, debt cases.
$5.95

HOW TO CHANGE YOUR NAME (California Edition) (Revised for 1979-80) Changing your name is cheap and easy. This book comes complete with all the forms you need to do it yourself. Full information on women's name problems with special attention to women who want to retain, or return to, their own name after marriage or divorce. This book is primarily valuable to Californians.
$6.95

CALIFORNIA DEBTORS' HANDBOOK - BILLPAYERS' RIGHTS (Third Edition): A constructive guide for those who find themselves over their heads in legal debts. Contains information on wage and bank account attachments, car repossession, child support debts, student loans, bankruptcy, etc. Also, detailed information on how to deal with collection agencies, including sample letters and agreements. Recommended by the Washington Post, L.A. Times, S.F. Examiner, Berkeley Co-op News and S.F. Action.
$5.95

PEOPLE'S GUIDE TO CALIFORNIA MARRIAGE & DIVORCE LAW: Vital information on community and separate property, names, children of former marriages, buying a house, probate avoidance, etc. Comes complete with a sample will and sample marriage contracts. Discusses divorce in detail and includes agreements for joint custody. Recommended by S.F. Consumer Action, Long Beach Press Telegram, Washington Post, Sacramento Bee and many more.
$6.95

HOW TO DO YOUR OWN DIVORCE IN CALIFORNIA (Seventh Edition): This famous book revolutionized the divorce field by making it clear and simple to the layperson. Tells you the practical things you need to think about and gives information and advice on making your various decisions. Shows exactly how to do your own. Over 200,000 copies in print have saved Californians more than $15 million in attorney fees. New edition includes 1979 law changes. (California only) $8.95

HOW TO COLLECT YOUR CHILD SUPPORT AND ALIMONY: An experienced attorney and collector tell you step-by-step how to collect all that back support. Includes sections on how to find people and their property as well as what to do when you do find them. This is one of the most valuable books we have ever published. There has never been one like it. $7.95

PROTECT YOUR HOME WITH A DECLARATION OF HOMESTEAD: Your house can be protected from your creditors up to $40,000 under California law only if you file a homestead. Here we tell you how to do it cheaply, easily and legally. An invaluable gift for the new homeowner. Third Edition with recent law changes. Also contains information and forms on exemptions for mobile homes and houseboats. $4.95

CALIFORNIA TENANTS' HANDBOOK: Sound practical advice on getting deposits back, breaking a lease, getting repairs made, using Small Claims Court, dealing with the obnoxious landlord and forming a tenants' union. Contains numerous sample letters and agreements as well as a Fair-to-Tenants tear-out lease and rental agreement. "...sharper than a serpent's tooth." ---Herb Caen, S.F. Chronicle (Over 60,000 in print) $5.95

HOW TO ADOPT YOUR STEPCHILD: By Frank Zagone. This straightforward guide shows you how to prepare all the legal forms necessary to adopt your stepchild in California. Includes information on how to get the consent of the natural parent and how to conduct an "abandonment" proceeding if necessary. Private and agency adoptions are not covered. $10.00

PLANNING YOUR ESTATE: This comprehensive book by attorney Denis Clifford contains a great deal of legal information about the practical aspects of death. Here in one place for the first time Californians can get information on making their own will, alternatives to probate, planning to limit inheritance and estate taxes, living trusts, and providing for children. A oerson's right to die and legal rights to have a funeral of his or her choice are also discussed in detail. This book will greatly increase the information the average person has about death. (Available September 1979) $12.00

================BOOKS DISTRIBUTED BY NOLO PRESS================

The following books are offered because we have used them and found them to be excellent:

LANDLORDING: A practical guide for the conscientious landlord and land-
lady. Covers repairs, maintenance, getting good tenants, how to do your
own eviction with the necessary legal forms, record keeping and taxes.
"A step-by-step guide to acquisition of business sense." ---San Diego
Tribune. This is a large book, 8½ x 11, 253 pages, produced by Express
Press and distributed by Nolo Press. $12.50

SMALL TIME OPERATOR: How to start your own small business, keep your
books, pay your taxes and stay out of trouble. Includes a year's supply
of ledgers and worksheets. This book is for people who have an idea, a
skill or a trade, and the desire to make their living working for themselves. By Bernard Kamoroff, C.P.A. Distributed by Nolo Press $6.95

IMMIGRATING TO THE U.S.A.: This is the best, moderate-priced guide for
non-lawyers who are interested in immigration. Written by an experienced
immigration lawyer who himself immigrated to the U.S., it discusses student visas, preference categories, marrying a U.S. citizen, work permits,
non-immigrant visas, deportation and much more. Immigration forms are
reproduced in the book along with instructions on how to fill them out.
                                                               $7.95

CLUING INTO LEGAL RESEARCH: Peter Jan Honigsberg has produced a readable,
easy-to-use book for people who wish to "break the code" of the law library
and do their own legal research. Much practical information as to how to
research cases, decipher code books and make use of legal encyclopedias.
Mr. Honigsberg teaches courses in para-legal studies for non-lawyers and
is an expert at demystifying the legal system. $7.95

===

TO ORDER ALL BOOKS

1 - 9 books: Title(s) of book(s), price, 6% tax & 50¢ postage per
                      book

10 or more books: Titles of books, price less 20% discount, 6% tax (we
                      pay postage)

Send check or money order to either:

NOLO PRESS DISTRIBUTING   NOLO PRESS-COURTYARD BOOKS
      Box 544   OR   950 Parker Street
Occidental, CA., 95465   Berkeley, CA., 94710
   (707) 874-3105   (415) 549-1976

===